Affinity with Night Skies
Astra Sabondjian's Story

by

Astrid A. Katcharyan

Gomidas Institute
London

ABOUT THE AUTHOR: Astrid Katcharyan was born in London of Armenian parents. She spent her early years in Venice, where her family still live.

Cover design by Arman Papazyan.

Cover quote from Antonia Arslan is from the Italian translation of *Affinity with Night Skies - Affinità con i cieli notturni*, transl. by Barbara Del Mercato, Portogruaro : Nuovadimensione, 2015.

This book was originally published under the imprint of Sterndale Classics in 2005. The present publication is a reprint by the Gomidas Institute.

© 2022 Astrid A. Katcharyan. All Rights Reserved.

ISBN 978-1-909382-71-8

05 04 03 02 01

Gomidas Institute
42 Blythe Rd.
London, W14 0HA
England
Email: *info@gomidas.org*

*To my wonderful mother Adriné
without whom this book could
never have been written*

Chapter Headings

	Map	6
	Foreword	7
I	The Subliminal Powers of Ancestral Wisdom	9
II	The Liberating Powers of a Formal Education	18
III	The Merging Forces of Destiny	30
IV	Secret Clues Hidden in Timeworn Traditions	43
V	The True Unveiling of Enchanted Love	54
VI	The Importance of Life's Ceremonial Handovers	58
VII	Fighting for Justice with a Lion's Share of Love	66
VIII	Exchanging Lives and Disillusionment	78
IX	Arbitrary Fortunes in Shifting Sands	82
X	The Transient Nature of Hopes and Dreams	89
XI	Capricious Times for the Great Healer	101
XII	The Welcome Clutching of Straws	119
XIII	The Unmovable Parameters of Dignity	129
XIV	A Need for Creativity and Independence	143
XV	The Wisdom of Expecting the Unexpected	149
XVI	The Need to Prioritise Emotional Perspectives	157
XVII	The Inspiration of Psychological Revival	162
XVIII	The Power to Challenge the Impossible	171
XIX	The Importance of Strategy and a Mother's Love	180
XX	Chance Favours the Brave	194
XXI	The Rewards of Endurance	200

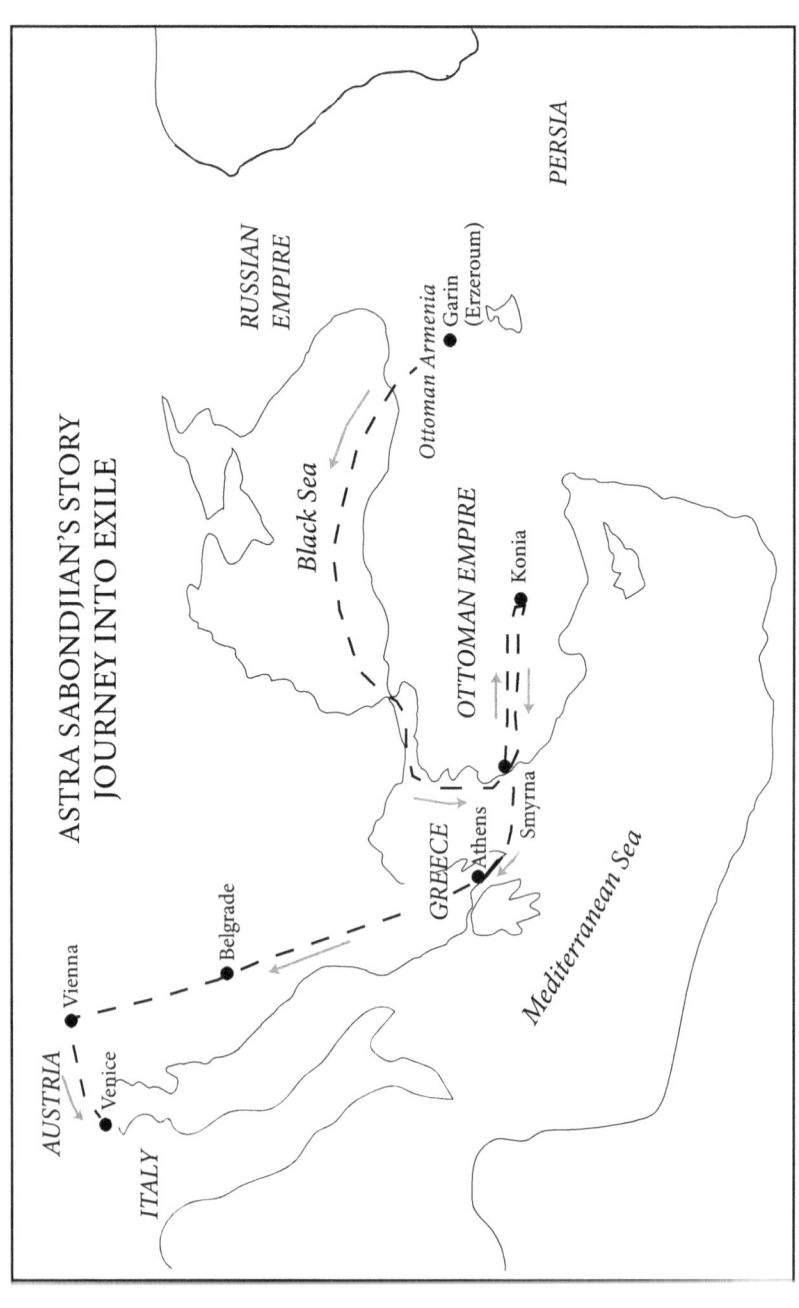

Foreword

The writing of this book is attributed almost entirely to my mother Adriné. Her gift as a three dimensional storyteller, coupled with her incisively wonderful memory, inspired me to always want to know more; and she would willingly oblige, seeing it as a loving duty to her mother, who she admired beyond words. Our family's tradition of ancestral story telling, which fed into this book, began with my mother's maternal grandmother, Peproné. Peproné would sit drinking tea, while my mother, interested since childhood, would ask questions about everything from their origins in Garin (Erzeroum) to how her mother grew up in exile. As time went on, I began to feel an increasing sense of self-imposed responsibility to pull these strands together and to do the story justice. "Have you started the book?" my mother would ask encouragingly, afraid, like me, that a true-life story of heroic proportions might be lost forever. Her death in May 2001 spurred me into writing.

I loved and miss the times when my mother and I would sit together, sipping strong coffee, spiritually, emotionally and mentally in tune, dipping enthusiastically into their shared histories and relive moments in their lives, while I scribbled copious notes, and asked ever more specific questions. Later I taped her accounts, but it was the drip feed of a lifetime of subliminal overview, inferred through her astute insights and colourful asides, which truly set the social backdrop. Whenever she was not completely sure, she would say so, preferring the accounts to be as true to history as she could remember, never happy with half-truths or embellishments. They were just the facts, pure and simple. It was only when I checked her accounts with established records that I fully appreciated how informed her knowledge and grasp of complex political and social history actually was. In case I needed it, this confirmed my complete confidence that I was right to rely on her personal accounts to be accurate to the same degree.

I hope my writing the story, as a series of chronological life changing events, will not affect the fluidity for the reader. I also hope my decision to keep to the facts will dispel any notion of fictional additions. Ultimately this book is a biography written as a novel.

My grandmother's story should be seen in its broader universal context, as she would have wanted. It is the life of one woman amongst so many other honourable, talented, and courageous unsung heroines, in their place and time, who triumphed over adversities of life. She died in Venice, where we would spend our summers, and where I knew her as a loving benevolent grandmother with a profoundly mysterious air. Now I feel I know her as a woman to be proud of too.

Astrid Katcharyan
30 June 2004

Chapter I

The Subliminal Powers of Ancestral Wisdom

I NEED to tell this story, for me, for all of them, but most of all, for Astra. Her story is our story and will not end with this book, her pages set in a distant frozen backdrop, melting and dripping its impact into our subconscious for eternity, for good or bad. The fate of our ancestors can weigh heavily on our psyche, their stories awakening us in dreams, ancient silent whispers treading time and space with startling proximity, as though an uneven blend of heart-bursting pride and heart-breaking guilt is gifted in invisible packages in indefinable proportions. And so we are left with them, those words and thoughts, which can never explain the psychological inheritance passed down generations as unwittingly as dark brown eyes or heart disease.

Astra Sabondjian was my maternal grandmother. I want to build a statue to her memory, for all our memories. I see her now, classic, heroic, noble, carved as a Greek caryatid carrying the temple of her family on alabaster shoulders. Her face framed with a golden globe of shimmering light, her eyes tearless, as if just wiped dry, her expression determined and purposeful, gazing beyond unknown horizons. She stands there timeless, upright and dignified, elevated on a granite plinth, a scroll chiselled with intricate precision slipping from her right hand, the part visible messages revealing wisdom, understatement, strength and love, the invisible, hinting tragedy and self-sacrifice. The Venus of Willendorf, the Venus de Milo, the Athena of Greece, and the Astra of Erzeroum (Garin) united in eternal spirit, forever as one.

I need to tell this story because not to do so would be to deny her, deny me, and all of them. I ask Astra forgiveness for understanding something of the reluctant heroine. I know too that her life was given and not chosen, even though she lived it with unerring acceptance.

How could a young beautiful free spirit not have craved for more? I ask her now to allow me the insight to reveal the glimpse of secret desires, hidden through necessity, from them, from me, but most of all, from Astra.

My childhood memories of her are wrapped in black and white images, naïve and glossy, crinkled with time. Others are visual and sensual. I'm running up tall marble steps, listening to feet echoing loudly as I walk up the cool dark hallway, so wonderful to be home. Long hot days of summers in Venice, sipping luscious cherry syrups and gulping ice cold tea, straight from the fridge, her never ending supply kept in tall clear bottles, made daily for all of us, and for the gigantic rubber plant living out on the balcony. Astra only wore dark colours after 1922, simple elegance, in black or dark grey, although I did wonder how she may have looked in bright reds or yellows. She had a penchant for cream lace and white stark linen collars, her only indulgence to fashion frivolity. The deep mysteries of her huge mahogany wardrobe, her bespoke black velvet hats, the astrakhan collars, and hand embroidered silk dressing gowns, and one pair of embroidered slipper covers, too large for her feet, unworn by her husband. Steaming pot roasts on Sundays and birthdays, deep silver trays of potatoes or macaroni, hot from the oven, making me hungrier than I really was. Her round cherubic face, sweet and kissable, covered in white flour as she focused on her task, the matriarch of the kitchen, surrounded by her ancient scales and weights, the magic alchemist, conjuring up the inimitable "nené's cake." Tall white walls and ceilings, slippery marble floors, long white curtains spreading in the breeze, tall fluted vases from Murano spraying red gladioli perched high on the piano, ancient ivory combs, ornate Byzantine gold and silver icons, her intricately worked bone covered prayer book, always close. But what can a small child ask about all of this? "I would die for you," she would say when we pleased her, and even when we didn't, while so much went unsaid.

As children she fed us on an invisible diet of love and discipline in exact proportions. Nené Astra could convey approval or disapproval with an undetectable flick of the eye. Lightening beams sent effortlessly across rooms, penetrating our thoughts, to ensure our best behaviour. She knew her power and used it well, targeting with discretion and appropriateness. I can still sense that intangible force emanating from somewhere inside her, even now. I remember thinking her moments of quiet time meant more than silence. I can still feel the silky softness of her long white hair as my small hands led the comb gently down her back, almost to her waist. I would catch her deep blue eyes gazing back at her own reflection from the large gilt mirror in her bedroom while she sat, still and emotionless, pondering on the life she had lived. I saw her wiping tears in private corners, which she would try to conceal with her enigmatic smile whenever memories gave way to sorrows children must never see. So why did her presence command such overriding respect? I had questions then too, though none I could voice, only clues to a mystery of a life gone by.

We would share innocent passions at breakfast time as the tired overfed house still slept. She would reach deep into the large refrigerator looking for tasty delicacies left over from a party the night before. It was our special private ceremony of cold "mille foglie" cake, baby quince in syrup, or her famous aubergine immam bayldi, always better cold, her favourite and mine. It was then, as we ate off silver spoons and precious china plates, in moments of shared indulgence, with the child in her and me, united in innocent frivolity, that I wished years had not come between us. We would sit opposite each other, she dressed in sombre chic, me still in my nightdress, across a wide table, swallowing delicious mouthfuls in silent reverence. She would watch me eat my favourite things while I watched her beam down gracious benevolence as she yielded to rare physical senses. And as we finished, and others came in to break the spell, I would kiss her hand and leave the table, wondering if in some small way I had helped to replenish her needy soul.

Some sixty years before, and a thousand miles away, Astra Sabondjian was safe at home in her first world watching the Cossacks arrive on horseback from Moscow. Days of riding over narrow mountain paths packed with icy snow, fighting hammering winds and blinding blizzards to stay alive and fulfil their purpose, all in the name of beauty. Peproné Sabondjian, her mother, had told them glorious stories of the Great Czar and how he loved to give his family and friends beautiful things, no matter where they came from. Astra imagined him kind and generous and would have loved to thank him for filling their house with shiny precious treasures, even though they were destined for other people she was never to meet. The Baltadjians, on her mother's side, were famous jewellers with a renowned reputation. As a child, Astra felt honoured to know these gifts were worth the journey across high mountains but asked why they would make such a treacherous journey. "Can't they make them in Moscow Dédé?" "Yes, the Czar has very skilled craftsmen in his own workshop, but our designs are different; they're very ancient, they date back from the kings of Mesopotamia and emperors of Byzantium," replied her grandfather; and so the special importance of beauty never left her. She knew that no matter the weather, or how high the snow had settled, the Cossacks risked life and limb to reach her home in Erzeroum.

On hearing their stomping hooves, Astra would rush to catch them charging down the valley, getting louder, larger, more threatening, coming ever nearer, galloping at break neck speed towards her front door. When the Cossacks were at the gate, Astra could make out their black fur hats, their huge leather boots, and their thick crimson capes, tinged with sable, still swaying as the horses were pulled to a thunderous halt, snorting and shaking their steaming heads in their cobbled courtyard. Peeping from the frost-covered window a five-year-old girl, hidden behind lace curtains, would watch and could not forget this. The men would stay on their saddles, waiting for her uncles to bring out metal boxes of precious cargo, impatient to start their journey home. Then she watched them busy at their task, tightly strapping boxes onto fringed saddlebags, looping and twisting strong ropes in swift ceremonious style, while Peproné offered refreshments to riders and horses knowing they would soon be gone. A few words and nods exchanged, the Cossacks waved behind them as they turned to race away, through the gates, down the valley, disappearing off into the mountains, heading back for Moscow till next time. When the roads were very treacherous, Astra noticed the horses wore thick woollen socks over their hooves. "They help the horses keep their grip on the frozen mountain paths where many riders have perished by falling down the black ravines," said her mother, conjuring up terrifying images of doomed horses and riders with their crimson capes splayed over the precious gems, lying frozen somewhere deep in the earths crust for all time.

Some days when the snow reached the windows and the light hung heavy, Peproné would take the children down to the cellar. They could choose one box each, not knowing what treasure was hidden inside. Then they would slowly climb the stairs to their mothers' bedroom and sit closely on the bed, each guarding their precious package. As if in a ritual, they would remove the lids with reverent expectation, before sharing in each other's "opening" in turn. They would imagine the recipient and wonder whether the gift was for a birthday or name day or some other special feast, or whether it was a gift for some dutiful deed performed, or just simply because they were loved. On sunny days the lacy icicles on the windows shone beams across the room, lighting up the precious metals, cut rubies and diamonds. Bright eyes catching flashing prisms of colour, indelibly imprinting the magic and memory of the moment.

She would be sad at the passing of her extended family, for her, for them, and for all of us, now reachable only through their voices echoing from a dark and distant place. "Bring them back," she would say to summon up precious interwoven relationships and so bestow invisible layers of non-teachable wisdoms on our future children. Much more than success or material wealth, she would wish we too were blessed with the beginnings that instilled intellectual and spiritual identities that must last a lifetime.

She was born in Garin (Erzeroum) in the ancient Armenia of Asia Minor, which is no more. Their house was the tallest in the city, just to the left of the main market street in the centre of town, set in a deep valley protected by a haunting landscape, and it filled her young eyes with awe and wonder. She would stretch up on tiptoe and rub the frost from her window to look out over high mysterious snow capped peaks as they threw out moody shades of indigo at sunrise and sunset across her town. From her roof garden Astra could count hundreds of flat roof terraces joined together so people could walk across town when heavy snows blocked the city streets in mid-winter. Behind dark-coloured stone buildings with their tiny windows she could just make out the paths carved by two main mountain rivers just before they spilled into seven gushing streams, the source of pure running water, which harsh nature brought so abundantly into their lives. When the scorching sun melted ice whites into luscious greens, hundreds of birds swooped down to drink from tall cooling fountains while she ran around the garden in search of fallen feathers to add to her collection of neatly combed shimmering home made pens.

It was a grand and joyous house, filled with understated plenty and fine, noble people. They learned from large gilt leather bound books and played gentle music. They ate fine delicacies off lace tablecloths, using ornate silver cutlery handmade by their ancestors who they always remembered in their prayers. Constant streams of visitors were welcomed any time of the day or night: Cherished relatives, friends, moustachioed professors, lawyers, politicians, newspapermen, and the occasional prelate, none of whom would ever leave without at least a taste of something special brought out steaming hot from the kitchen. The formal and familiar were never addressed by first names, it was always "Baron" this or "Madame" that, even Astra's mother's closest friend was always "Mrs. Pigeon," her first name kept secret in unspoken respect, part of social etiquette of a time gone by.

Passionate after dinner debates started with the serving of brandy. Compliments on that night's food offerings followed with sated guests airing views on a myriad of issues, education, religion, law, often ending with national or world affairs. It was hard to sleep when voices seeped through walls and corridors, reaching secret hiding places under stairs, making their subliminal impact on young fresh ears. Astra and her siblings were often discovered wide-awake, eves dropping, to be then called in from hiding places to meet the guests. Sometimes they would be asked to perform some literary piece, recite a poem or sing a song, to a wave of spontaneous clapping, noisy laughter and much hair ruffling. Astra was seven years of age when she had already lost count of the times her hair had been ruffled, each appreciative hand tapping in an inner strength for what was to come. Some memories must last a lifetime.

Astra's parents were good people. When Peproné Baltadjian, fresh out of the Parisian College in Erzeroum, married Setrag Sabondjian in 1885 she had all the hopes of any young bride who had fallen in love with a man of principle. When Astra's father, Setrag, a young idealistic lawyer began his career in the legal offices of the local *millet*, under the direct auspices of the Ottoman government, he had already contrived his downfall. A man of unshakable honour and deeply offended by injustice, especially where money could not buy favour, Setrag soon began to make enemies. Thinking that justice favoured the brave, he would speak out daring to question official decisions, but still the rich became richer and the poor became poorer, but no one would ever change things. But Peproné and her family urged him on. "Don't work for them, work for yourself, we don't need the money," they said. So he worked for free, challenging officialdom on behalf of the deserving underdog.

And so Peproné loved him all the more, though sometimes she would tease him. "So what did your clients pay you with today?" she asked, slipping her fingers into his empty pockets. "Well you know what they said. They said, 'Thank you very much Mr. Sabondjian.'" "Oh did they indeed, well tell them you brought the 'thank you very much' home, put it on the table, but your children couldn't eat it." But they didn't need for more. It was easy to have principles if you could afford it, and luckily they could.

And so for a few years Setrag Sabondjian fought unfairness in society under a shadowy existence, right up till that morning. Setrag was climbing up the stairs to his office when a bullet pierced his back and ended his life just thirty years after it had begun, leaving his children to carry the torch. Astra remembered that black day. She was nearly eight years old. Five children now left fatherless looked to their mother for answers but there were none that she could give. Fear and silence permeated the house where French became the language of secret whispers. Peproné's father and brothers had excelled in languages at the famous Sanassarian College, and it helped spare the children for a while. There was no trial, no pretence, no justice, just the predictable government cover-up Setrag had fought so hard against and it spelt danger for them all. Accused by close association and moral affinity, they had no choice but to flee for their lives.

They would never return. Within two months of their escape, thousands of others were to be killed by the sword in what history now calls "the small massacres," small in that the numbers killed were in the thousands rather than millions. And so it had begun, the tragic fate of Armenians forced to die or leave their beloved homeland forever. Armenians called it Garin, now others call it Erzeroum. The Jewel City, crowned capital after a devastating earthquake destroyed the medieval capital city of Ani, six hundred years before. Armenia, the cradle of their civilization, a land with mythological dimensions, crossed by four rivers, home to the Garden of Eden, home to Mount Ararat, home to them for more than three thousand years, was ripped from them as a nation was sleeping. But this is not a political story. None of it was ever her war. This is the story of how someone can be born in the right place but in the wrong time. She was intelligent, beautiful and talented, a strategist and peacemaker, but above all Astra was a survivor who used everything at her magic fingertips, for her, for them, and for all of us.

Our secret dreams of ancestors wise and strong help to comfort our needy souls: our lives given, not chosen. As they left Erzeroum, they cried. Eyes looking back at well walked streets, leaving dear friends and their house on the hill. Walls and people, crumbling or dead, left behind, trying to understand the reasons. Strange what you are left with when all that filled life drips into a watery blur from your frozen cheeks. Peproné, her 5 children, her sisters, and mother went one way; the uncles went another, a family divided to safeguard their protection. Granddad Baltadjian had died three years earlier, wealthy and happy, of old age. It would not be a fate allowed many of his descendants.

In their panic to escape the sword, they ran down to the cellar, smashed open tall pots of gold and silver, poured what they could into pockets and velvet drawstring bags and fled for their lives. It was a sudden and hollow exodus, silent and final. Peproné clutched her youngest child Zevart, while the others pulled her skirts in panic. "We must walk in a line, the paths are narrow," she said stooping down to pick up a sharp piece of black obsidian vitreous rock, symbol of her ancient homeland with which she pierced her arm. The cut went deep but physical pain satisfied her heart knowing she was trailing her lifeblood where it belonged. It bled while they walked, through treacherous mountain roads, towards the distant seaport of Trebizond. Peproné pressed her veins as her arm hung down, forcing warm fresh blood to trickle onto icy snow, making sure part of her earthly being would be part of that sweet frozen earth for all time.

From Trebizond they took a boat to Smyrna, which in 1905 was still a safe Christian corner at the western most tip of the Ottoman Empire. Here Greeks, French, Italians, Turks, Americans and Armenians lived side by side albeit each within their own national quarters. It was a prosperous international city where education and culture were allowed some freedom of expression, at least for a while. The family moved into a house in the Armenian quarter, and soon felt able to absorb life as new immigrants. The theatre, wide avenues, shops, libraries and reading rooms helped to integrate the family whilst allowing them the freedom to maintain their national identity. At ten Astra had already learned it was best not to look back. Her family was forward thinking, and by the age of eleven she had started to embrace their new homeland as a positive experience in cultural cross-fertilization. She had heard her mother talk French with her uncles, Greek with the Greeks, and Turkish with the Turks, polyglots, all of them.

She often accompanied her uncles to the reading rooms where men and women talked earnestly about the changing philosophies of their time, about new progressive publications, and news from around the world, even when it did not touch them. Astra would sit and listen to her moral guardians, silently twirling her long blond curls while copying out pages of written text to improve her handwriting, but it did much more than that. She soon developed an ardent interest in discussions and her potential did not go unnoticed. At a local meeting at the American School, a lady governor persuaded Peproné that an American education would enrich her daughter's eager mind and offered Astra a free sponsorship at the American College. "I can't let my daughter walk the streets alone," said Peproné, worried about her safety. "She can stay as a border, everything will be paid for." Even this family who had bowed down reverently at the altar of learning for generations could not have known the importance that an American education would have for her, for them, and for all of us. Some years later, her ability to speak English like an American native would in a very literal way save their lives.

Chapter II

The Liberating Powers of a Formal Education

THE ground beneath the house seemed to quiver when Astra came home from college. No one expected her to just fit in as though she had never left, but three months away seemed to have changed her more each time. She never stopped chattering and bubbling with ideas whilst dripping an aura of increasing independence wherever she went. It scared her mother, not that her status as a dutiful daughter was ever in question, but her family could not help but notice that education seemed to agree a little too well with Astra. At times she sensed it and tried to moderate her enthusiasm, while noticing that her ideas were more accepted by the men rather than the women of the family, young or old. She had heard Aizemnig, her oldest sister whispering criticisms to her mother. "Astra is becoming too opinionated. Don't you think college is making her selfish? She'll never find a man to put up with her."

Astra remembered her sister's wedding day. At fifteen Aizemnig had seemed even to her not much more than a child and her husband-to-be, Karekin Ounanian was twenty-five years her senior. "How can she want to marry him?" she asked herself while her sister rolled large blue glass marbles along the roof of their house in Erzeroum. She had stood and watched her sister wearing her medieval red velvet wedding dress pulled up over her knees and her lace-wedding veil pushed back over her head. "Why were they marrying her off?" she wondered. Already Astra had became aware of a strange intellectual conflict with tradition. "She's still a child," she thought, as she listened to the guests gathering downstairs. Then the bishop became impatient and the bride was nowhere to be seen. Astra knew where she was. She slipped upstairs to join Aizemnig, to tell her to escape, or to carry on playing marbles, to sing more songs, anything to keep her sister with her for a few more years. Then their eyes met and Aizemnig stopped singing. She slipped the marbles into her lace cuffs and skipped past her down the stairs. Astra could not stop her and that day Aizemnig married Karekin Ounanian—rich, benevolent and impotent. Whether it was a gift or a burden, Astra began to realize she had an ability to glimpse into the future, but intuition came at a price, so she decided it was best for everyone to keep it secret.

Her mother and grandmother were classic examples of the old order. Armenian girls were educated and moulded for their future destiny as respectful wives and mothers, ultimately aspiring to the role of matriarch. It had worked so well for them all. An honourable ambition based on the social structure she knew and respected and, till then, had never questioned. She had never doubted the appropriateness of the self-sacrifice. But it was a forced destiny, and she hated that. She dreamed of shedding that protective maternal skin and one day break out of that imprinted emotional pattern, for good or bad.

Astra's uncles took it in turns to accompany her home for the Easter and Christmas holidays. Her heavy books would keep slipping from her icy fingers but she would always insist on carrying them herself, her precious books. A few streets from home, she would start to feel guilty. Of course she had missed them, but she knew they would have missed her more, but it didn't mean she didn't love them. Her homecoming was a ritual they all shared. Her youngest sister Zevart was always first to the door, quickly followed by her mother. Astra would squeeze them till her hands went numb, letting the flow of emotion fill the space of words. Seeing Zevart growing lovelier each time took her breath away. Then her brothers would rush down into the living room, their arms outstretched, saying her name again and again. Hagop, wise Hagop, the dad of the family now, would not be sure whether she was too grown-up for kisses, so she would kiss him first. Then she would see her baby brother Haroutioun, with dark brown almond eyes waiting for his turn in the pecking order. Aizemnig and her husband would join the celebrations later but Astra felt a distance growing between them and she knew why. Her sister believed in the status quo, and there she was, this free spirit, back home to challenge everything her own life stood for. At supper Astra would sit in her usual place, next to Aizemnig, everyone pretending it was like she had never left it, but she had. Reaching for her sister's hand Astra sensed anger in those large green eyes and each time it was becoming more apparent. This was not the time to update them on her term's academic achievements. She had been awarded gold prizes for English literature and chemistry. The Principal had presented her with a medal for her solo piece at the organ recital at the Christmas concert, and she had captained the inter-college championship basketball team. "I'll tell Mama later," she thought, "when it's just us." Her sister's love meant more to her.

Her heady college days of American independence, as she started to call them, made her resent terrible restrictions forced upon young women in the Smyrna of 1908. Girls were never to walk alone, anywhere or any time. She saw it as a terrible infringement of liberty and unnecessarily over protective. "Horrific dangers are lurking around every corner, Astra. So many young girls just disappear, even when they're just popping out to visit their neighbours," her mother had warned them so many times. Then one day, outside her house, she caught sight of his evil eyes and her very soul shivered in the warm morning sunshine. The proof she never expected to see was staring right at her, holding the evidence of unspeakable acts committed against young girls. The chilling image never left her. He peered shamelessly, assessing a potential addition to his gruesome collection. Astra sensed his evil trying to grab her sickened heart. Frozen to the spot, she watched his gnarled filthy fingers playing with the evidence; a long string of worry beads threaded from end to end with the dried nipples of young victims who had fallen prey to his deranged power and savage sword. Showing no reaction, she walked backwards inside, and slammed the door to shut him out, but his dark satanic presence seemed to follow her inside. That sinister smile, those perverse eyes, the imagined deeds, which preceded that piece of macabre history flicking through his hands, left memories to last a lifetime.

Late that night she heard her mother still busy in the kitchen. She wanted to run down to unburden her heart and tell her what she had seen. She prayed for the souls of the girls who had seen his face and felt those gnarled fingers devour their young bodies before they died. "Oh God please let it have been quick," she prayed. She sat on the stairs craving her mother's loving arms to cocoon her from the cruel world outside, but time and dark silence made her reconsider, "No, I can't tell her, it will only make her worry more." As her terror turned to seething anger she felt a powerful urge to be close to little Zevart. She sat by her sister, watching her sleep, passing protective energies to permeate her dreams. Years later she would try to dismiss it as a natural reaction, refusing to believe it was her prophetic senses at work. "Why?" she asked herself, taking her turn behind millions before her who had all asked that same primordial question, never finding the answer.

Although Astra had never met Miss Jennings, she had developed a real affection for her benefactor and long distance soul mate. Florence Jennings had returned to America in 1907 but kept an active involvement in Astra's progress from afar through a flamboyant correspondence which had developed between them. Florence Jennings saw herself as a woman with a mission; a shining light in the dawn of female suffrage, an international missionary for social change, and her ideas were rare music to her protégé's ears. The influences on Astra had started in childhood while listening to her father's idealism, hidden behind the living room door, when they thought she was tucked up in bed. "He was a social philanthropist born into a savage society" was how she had described him in her letter, and proudly read it out to her mother before sealing the envelope. Astra had often asked her mother about the background to her father's murder. Her mother had explained it with some reservation; history had a nasty way of repeating itself. After all, it was a mother's job to protect her children, but she stopped short of burying the truth. They had a right to know what type of society they were living in. She had taught her children to believe in equality, but an unjust world has its favourites. "Your father believed in justice regardless of nationality, wealth or position. We all do so, but the problem was he shouted it from the roof tops." Her daughter needed to face the fact that Miss Jennings' ideas were too radical, even dangerous, and a million light-years from the real lives of women in the Ottoman Empire.

Peproné had started to dread the letters from America but would hand them over to Astra against her better judgment. She had almost thrown them into the fire so many times, but could never do it; they were her daughter's letters after all. Some were packets rather than letters, large and mysterious, tied up with thick rope and sealed tightly with red wax, probably to keep their secrets hidden from her, and those were the ones that worried her most. Peproné guessed that they contained political or feminist articles and those tempting photographs of life in the New World, and mostly she was right. Astra would read them in her room, late at night, censoring any articles, which her mother might find too extreme. Then she catalogued them before placing them into a large wooden box under her bed. Next morning she would bring down the photographs hoping to stir some of the same passion in her. "Mama, you must agree America does look exciting. It's budding with newness and hope," she said, quoting her benefactor. "Maybe we could go there one day. I've heard of whole families emigrating." It was her dream. She had never mentioned that Miss Jennings had already invited her to stay in Boston. "My mother needs me here," she had written, politely declining the offer. So while they tucked into fried egg and cheese, Astra drooled over impossibly tall white buildings, wide sunny avenues, and the vast panelled meeting rooms from where Miss Jennings always smiled back benignly. "Mama, it looks so much brighter than it does here. I wonder why?" Peproné blamed the camera. "It's the type of film they use." But the clothes were nicer, and the hats; her mother had to agree with that. Astra reflected that for all her political fervour, her benefactor took great delight in wearing the most elaborate of outfits. "Astra, how does such a busy political activist find the time for so much shopping?" asked Peproné. "It's important to wear the latest fashions if your ideas are forward thinking, and anyway you always say it cheers you up when people look nice." "It's not like her to be on the defensive," thought her mother.

She and her people had always appreciated aesthetics in any form; the creative arts had been in their blood for centuries. By the age of fifteen Astra had already grown into a young woman who dripped classical elegance with effortless ease. Diminutively statuesque, she was blessed with a long neck, straight back and shoulders, a heart shaped face, spellbinding almond shaped blue eyes, a full shapely mouth, a strong neat nose, immaculate fair skin, and long flaxen flowing hair down to her waist. After basketball games her college team friends would sit discussing future match tactics while taking it in turn to brush her hair into different styles, but she preferred to pull it back into a neat plait above her head to make life easy. Her looks were not something she considered greatly. Admittedly she was pleased that she needed the minimum of maintenance to look presentable but it was completely unimportant in the scale of things, and even irritating at times. "We don't have to read your coffee cup to see you'll find a rich husband," her nosey neighbours had said before whispering something about her lips being so red she must be wearing rouge. It was nothing less than a scourge on her honour; no self-respecting young woman should be wearing face-enhancing products at sixteen. Smiling knowingly at her mother, she ran on ahead, took out a lace handkerchief and rubbed her lips and cheeks right there in front of them. "I'm not looking for a husband! Now please stop gossiping about me," she said holding up the handkerchief, which showed no trace of colour. The neighbours laughed nervously, fumbled a few shallow compliments and made their excuses to rush on while mother and daughter strolled on behind, smiling smiles of the vindicated. Astra never wore make-up, not even on her wedding day.

Mother and daughter shared the closest of bonds. Astra was in many ways Peproné's confidant but not all problems were for sharing. Her sister, now married for seven years was still childless, and all the money her husband lavished on her and her family meant nothing to her. She was desperately unhappy. She resented Astra's freedom. She resented her childlessness. "How could you have made me marry him?" Aizemnig's voice spat out venom. Astra never did witness the true force of her despair as she kept her outbursts for whenever Astra was away. "Mama, I didn't chose Karekin, you did, and now look at my life!" It was true; Aizemnig had seen her husband's face for the first time at the altar. Peproné tried to remember the reasons. Karekin was a good man, from a respectable wealthy family, but he was 25 years her senior, and those were difficult days. She was still in mourning for her husband, their future was uncertain, and her family had been used to plenty—so Peproné had looked to financial security as her way of putting things right.

Now, with hindsight, she was full of remorse and no words of comfort could ever undo her eldest daughters' fate. She wondered if her childlessness was a curse for the sins of the mother. So Peproné took to going to church every day to kneel before the Virgin Mary. "Forgive me, I am not a greedy person, I did it for them all," she would say, lighting candle after candle, hoping for a miracle. She looked to the heavens promising solemn oaths, denying herself the smallest indulgences in an effort to make amends, but nothing changed. Still, her religious belief remained unshakable. Powerful strands of Christianity, woven tightly with sacred thread, could never fray, but shone through ever more brightly with the blinding light of wisdom gained too late, even as emotional daggers kept stabbing at her faith.

In 1911 Astra was in her last term. Five years at American College had helped her develop into an independent and accomplished young woman. No one could deny that fact, and she had Miss Jennings to thank for it all. Before packing her case and collecting her certificates, she wrote a heartfelt letter to her benefactor. She listed her achievements to share them with her. She ended the letter with words of genuine gratitude. She waited till the last paragraph before promising to visit Boston one day, before too long, but it was really more a wish than a promise. "I will never be able to repay you," she had written, but Miss Jennings had never looked at it that way. For her it was a privilege to educate a bright young mind. For her the rewards would come later and so far her protégé had surpassed all expectations. Happy college days ended on the 26th of July, two days before Astra's seventeenth birthday, when it suddenly struck her: what now? Most of her friends were going home to far-flung parts of the Ottoman Empire; she wouldn't see them again, except for Anoushka, who was as dark and sultry as Astra was fair and dynamic. Anoushka lived close by, but then neither girl had any idea of how their lives would soon be ripped apart.

Astra returned home, laden with certificates and uncertainties about the future, as Peproné fussed about her daughter, relieved and delighted that it would be her last college homecoming. Sweet Zevart had prepared for her return in spectacular fashion. When Astra took her case upstairs she stood at the bedroom door stunned and speechless. The room had been turned into a fantasy of red and white flowers and ribbons, bows and swirls swayed in the warm summer breeze, and on her bed lay a gorgeous powder blue silk evening dress. She recognized the fabric immediately from that time when her mother had taken her to visit Satenig's famous fashion house by the main port. Satenig and Peproné were old friends, both widowed at the hands of cruelty, that time in Erzeroum. Next evening Astra wore the dress at her welcome home party. It all seemed so perfect except that her senses were telling her otherwise. As the happy gathering stood clapping a few friends performing a folk dance around the living room, she sensed an ominous atmosphere brewing in the corner. Pinpointing her focus, she was just in hearing range, "Be quiet, don't start, not now please Aizemnig! Did Hagop really say that? No, of course she's not going to America!" Up till then it had seemed almost possible, why not university in Boston? But she knew her sister would never approve, so her mother would have no peace. Her mother's love meant more to her.

But they did talk about her future that summer. Her brother Hagop was always the giver of good advice, but this time she knew she could not take it, and he understood why. It was her moral conscience winning over desire. So she said she would learn to cook complicated Armenian specialities passed down for generations, and help her mother around the house. She wanted to spend more time with Haroutioun and Zevart to teach them English. It was beginning to sound like the life of a governess. "No Hagop, going to university in America is really out of the question. Aizemnig is so against it and I won't put Mama through it. She's had enough telling-offs from our big sister. I'll stay home for a while, but who knows, maybe one day, it's not running away!" But her brother had another idea. "You know Astra, if you're not going to university then why not do some research work for the newspaper I work for? We do need someone to scan British and American papers." Her eyes lit up. "I'll bring everything here so you can work from the house." "I would love to," she said jumping up to kiss him. "So then it's settled!" Hagop was the first journalist in their family but he would not be the last.

Hagop knew that marriage was the last thing on his sister's mind. Since leaving college potential husbands had been buzzing like bees around a honey pot. She was at that marriageable age but with no father around suitors had to approach him, and so far he had warded them off, following her instruction to the letter. He resented family pressures that had caused her to set aside important personal goals and was not about to add to her problems. They had a rare affinity, which took them talking late into the night, chattering away about the new concepts of morality, the changing social order, and ways to liberate individuals trapped by forces of convention. They visited reading rooms and took their place around tea tables and led debates where Astra could offer herself up as a living, breathing example of how moral obligation can conflict with individual desires. She had developed her confident style at the College Debating Society, staying calm even when it was personal, genuinely listening to opposing views, not jumping in, waiting for the heat to drop before replying with alternative opinions and opposing facts, always making herself hold back on passion, even though she was passionate about almost everything. Humanitarianism, equality for the masses, emancipation of women, ending racial persecution and the glib unfairness in the Ottoman Empire stirred her beyond words. She was always extra vigilant never to be seen as a table slammer. But these were things she had felt on her own skin, as a daughter, as a woman, and as an Armenian. Even though fervour was justified, this was definitely not the place to express it. You never knew who might be listening.

A network of auditoriums had started springing up around the *millets*. Smyrna, a cosmopolitan town, appeared to accept the need for people to come together to try to settle local issues. Later they developed into lively forums for raising national awareness and open political debate. They reached their peak between 1908 and 1914, at the dawn of a new era, for good or bad. They were also social venues, an opportunity to meet family and friends and to listen to well-known intellectual orators of the day. Congeniality and good food precariously masked the underlying life and death agendas. Sunday evenings always had the best turn out, when discussions were liveliest, and in the main still innocuous. But soon the atmosphere began to shift, people started getting angrier as daily issues became more serious. A dangerous unease had started to affect non-Muslim minorities. The repressed wave of nationalism, which had started its ripples in Europe, was about to lash out with devastating violence on the shores of Asia Minor.

Astra kept her promise. She learned to cook and taught English to her little brother and sister, even resorting to bribery to keep their attention during lessons by keeping a large tin of sweets by her at all times as reward for genuine interest. She kept the lessons short, believing education must come from the heart. Haroutioun was usually the first to drift into glazed oblivion, preferring to fantasize about becoming a famous hero before falling asleep. "Alright, that's enough for today," she'd say, giving her little sister the nod she was waiting for. Instantly Zevart would rush out to pick flowers or to draw tiny sketches of the birds in the garden. Birds held a special place in all their hearts. Peproné had given over much of their garden to a huge aviary. It reminded her of her beloved Garin. Garin, the ornithologists' paradise, home to 170 types of birds, and home to memories of her young husband running across those vast plains trying to catch them as she stood mesmerized at the sheer numbers and varieties flying between mountain peaks in the distance; an iridescent kaleidoscope, gliding a myriad of colours into a dusky horizon.

Astra adored pomegranates and they grew in abundance in their back garden. She would sit with Zevart and teach her how to open the tough skin and peel each segment with delicate precision so as not to drop even one seed to the ground. The peeling of the sacred pomegranate, symbol of fertility, had become a real sport amongst the young girls of Smyrna. She held the local title, testament to her dexterity rather than practice: nimble fingers, and a sharp brain. Juicy crimson fruit, cherished friends and sweet Zevart, whose life was to be cut down, like the flowers in her hair. Sweet frivolous memories, unforgettable for their very insignificance, stored in her bank of images, to use again and again, as powerful emotional antidotes from the venom that life was to spit at her.

Needlework was a million miles from her dream career but it had been Aizemnig's idea, and her mother seemed to agree. "It's always a useful skill to have, especially for you. You love nice clothes," said her sister. That part was true, so she agreed to the idea as a temporary obligation, as peace keeper and dutiful daughter. Aizemnig had stepped into the role of careers' adviser at one of her many dress fittings at Satenig's atelier, and suddenly it was arranged. "I can only do two days a week," she said, reminding them about her work for Hagop, and the English teaching, "but I will try to enjoy it," she added. Astra was heart and soul. She needed to enjoy whatever she did.

From the moment she stepped into Satenig's workroom a powerful surge of recognition sent vivid sensory flashbacks of her uncle's workshop in Erzeroum. The twinkling colours, the satins, the velvets, the silk taffetas all draped loosely across chairs and long tables, the rows of small brown boxes with open lids showing gold, silver, and mother of pearl buttons. Large vases of sequins caught the light as she walked past. She bent down to examine the tiny stitches of a half-finished dress, impressed by the talent, which put them there. It was Sunday and the girls were not at work. Even with all of this the room felt empty and silence helped her recall every detail. The Cossacks would have waited in the courtyard, on steaming horses, before knocking at the door of the empty house. Her mother had dragged her from her bed to rush down to the jewel-studded workroom and they grabbed whatever they could, but most of it was left on long tables never to be finished.

She soon settled into a balanced working week of sewing, teaching, cooking and journalistic reviews. Hagop made good use of her translations. They gave a global picture in contrast to what was being printed in the Empire where everyone knew censorship was rife. On Sundays her mother would insist on everyone going to church. Astra always went, although for her the temple of God was in her heart, but it was more than that. She felt uneasy testing religious intolerances of her Muslim neighbours. Foreign newspapers reported unrest brewing in all corners of the Ottoman Empire. Thousands were dying and unfair taxes were crippling the living. They said religious divisions and ethnic fervour were to blame. The papers were really depressing so she would rush through these stories to concentrate on less distressing news. There were plenty of other things to translate, articles on dynamic women writers, new discoveries, education, social change, but it was all happening somewhere else and that upset her.

Four months later Hagop had started to question his decision. His worries were well founded, not everyone could read about daily horrors and report on them without being affected; some souls were too sensitive. Astra found that reading about her compatriots in the world press was pulling too harshly at her heart strings. Her nightmares were so vivid they were waking up the household. Zevart was closest so it was up to her to shake her free from night terrors. Hagop felt responsible. "Look, you know what the press is like. They love to exaggerate. Lots of these stories are just sensationalism," but she knew they weren't. "Hagop, thanks for trying, but please don't use censorship on me, I'm not some delicate little flower." But she was. Her visions sapped her strength though she could never tell them what she saw. It felt like a prophecy; half dead emaciated bodies filing past human remains somewhere in a desolate forgotten desert.

Her days at the atelier became a welcome escape from a brutal world, not that the work was easy. Some clients were impossible to please. It came as a real revelation that the richer they were, the less willing they were to pay for hard work, often demanding complete alterations from the original design, and it was no use arguing. Satenig would curse silently under her breath as she handed a dress back to her girls for remodelling. But Astra felt surprisingly at home in the hustle and bustle of a busy workroom. Some girls, from rich families themselves, came to learn lace making and fine sewing skills. It was a type of creative finishing school. They reminded her of a happy young family where there was always time to laugh and share secrets. They would pass idle comments on the clients, about their funny shapes or affected mannerisms and laughed so much that their stomachs nearly burst. It was harmless fun, which Satenig would try to curb by the occasional shouting spree, but Astra caught her looking out of the window quietly laughing with them nearly every time. "How strange my life is," she reflected. "One day I'm reading and writing about death and destruction, and the next I'm sewing beautiful dresses, and both seem just as important!" She needed the diversity and realized she actually quite liked sewing, particularly pattern cutting, and was surprised to find she was exceptionally good at it.

Chapter III

The Merging Forces of Destiny

BY 1912 Setrag Tokadjian had a growing reputation. Aged twenty-four he was already an outstanding orator, writer and political commentator. He was a star speaker at the forums around town and Astra had seen him, from a distance. Hagop had met him on a number of occasions through journalistic contacts, originally wary of his motives having heard something of his past. Setrag Tokadjian had been labelled a revolutionary at the young age of seventeen but lately people had started to believe his motives were justified. He and his brothers had put a bomb in the Ottoman Bank in Smyrna. It was set off in the early hours of a Sunday morning in 1905, when the offices were closed. No one was hurt. Setrag was part of a band of young passionate brothers, driven to act by nationalistic despair, with only one aim in mind, to draw world attention onto an abandoned stage. Thousands of their compatriots, family members and friends had been the victims of bloody massacres since the 1880s and the government had not only turned a blind eye, it now seemed they were implicated. Central government was adding to the cruelty in the form of unfair taxes and crippling social policies. Armenians, who had been known as the faithful *millet* began to feel abandoned and alone. Then, when thousands more were massacred in their hometown of Erzeroum, enough was enough. The Tokadjian brothers were moved to action. Astra's brother Hagop Sabondjian had begun to feel a strange affinity with Setrag Tokadjian. They were both journalists, they were both from Erzeroum, and both their families had been forced to migrate west to Smyrna for the same reasons. He liked the name Setrag. It was an honest name, it was his fathers' name.

Almost immediately after the bomb incident, fingers of blame were pointed at the transparent young brothers, so they fled to America, which offered a hand of sympathy to freedom fighters still wet behind the ears. Setrag settled in Boston and started his journalistic career writing for *Hairenik Daily*. He was young but an exceptional scholar, mature for his years and extremely well read. Like Peproné's brothers, Setrag had been educated at the famous Sanassarian College. He was born into a modest family but Setrag had also impressed a rich benefactor at a young age. At sixteen he had written plays and had them performed and soon started his own theatre company called the Adam Players who forwarded all profits to help orphans from Erzeroum achieve a good education. He was well versed in the classics, world literature, ancient and modern philosophies and world politics. His flamboyant speeches impressed audiences, even though many of them were not fully able to grasp his intellectual nuances. He was well-travelled, well read, and could speak persuasively on local, national and world issues. People had started to queue to ensure they found good seats at the forums whenever his name was on the guest speaker list.

One Sunday evening Astra sat with her brother Hagop analysing his delivery. She was intrigued by his style. She followed his well-polished nails wrapped tightly around a batch of speech notes, as his knuckles grew whiter with conviction. She had to admit he had something, which drew her interest. Glancing around the auditorium she saw the audience was gripped; rows of eager listeners, wide-eyed, affirming, nodding; the crowd tangibly in his frame. She sat back and observed him play to the crowd as he pitched his voice to maximum affect, at times decisive and animated, interspaced with deliberate pauses, then continuing at a slower more deliberate pace as his tone became more gentle and reflective. She noted an unusual air of authority in one so young, considering his powers of persuasion before reviewing his choice of outfit. "What is it with these radical reformers that they dress like they're going to a fancy dress party!" He wore a red and green satin waistcoat and matching bow tie tied round a dazzlingly white upturned collar. "Somewhat overdressed," she thought, quickly dismissing the parallel with her benefactor.

They were sipping tea at the interval. "He's so knowledgeable and committed," said Hagop full of admiration. But Astra offered a different perspective. "Of course we're bound to agree with most of what he says. He is preaching to the converted. I admit he is impressive, fluent and confident, you could even say he's unconventionally handsome, even though his flamboyant dress sense and over waxed moustache do detract somewhat from his credibility." As far as she was concerned it all seemed a bit too easy. "I wonder if he thinks good looking people have an easier time in life?" But she did agree with him. Like her, he was an ardent socialist and humanitarian; like her, he saw education as a true liberator. "I agree that for a man who is not particularly large in stature he does exude an awesome power." Setrag had made an impression. His parents, Anna and Krikor Tokadjian had been sitting in the front row, glowing with pride, entranced if somewhat bemused. They were simple peasant folk, who somehow, through the miracle of genetics, had managed to produce four exceptional sons, and Setrag was their shining light.

His newspaper career had started very early. By the time Setrag had left Boston he was already the assistant editor on *Hairenik Daily,* a newspaper with an international circulation. Astra had read some of his articles. 1908 seemed to be the dawn of a new era of liberation for minorities in the Empire, and with electoral reforms and promises of a fairer government—and with the bombing incident all but forgotten—the brothers headed back home to Smyrna. They had saved every penny for three years hoping for such an opportunity and could afford to start up a bookshop in a prime location near the port. Within a year Setrag had started his own newspaper right next door. He cleared a large empty depot at the back, swept up filthy wood shavings, washed the floor and walls, found some desks, three old typewriters and a second hand printing press. Soon he was in a position to employ a printer and distributor. For two years Setrag hardly slept, running the publishing house almost single-handedly. By 1911 his reputation as an orator had helped sales rocket through the roof. He called his newspaper *Ashkhadank* (Work), his synonym for life. Within a year, acclaimed journalists and avid readers were upping the circulation, hooked by its broad range of topics, it's honest reporting, its international comparisons, and Setrag's incisive editorials. A young visionary was in the process of capturing hearts and minds everywhere, Astra's included.

Next Sunday was Easter, the most important day in the Armenian religious calendar, and everyone spent it in the same way;

going to church in the morning, sharing massive amounts of food with family and friends, and everyone and everything looking perfect. Astra pulled her hair off her face and tied it tightly behind her head and slipped a few long pins to hold it in place. Then she went downstairs and put water and tea in the samovar. There was a lot to do before two o'clock. Mass started at eleven but before that the house had to be spotless and the table ready. "I should wake Zevart to pick the flowers and decorate the napkins," she thought. It was seven o'clock and Hagop had already left for the bakery to order bread, cakes, pastries, and two large legs of roast lamb and she could almost smell it. They would pick them on the way home from church as a well deserved reward for forty days of strict fasting.

Astra loved Easter mass. The church would be decorated with white and cream flowers, the children were dressed in their new spring clothes and the weather gave promise for more sunny days to come. The choir sat close, singing melodies in the minor key which never failed to move her to tears, though she couldn't say why. After two hours, when the mass finally ended, a hungry congregation would spill out into the bright sunshine, while taking deep breaths to clear their mouths from the pungent smell of frankincense still in their lungs. Then everyone would burst into convivial chatter, kissing and hugging and shaking hands in a spontaneous release from the reverent worship they had shared.

Mother and daughter had been starving while preparing mouthwatering delicacies the night before, but no one ate anything till after mass. Astra had picked out best serving dishes and lined them up in order on the kitchen table ready for filling. All that was left to do was to cook two large metal trays of potatoes and macaroni in the oven. Zevart had spent hours decorating eggs, painting them with tiny flowers and birds while her mother dyed twenty with dried red onion skins. "We can start with the red ones first, Zevart's are too pretty to smash," she called to her mother. Gotch-gotch was the first thing they did when they came home from church. Taking an egg, Peproné would wrap her fingers around it and tap the top of her egg onto the top of the egg of her challenger. They would tap each other's in turn and whoever was left with an unbroken egg would win a prize, and the promise of a lucky year to come.

With the house gleaming, it just left the windows to be done. Astra stood up on a chair and started wiping the tall panes left to right with an old copy of *Ashkhadank* dipped in water vinegar. She swirled her arms in rigorous rotation, until the glass sparkled. Balanced on the chair in her dressing gown with sweat dripping from her forehead and with her hair dragged loose, she had a strange feeling someone was watching. She stopped and peered into the street; there was someone, just a few feet away and he was smiling right at her. She jumped down and drew the curtains tight. Soggy clumps of newspaper dropped from her hand while she summoned up her powers of recognition. "Oh my God, I know that face, it's Setrag Tokadjian, and I look such a fright." But he didn't agree. He had never met her, nor knew her name but in a street like any other, an angel had lifted his eyes and placed them on her heart. That was it, love at first sight. He had no idea how long he had been standing there gazing at her face, but he didn't care about the rights and wrongs of social etiquette. He would quite happily have stood and stared at her for hours without ever needing any formal introduction.

Hagop Sabondjian was almost back home when he noticed a young man wavering outside his house. He recognized him immediately and watched as Setrag peered over his shoulder as though saying goodbye to someone, but the street was empty. "Good morning Setrag, you're out early," "I'm just off to put in our order at the baker," "Well you'd better hurry, they're so busy they're running out of lamb." Setrag watched Hagop climb the stairs of that very house. "She must be his sister! The Gods are really smiling on me today," he mused. This was his chance. "Hagop we really must meet up soon and sign you up as a formal Dashnag party member," said Setrag, not really thinking about politics for once. "Yes, and the sooner the better. Would you like to come to dinner tomorrow?" asked Hagop. Setrag opened his tiny pocket diary, pretending to check for conflicting commitments. "Yes, that's fine. I'll look forward to it, about eight o'clock?"

Setrag knew his family would be getting ready for church but he had an urge to chase the wind down the wide beach road and dive into cooling ice-cold water. He was a strong swimmer and within minutes was a long way from the shore. As he surfaced for air he was euphoric. His eyes searched for the house where he would sit by her at dinner and hear her speak about whatever she spoke about; he didn't care, whatever it would be, it would be the sweetest sound in the world. Setrag had fallen in love with a woman he had not yet met, but somehow it seemed the most natural thing in the world, so he felt no need to ask himself how or why. Then he swam back to the shore, stumbled into his clothes and ran home. As he turned the key he saw his mother crying at the window. Anna always worried when her boys were late, even a few minutes would send her heart thumping. The same scene always came back to her; that last kiss she had placed on the cheek of her first born son, still damp as the soldiers marched him away, with others like him, to their deaths in the mountains of Erzeroum. How could she ever forget it when her precious Setrag had become so famous for speaking out and in full view of the authorities? She thanked God every time he came home.

The Tokadjians were late for church. As Anna pushed her way through to light a candle for her dead son, Setrag sensed vibrations drawing him forwards well before seeing her sitting close to the front between two well-dressed children. She was too far away for his liking but he studied her strong profile, as her mouth moved silently, deliciously between them. Zevart and Haroutioun were being annoyingly curious that day. "Sshhh, keep your voices down," she said between whispering explanations of an ancient liturgy as mystical rituals of the first Christian nation were being performed within touching distance. Then, as the velvet purple curtains swished across, separating the altar from the congregation, she sensed someone calling out to her. She turned round to see, but the church was packed with large brimmed hats and shiny balding heads. Then, as a gentle breeze stroked her neck and a powerful surge of adrenaline pumped through her veins, she somehow knew he was there.

Setrag pushed his way through a throbbing church courtyard saying, "Hello Hagop, we meet twice in one day!" Astra wondered what was coming next, something about cleaning windows perhaps. "Very pleased to meet you," he said, desperate to touch her hand for the first time. "May I introduce you to Setrag Tokadjian? He's joining us for dinner tomorrow," said Hagop with a hint of hero worship, which Zevart picked up on. "Mama is he famous?"

"Apparently he is, but there's more to it than just that if you ask me," she said. Peproné sensed cupid's arrow following Astra all the way home.

Setrag was a high-ranking member of the Armenian Dashnag party, a fast growing political federation with strong socialist ideals based firmly on the needs of the people. Hagop and Setrag had often talked politics and Setrag had recognized his potential well before the window-cleaning incident. The Dashnag party believed in political compromise as a way of promoting a fairer judicial system. They saw it as the only way to stop Armenians being massacred at worst or being stripped of their livelihood at best, all with the obvious connivance of the Ottoman government. In 1909 the Dashnags had signed a treaty with the Young Turks, which to some degree helped counter the view that Armenians were pushing for national independence outside the Empire. Setrag's party believed passionately that trust and fairer laws would make way for an autonomous Armenia within it, hoping that political consolidation would demonstrate that at least one non-Turkish group in the empire was prepared to support them. Setrag the idealistic patriot preferred to fight for justice with the pen and reason. Even when blood dripped through the pages, he would never accept the sword was mightier than the pen.

For all his accomplishments Setrag was very inexperienced when it came to matters of the heart. By ten thirty the next evening, he had sat opposite the girl of his dreams, made her blood boil for all the wrong reasons and had already left with her brother, apparently for the Dashnag party offices. Peproné said nothing, remembering her dead husband Setrag and his well-meaning ideals. "Maybe it's something in the name," she wondered. Astra couldn't keep quiet any longer. "What was he thinking of, dragging Hagop out to his beloved party offices at this time of night! Why couldn't they have gone tomorrow? Setrag Tokadjian is obviously used to having everything his own way." She would normally have started clearing up plates by then, but she was still seething. "Look, he hardly touched his food and after all your hard work! All I can say is he's definitely better from a distance." Then she needed to be busy and rushed in and out of the kitchen mumbling a tirade of accusations ranging from ingratitude to chauvinism. Peproné knew better. "I thought he seemed very pleasant, if a little shy perhaps." "Shy? Him? Never! He wasn't interested in a word I had to say. Did you notice his demeanour when I was talking about women's rights? He didn't even have the decency to look at me! He behaved just like those ignorant men in the reading rooms who think a woman's place is in the home. I don't know what was more annoying, his silly moustache or his pompous manner!" But Peproné, the wise romantic, knew nothing else could possibly have made her daughter become so angry with a man she had just met, except for one thing. For good or bad, she knew Astra was falling in love.

Setrag had never been in love before and sitting so close to her had tumbled his senses into turmoil and he knew he had made the worst possible impression. The minute she had sat down and looked at him with those captivating eyes he had an urge to declare his love right there and then. But instead he looked at the floor, at her mother, at her brother, at the cream lace tablecloth till the pattern began to blur his vision and made him nauseous. He looked everywhere except at her. He had decided to lean back to create more distance between them when suddenly he caught his own glazed expression in the mirror. It was then he contrived a reason to escape. Before they reached the party offices Setrag decided to come clean. "Hagop, your sister seems to have had a devastating effect on me. I want to apologize for my rudeness, I behaved like an idiot." Hagop wondered what on earth he meant. "I saw her for the first time on Sunday, when she was cleaning the windows and something unbelievable happened to me. I can't explain it any better than this. I fell in love with her and ask your permission to marry her." Hagop kept walking. "Setrag, I'm not the one to have to give you permission. Weren't we just listening to her views on the ethical wrongs of arranged marriages? Astra will make her own decisions about who or when she marries, but perhaps in time you could ask her yourself." Setrag, the impatient lovesick editor found it hard to sleep that night, wondering how one woman could shake his equilibrium when he was completely in control with huge crowds hanging on his every word.

When something is meant to be, the forces of nature seem to converge. Satenig had known Anna Tokadjian since childhood. She had been with her at the birth of her children, way back in Erzeroum. She was there when Setrag had slipped into the world, his eager eyes already wide as his hungry mouth searched its first suckle. Satenig had never had children, but had "adopted" Setrag as her own. She had formed an instant bond with this chirpy lad who thrived on humour, relished the flamboyant, both of which were sadly missing from his home. Her involvement had helped his mother cope with life's on-going struggles. The two unlikely soul mates had remained good friends, and now that he was grown they shared similar interests, especially the theatre. Satenig had even acted in one of Setrag's plays. Her husband had died in the "small massacre" of 1905 and after mourning him for seven years Setrag knew she was starting to remember the blessings of a warm marriage bed.

Setrag knew everyone, through his newspaper, through public speaking, through his theatre company called the Adam Players, and through his natural ease of communication, except of course with the woman he loved. He felt as comfortable with politicians and academics as he did with barbers, fishermen and shoeshine boys. The early mornings were richer for the knock-about repartee exchanged between them as he strolled cheerfully to his office, when he would put aside serious projects buzzing in his head. That morning love was in the air and he was determined to set matchmaking plans in motion. His friend Karin, also widowed and extremely eligible, had started him thinking: "Satenig, now she's a good looking woman." The more he thought about it, the more he was optimistic about the prospect. "Satenig and Karin, sounds nice" he mused, whistling his way through back streets as he headed for her workroom.

Apart from requiring a crash course in romantic courtship, Setrag had a lot to feel good about.

The Tokadjian brothers had done well since their return from America. Business was booming. Multi-cultural townspeople and local intelligentsia would come to buy or just browse, often deciding to place orders for books and periodicals imported from all over the world. It was the only shop in town with such a broad range of publications. Not only that, but the circulation of *Ashkhadank* was at an all time high. Setrag had to pinch himself, it was all going a little too well. They had just moved to a much larger house on a long quiet road facing the sea at Cordelio. Their neighbours had welcomed them in true Armenian style, but best of all, the large cool cellar was ideal for storing. Anna Tokadjian thanked heaven for some space, at last, which was not piled high with towers of newspapers or stacks of books, none of which were of any real interest to her.

Every morning Setrag would catch the early train from Cordelio, and after ten minutes of incessant juddering on a hard wooden seat, jumped off before it pulled into Smyrna Port. Then he would run along the harbour, cocking his large hat at tired fishermen sorting their nets before heading for bed. Raising an eyebrow, he would whistle at the size of their catch, as they whistled back at his flamboyant attire, pointing to a new shirt or shiny velvet jacket. Setrag had a strong sense of the theatrical. The theatre was his passion and he made no apologies for it. It pervaded every bit of his life and even on days when newspaper deadlines kept him at work for fourteen hours he always dressed the part. As editor, he would send his brothers home and write late into the night and, next day, they would open the door at eight thirty to see him fast asleep across the desk surrounded by newspaper bundles tied up in packs, ready to go. But this was Tuesday and he had other things on his mind.

Eating humble pie didn't come easy, the result of spending his developing years surrounded by learned academics, none of whom had taught him about women. Just then a glaring contradiction smacked him in the mouth: his romantic concepts were just that, theoretical, abstract, idealist notions he had read about in stuffy books and had nothing whatever to do with the thumping, pumping emotions he was feeling now. Anyway, he would never want a woman who longed to be swept up by a knight in shining armour. By the time he stepped into the fashion house a new kind of heartbeat was pumping through his veins.

Satenig was busy fitting a capricious overweight client with notions that her money could buy a perfect figure. The evening dress had been moulded and remoulded, taken in here, let out there, shortened, and lengthened, but even Satenig was no miracle worker. If your were fat you were fat. "Patience is a virtue," she repeated, biting her top lip to stop herself uttering obscenities. That was the surest way of guaranteeing no payment for the hours of painstaking work, but it was beginning to feel worth it. Setrag had been shown into her small untidy office with a large window into the workroom. He sat by a square white pillar and noticed it had been scribbled on from top to bottom. He laughed as he read the names of clients, delivery addresses and deadline dates. Even body measurements were scribbled anywhere she found a blank space. "Now that's a good idea! You can never lose important information if it's written on a wall!" Her delicious eccentricity was her most endearing quality. Satenig could not be less like his mother, who was the epitome of traditionalism and propriety. She would not approve of his matchmaking plans, so Setrag hadn't told her. He didn't share her views that you only get one chance at happiness.

Looking out into the workroom the atmosphere was quiet but industrious. It wasn't always like that. The girls knew they had a celebrity in their midst. "Creature comforts are obviously not high priority for Satenig," he thought, perched high on a hard wooden chair like a prized peacock in a birdcage. He felt awkward, trying to fluff up his dignity feathers as their eyes flickered up every now and then. "Oh my God," he gulped, recognizing those eyes as Astra shot them back down. He had no idea she worked there. He jumped down and diverted his eyes to his pocket watch, trying to regain his composure. Just then Satenig threw the door open and almost sent him crashing through the window. "What are you doing here my precious boy?" she said, helping him up before mumbling joyous greetings with dressmaker pins still in her teeth. She had never seen him blush before. "You're obviously not used to being surrounded by women. They are a little fierce I admit," she laughed. "Satenig, I have something rather delicate to ask you, could we go somewhere more private?"

There was nowhere else more private so they talked in whispers. Astra couldn't resist observing their body language. It spoke volumes. "Perhaps he's her nephew," she wondered, watching him lean forward and kiss her hand with a certain familiarity. She had never seen Satenig so pliable. He certainly brought out a side in her she had never seen and his persona bore no relation to the pompous ass of last night. He was so affectionate and couldn't stop talking. What on earth was he telling her? Then, yet more kisses and more intense eye contact. Then the mood changed as Satenig reached for her fan and pointed straight at Astra. After a few more words Setrag kissed her hand again, picked up his papers, and the next thing Astra knew was that he was standing by her table. She took her time before looking up, needing a few seconds to prepare for battle.

"Good morning Astra, I had no idea you worked here." "Oh didn't you? Well you should have guessed. It is women's work after all," but it was unnecessarily sharp and she regretted it. Setrag refused the bait. "I am so glad to see you. I wanted to apologize for having to rush off last night, but I wasn't feeling too well and please thank your mother and pass on my sincere apologies to her. What a lovely lady she is." His manner was so different that Astra began to think she may have misjudged him. "I'm making a period costume for a theatre production, it's for Ophelia," she said attempting to make amends, especially to the girls still sewing beside her. "Do you like Shakespeare?" he asked. "Yes, Hamlet is one of my favourite plays." "Would you like to see it? Perhaps Hagop and your mother would like to come too, but I hope to see you before then." Astra sensed an imaginary white flag waving away the memories of their bungled first encounter, even without having heard that conversation behind closed doors.

His matchmaking plans had been well received. "No of course I don't mind meeting him, just as long as I meet him in company," Satenig had said, hugging him for his genuine interest in her happiness. Then it was his turn. "You see that lovely girl over there? I'm in love with her!" "Do you mean Astra?" she said pointing with her fan. He nodded and began to open up his soul. Her advice was simple. "All I can tell you is to be honest and let things develop. Don't be embarrassed about your feelings; it's what makes the world go round! Remember it does no good to be proud, so don't go putting on silly airs or graces! Just be yourself and she won't be able to resist you." She paused to reflect. "Astra is a free spirit, she won't suffer fools gladly, and whoever she chooses must meet her half way. She exudes a high voltage energy which fires her. See how she's holding that needle in her hand? She's driven, just like you! You can never try to win over someone like that, not with all that electricity flying around, that's a sure recipe for disaster." He caught every word as if pearls of wisdom were dropping from the mouth of his personal soothsayer. "I'll start right now if I may. I know she's seen me." "But certainly my boy, but keep it short this time. Build bridges first and walk across them later, and I don't want the girls gossiping about you all afternoon, we're busy!"

When Setrag left, Astra was summoned in to see the boss. All she could think was that Satenig must have heard her denigrate skilled dressmaking, as though she too was now part of the conspiracy, which underrated sewing as demeaning "woman's work." Instead she was being offered a cup of tea and an invitation to a night at the theatre that coming Saturday. "Setrag is trying his hand at matchmaking and thinks he knows just the man to make me happy again. I don't really want to meet him alone, and I know you love the theatre, so would you accompany me for some moral support?" What she didn't tell her was that it was to be the opening night of Setrag's play or that romance was as much in the air for Astra as it was for her.

Setrag had been writing since the age of thirteen, but this three-act play was his most ambitious yet. Each act depicted one day in the life of an ordinary couple at the start, the middle and the twilight years of marriage, as love helped them deal with ravages of life head on. It was a poignant study of enduring emotions and shifting philosophies as time lays down changing priorities. The characters had aged convincingly, more a tribute to their acting than grease paint but no one, not even Satenig, was expecting the twist before the curtain came down. The characters stood statue like, held in a moment in time, as Setrag stepped out on stage. He read out two scenarios, offering the audience a choice of endings. The audience shouted loudest for the happier ending and the play write prompted his players to perform one last scene. It was proof of the audience's affinity with the characters and a reassurance in the innate goodness of the human spirit. Then, as the lights went up, Setrag stepped out to join the actors in taking bows to thunderous applause, and he saw her. Astra had tears in her eyes. Her hands were stinging, but she clapped harder as a form of penance. "I'm amazed that Setrag has such emotional insight," she said. "So am I," replied Satenig, "and look, the safety curtain is coming down. Astra, let go of his eyes now or he'll be decapitated!"

Chapter IV

Secret Clues Hidden in Timeworn Traditions

ASTRA or Asdghig as she was christened, had no specific name day. She had to share in the general celebrations with others given non-saints names on Shrove Tuesday, the eve before Lent. Ancient Armenian Zoroastrian traditions dated back three thousand years, and Peproné was not one to go against the flow. She glanced at her daughter named after the pagan goddess of beauty and humility. "Perhaps a little more humility and a little less beauty would make for an easier life," she thought, but she knew her God given proportions were pretty much perfect.

Setrag started visiting the Sabondjian household a lot more after that night in the theatre. It was Shrove Tuesday, February 1912 and Peproné Sabondjian was expecting guests, but the Tokadjians had cordially declined. "Setrag, why must you tell your mother every little thing? You just have to breathe differently in this town and everyone's tongues start wagging," complained Astra, sensing her reputation was becoming mud in the locality. She imagined Anna Tokadjian's accusing finger shaking pointedly at her son, disapproving of his choice of intended and praying for someone more in keeping with Armenian tradition to catch his eye. But Setrag had decided that there must be no secrets between them. "Astra, try to understand, it's nothing personal of course, how could it be, you've never met each other. It's just a question of upbringing; she believes women should not be writing politically sensitive material even if it is for your brother and done from your respectable living room, and all her like-minded friends happen to agree with her!" She loved the way he could turn a serious discussion into a light-hearted exchange. He wasn't being disloyal to either woman. "Being forewarned is being forearmed" was his philosophy. But Setrag was an unshakable optimist and believed that once his mother and father had laid eyes on Astra all the ice would melt at her feet.

Soon they were becoming inseparable. Setrag and Astra adored stuffed mussels and he knew the best place to eat them. "Satenig, why don't you join us for lunch today?" he asked. "No, I can't eat a big lunch twice a week and still get into my clothes. Anyway, where were you? It's late, and she's been like a cat on hot bricks." The restaurant was minutes away on the quay, the owner was a good friend, and best of all, he always gave them the same table at a discrete corner at the back. Satenig drew straws to see who would chaperone them each time. "Oh no Madam, not me again, I went last week. It's exhausting sitting with them, listening to their endless chatter. They never stop talking! The owner puts them right at the back so other customers can't hear them." It was true. Astra and Setrag had to put aside all thoughts of physical passion and did this by channelling every pulsating vein into heated one-hour sessions of highly charged conversation instead, and it seemed to come so naturally to them. "First they devour their mussels, then it starts. Politics, art, law, books, architecture, philosophy, religion, animals, travel, you name it, and they talk about it. Peas in a pod! You'd think they've known each other for twenty years."

One day the following week Satenig had agreed to join them and it gave Setrag the impetus to ask Astra something rather radical. "Astra, would you have time in your busy schedule to consider working for my paper? It will depend of course on you showing me some of your work, but Hagop recommends you extremely highly. I thought as you've got so much to say you might as well tell my readers as well!" Two days later she arrived for an official interview for the position as a freelance weekly feature writer for social policy and education. As Setrag scanned through her work he became genuinely impressed. She had a special way with words; she was persuasive and succinct but a little too emotive for his liking, but that could be tempered. "You will have to adhere to my editorial guidelines, and I warn you I am ruthless! I think it's important to give my readers time to absorb new ideas and of course we can't forget what neck of the woods we're living in. Equality for women and education for the masses are new concepts in the west, never mind in our backwater." She nodded knowing that he didn't like it any more than she did. She also knew some of Setrag's history. He had never spoken about it but she understood his underlying fear that at any moment he could be relabelled a revolutionary. Their lives were stifled by a brutal regime and only a complete fool would ignore the political sword of Damocles hanging over their heads. "I accept your terms fully," she smiled. "Then I'm delighted to offer you the position. When can you start?"

She worked mainly from home, sifting through articles from American and British newspapers, translating and précising accounts, hoping to shift attitudes rather than challenge the Ottoman regime, her angle being news rather than views, although her editor did allow occasional personal observations if they backed up accounts. The first time she saw her words and name in print, excitement got the better of her and forgetting formalities she ran and flung her arms around his neck. "I don' t bite," he said as she jumped back almost as quickly. That night she folded her page and put it in a letter to America. "Miss Jennings, I did it, I'm a bona fide journalist! We live in such different worlds but our dreams and hearts are now closer than ever."

Two weeks later she was due to meet her future in-laws, a day she had been dreading, but it had finally come. That morning Astra had spread her papers across the dining table, polishing off her article "The importance of music and sport in a comprehensive education system." She always toned down her first draft, aware that her style tended to be over-exuberant and so potentially liable to Setrag's editorial censorship, but as her mother was hovering, she decided to make last minute changes later. "Astra, hide the evidence, we don't want to start off on the wrong foot!" she said and Astra did as she was told. "Mama, I hope they don't bring all this up today. Anyway, whatever they say, I'm still going in tomorrow, I have to, my editor in chief wants me to check my article layout before it goes to print. It's not my fault that I'm the only woman working there, and anyway, Hagop is coming in with me." Hagop had reorganized his own schedule to give his sister a fighting chance at fulfilling her male dominated career ambitions even though that might anger the narrow-minded traditionalists coming to tea. Peproné had no time for snide gossip or bourgeois tittle-tattle. "It's just petty ignorance my dear, try not to take it to heart." She looked to heaven and squeezed her tender feet into her best black shoes. "The sooner they formally announce their intention to marry the better for everyone." Standing all morning on a stone kitchen floor had made her feet swell up two sizes but to her it was just a mere fashion inconvenience and well worth every twinge, so long as the food went down well, and everyone enjoyed themselves.

They were late. Astra tried to hide her nervousness as the clock ticked passed four. They should have been there an hour ago. She had tied Zevart's hair in bunches, then into plaits, then combed it loose and now she sat perched on the edge of a dining chair trying to read Hamlet while twirling the long corner of their best tablecloth and wondering if it was all off. This "surprise visit" as it was called, had been arranged a few days before. The Tokadjians were expected to drop in "unexpectedly" for the first time to meet their new neighbours. In fact they weren't strictly neighbours at all. Setrag lived four streets away, on the sea road, but that was the formal reason given for coming to visit. It was the way of her world, full of strange traditions and Astra had to accept them even though she despised the pretence. Setrag would not be with them, just parents and godparents, all coming to scrutinize her every move, her features, her manners, her child bearing hips. Her contribution would have to be minimal, she would say "good afternoon," play a turgid piece on the organ, serve coffee and cakes, while keeping her head bowed at all times, and nothing more. Then they would start discussions about nothing important while she would sit passively in a corner as the guests assessed her suitability. "That's the usual programme but once it's over with the fun can begin," said her mother, wondering if she'd been a little too graphic with the explanations. "How on earth can they tell what type of person I am if I am not allowed to say anything?" she asked and her mother had to admit there was no logical explanation. "It's tradition my dear, and you'd be surprised how much people can pick up just by being in the same room with someone for even an hour." Astra took the flippancy in her mother's voice as her way of detaching herself from the contrived ceremonies to come. "Just be natural and they'll love you." Suddenly she remembered her own "surprise visit" when five sets of critical eyes bored into her back as she went flying into the fireplace. It still made her giggle but she decided to keep it to herself. It had all been going rather well when just a few minutes into the proceedings she tripped over her petticoats and sent the heavy silver tray packed full of sticky sweets right into the lap of her future mother-in-law. But somehow it had not gone against her. The Baltadjians were very wealthy people after all.

They had almost given up hope when at last they arrived just as the clock struck five. The haughty looking strangers stepped inside offering neither apology nor a pleasant greeting, and left a short time later almost as suddenly. Astra watched as the entourage walk down the street trying to make sense of it all. She had done everything by the book. She had played her turgid tune note perfect; she had passed round the heavy tray with the submissive femininity and refinement of a geisha. Nor had she uttered a word out of turn, nor dared to look directly into the eyes of her examiners. So why had they bothered to come at all? All she knew was that whatever happened she would never put any child of hers through the same humiliation, not even if they were expecting a surprise visit from the king of Siam.

Peproné was speechless and in obvious pain so Astra knelt down and after a struggle managed to free her mother's ever swelling feet from her ever shrinking shoes. Peproné stroked her daughter's hair as she tried to find words of comfort, but there were none. "My dearest child, you must put this behind you, maybe it's not meant to be." That was the best she could come up with. "Mama, was I hearing things or did she say my hair was too long?" "Yes, that was almost all she did say!" It had not started well: after initial introductions no one could think of what to say. They ate and drank in embarrassing silence, interspersed only by Krikor Tokadjian's compliments to the chef, "Mmmm, may your hands be blessed, the spinach pie is very, very tasty," he said accepting another piece. Then in one misguided moment Astra's well-meaning godmother decided it was time to lighten up proceedings. "Don't you think she has such beautiful hair, but it is a shame she always wears it up," she said picking out eight long pins and shaking it loose. She waited for appreciative nods but none came, and when Krikor Tokadjian tried to sneak a smile, his wife's eyes flashed disapproval and he raised his eyebrows in defeat. Astra sat staring at the swirls in the dark blue Persian carpet while Setrag's mother brought up the sin of vanity. "Actually I think her hair is too long to be practical. I always say that if hair had power, goats would be prophets! Don't you agree, Mrs. Sabondjian?" Peproné did not honour her with an answer, knowing her daughter's hair had nothing whatever to do with it. Mercifully they left soon after. No follow up meeting was mentioned and everyone took this to imply an outright rejection of Astra as a future daughter-in-law. "She might as well have slapped me in the face. These ancient traditions are cruel and demeaning. I swear I will never ever go through that again, never, even if it means I die a spinster."

On the way home Krikor Tokadjian had much more to say than usual. He walked slowly, his hands behind his back with his head turned pointedly towards the sea as a testament to his bursting anger. "I will not let your silly old fashioned ideas break our son's heart. I thought she was a lovely girl. If he wants to marry her we will not stand in his way, do you understand?" Anna looked shocked. "What are you afraid of Anna, that the girl has a mind of her own?" Krikor, uneducated but abundant in age-old wisdom and simple common sense had recently begun to question some of his own life choices. He was frail, and tired, and he knew his life was drawing to a close. For years his need for domestic peace in politically troubled times had urged him not to upset his wife's apple cart, but now time was precious. It was too late for him but he was determined not to leave this world denying his son his chance for true happiness. Their son who had asked for so little and given them so much deserved nothing less.

Before they reached home Krikor had told his wife that barring a miracle he would not expect to be alive by Christmas. "Oh my God, Krikor, how do you know that? No one knows when we will be called to our maker." Her regular and sudden attacks of the vapours were usually followed by melodramatic fainting fits, feigned for effect, and invariably ensured Anna had her way in most things, but not this time. Krikor knew she would have to grant her dying husband his dying wish because not to do so would not bode well for her eternal peace, but he kept it short, "I hope to live long enough to see our son married, so I suggest that you start by making amends before it's too late. You have to go back to see Mrs. Sabondjian first thing tomorrow with some excuse, I don't care what, and offer an apology to repair the damage you caused. I just hope the good lady will allow your foot in the door after your performance today." True to form, Anna feigned a swoon, but Krikor walked on even faster, keeping his eyes fixed out to sea, fully aware of his wife's theatricals, but this time he was having none of it.

Next morning Anna swallowed her pride and made a concession to her husband's wishes, but she managed to persuade Krikor to go with her, on his condition that she should do most of the talking. "We may not be very welcome, and I'd rather not be the only one who has the door slammed in my face," she said and he agreed. The visitation proved easier than they both expected. Peproné was far too polite to bring up the fiasco of the previous evening and luckily everyone else was out. Haroutioun and Zevart had just left the house in search of mussels on the beach. "Media Dolma" or mussels stuffed with onions, pine kernels, cinnamon and rice took hours to prepare, but her two youngest had already asked their mother to spend another long day in the kitchen. "Oh go on Mama, please, it's Astra's favourite, it will to cheer her up." Peproné had decided not to wake Astra up that morning, thinking a day at home would help to soothe her puffy eyes, but she had already soaked them in camomile tea before the sun came up and left in a surprisingly good mood. As Hagop left his sister at the door of the fashion house, he only had one thing on his mind, to go to Setrag and give him hell, but Astra read his mind "No, you must not tell him a thing about it. I'm sure he has no idea what happened." Something was stroking the back of her neck, making her feel warm and safe, and she knew they would be together before sweet red apples fell off the trees.

At much the same time Peproné, Anna and Krikor were sipping cinnamon tea. "We are so sorry to have left so suddenly yesterday, before the real business of our children's happiness had been discussed. You see my wife Anna suffers from blinding headaches, but we were thinking that July would be a lovely time for a wedding," said Krikor, never one to stand on ceremony. Anna kept her lips tightly pursed but eventually she contributed to the discussions. "We must follow the pre-nuptial traditions and take Astra to the baths. Gayené my only daughter would come too." Peproné knew that after yesterday's fiasco Astra would never agree to the ultimate indignity of being examined for physical abnormalities by the groom's women folk under the guise of a pleasant day out! Peproné used her upper hand to best advantage. "Oh, that is so very old fashioned and completely unnecessary these days. As you can see Astra is graced with great beauty and do take my word for it, everything that you don't see is perfect in every way!" She continued, "And she's so busy, what with her work for *Ashkhadank* and the fashion house, and what with her translations for Hagop's paper she has no time to waste on such unnecessary silliness." It was a reply she relished for months to come and just wished her daughter had been there to hear her in action. Peproné was on a roll and in one breath managed to negotiate a wedding package her daughter would be thrilled about. None of the old traditions would be adhered to. Krikor nodded while Anna held back objections, feeling regular sharp kicks from her husband's pointed shoes under the table. "I can't speak for her you understand, but Hagop will come to see you this evening with her answer." They shook hands on it and left, wondering which one was the more radical, the mother or her daughter.

Astra and Hagop came back to see the Media Dolma cooling on the dining room table. "Leave them, wait for dinner," called their mother from the garden. They found her perched upright in a whicker chair under the apple tree performing a delicate operation on Sima, the best loved of their five chickens. Sima was a prolific egg layer with an unfortunate habit of chewing a large hole in her own neck for idle fun. Whenever the hole got too large Peproné would take a long thin needle and thick cotton thread and sew her up, normally every three months. It never bled or appeared to cause the slightest pain and the chicken sat resigned and unflinching, waiting for her operation to end, after which she would flutter her wings and jump off before starting to peck it open again.

Peproné had done a lot of thinking that day and much of it had tempered her initial exuberance. If Astra married into the Tokadjian family she would have to live with a mother-in-law who, to say the least, was old fashioned. If Peproné had her way, both bride and groom would live with her, but this was completely out of the question and an insult to Setrag, so she didn't consider bringing it up at the marriage negotiation table. But Peproné knew she must say something. Having her eldest daughter's childlessness on her conscience was burden enough. But first, Peproné staged her story of how the Tokadjians had come, this time genuinely unexpectedly, almost on their knees, begging for Astra's hand in marriage. "Mama, you have such a way with words, I can just see them now, their shocked expressions in every detail. You know, you really should have been an actress." It was what Peproné liked to do best, to make people laugh.

Her animated performance reminded Astra of those icy nights back in Erzeroum, when the fire roared and the wind screeched through the thick stonewall. As shadows crawled across flickering candles her mother would put her arms around the children to gather them close until the mood felt right. "Oh mama, please tells us the stories of the Perrymen." The stories were different every time, new monsters, new magical worlds, all her own improvised versions of mysterious folk tales and fables she had heard when she was young. Their eyes would grow wide, their breathing would stop till her hearty laugh broke the spell and dragged their minds to the here and now. Their favourite stories were of the evil Perrymen whose feet faced backwards. "You have to see their bare feet to know if they really are the Perrymen. You can't tell if they have their shoes on," she whispered. Astra recalled wondering if the huge archbishop who came a little too often was a Perryman. His long black robes and pointed black headdress terrified them, but as he always wore shoes, they were never quite sure. On hearing his thunderous voice, the children would all run upstairs and send prayers to the Virgin Mary, crossing themselves again and again in true Orthodox style, until both of his huge feet stomped out of their front door.

"Astra, are you listening? This is important!" She sat and pondered over her mother's anxieties but she trusted Setrag. After all, he had told her it wouldn't be easy, but as he would be there to mediate, it wouldn't be a problem. She remembered the time when she had seen his parents glowing with pride after his speech that Sunday evening. He was the apple of their eye. "Mama, I thought about it too, but it won't be forever. Setrag's two brothers will probably be married soon and we'll have to find our own home then." Peproné nodded. Astra made a wish that within two years, barring a catastrophe, they would be settled in their own home, alone. Just then an icy breeze brush her neck, but March was like that. Taking her mother's hand she said, "Come on, let's go inside, I am really starving."

Astra felt much better after dinner. She was never a big eater. There was always too much else to do, but that day her body needed reviving. A huge pile of blue-black shiny discarded mussel shells toppled off the edge of her plate. "Zevart, I think it's your turn to clear up," she smiled, not able to move after her over indulgence. Astra had heard her mother exonerate herself from possible negligence, painting a dire picture of a new bride trapped in the clutches of an interfering mother-in-law. "Mama, how do you know all this? You've only met the woman twice!" said Hagop. "I wasn't talking about Mrs. Tokadjian specifically, but some women make difficult mothers-in-law, that's all." "Mama, now that I've listened to all the things a new bride has to put up with, would you permit Eros, my winged messenger to do his brotherly duty?" "Are you sure?" Hagop asked. "I've never been so sure of anything in my life," she replied. So he kissed her hand and flew out of the house on a proud mission of love and happiness and everyone breathed a sigh of relief.

After shivering in the garden, Astra was almost expecting it. That night she hovered weightlessly above that same recurring dream; the grey bleak desert, the emaciated bodies piled high, pyramids of limbs and bones and half living faces left abandoned in that terrible place she prayed could not exist in a waking world or any world, ever.

Within days the pre-nuptial propaganda machine was in full flow. The girls in the workshop, weighed down by rolls of velvets, chiffons, silks and satins were in the throes of preparing for Astra's dowry and as Lent was always quiet, the timing was perfect. "My wedding dress is nearly finished," she told her brother on the train home. "Well, why are you waiting then? You could be married by Easter," he said, eager to have a famous brother-in-law. "Setrag needs time to prepare important domestic ground rules before I move in and anyway it gives me time to establish myself as a writer. Setrag has started to read his mother some of my articles and she seems to be coming round." "A serpent changes it's skin, not it's nature," he replied, hoping that the wise words of their poor departed grandmother would not be proved right this once. She came back with "Yes, but they say that a cut from a sword heals quicker than the curse from a tongue, and that patience is a virtue. I would rather wait."

Chapter V

The True Unveiling of Enchanted Love

KRIKOR Tokadjian stroked his prickly grey moustache in fatherly pride knowing that all but one of the necessary preconditions of the wedding had been satisfied. All that was left now was the preparation of the "Hina tray" ahead of the wedding ceremony, just three days away." Please lord, give me life till sunrise on Monday, and I shall be forever grateful," he thought chuckling at the paradox. "I think we should give her my mother's wedding ring," he said, already polishing it. Anna had hardly ever worn it; she had preferred to wear her mother's ring and didn't approve of over-adornment. "Krikor, can't you see it's too small for my finger?" she had said, dismissing her husband's disappointment as sentimental hogwash. Now with thirty years of hindsight he knew that in that one sentence she had set the tone of their union from the start.

Now he was smiling secretly to himself, knowing that Setrag would see it every day and night on Astra's lovely finger. It was an understated, even modest ring: a small cut diamond, surrounded by a circle of golden spheres, which encased the setting. He knew Astra would have far more beautiful rings, her family had been jewellers for the Czar after all, but he knew her well enough to know its symbolism would deem it priceless to her as it was for him. He placed the ring on top of her wedding veil to form the centrepiece of the tray. Then he took out the square lace place mat which his mother's dainty fingers had embroidered so painstakingly and covered the sweets, nuts and dried fruits. The tray was ready.

As the wedding day loomed ever nearer Anna Tokadjian began to feel attacked from all sides. She had been subjected to the same unimpressive arguments ever since the wedding was announced. Setrag had seemed to start his every sentence with the exact same words, "The world has changed Mama," but she had serious difficulties in trying to understand any of the advantages. "Don't they think I can see what's happening with my own eyes? I don't like any of it," she would mumble to herself just out of earshot.

She had started to take to her bed whenever Setrag came home. It was becoming the last bastion of peace and quiet left within her four walls. "Krikor, I have a piercing headache today, please would you mind sorting out the Hina tray?" It was hot and her blood pressure was pumping so she lay down, closed her eyes, and fanned herself frantically to catch whatever air was out there. "It's all done and ready my sweet," he called up, still cheery from having performed the honour all by himself.

Well, that morning she had heard it all! Her future daughter-in-law was still going to be paid for working at the paper, even after the wedding! "What will she need money for, tell me! We will feed her, what more does she need?" Setrag knew his mother would refuse to grasp the concept, but tried again. "Mama, it's not about the money, it's about her independence and self-respect, and because it is the right of all workers to be rewarded for their skills and effort, no matter who they work for." Anna threw up her hands in disbelief, "Well, is this what the world has come to, that your own husband has to pay you for helping him. I just can't understand any of it." "Mama listen! Astra will give everything she earns to you, I told her not to but it was she who insisted." "Well then, why can't you give the money directly to me in the first place, and save her the trouble?" The gloves were off and her imaginary battle for domestic supremacy had well and truly started. "Mama, you must believe me, Astra has the heart of a saint, and she would never threaten the balance of power in your house." Anna looked baffled. "Why must you always talk to me in riddles? It's just like when I'm sat there and you're giving one of your speeches." But his startled expression made her realize this time she had hit a nerve and quickly changed her tune. "Oh Setrag, I am sorry, I didn't mean that, it's just that my headaches make me say silly things. I know she's a good girl, let me talk to her. I'll tell her she can buy anything she likes with her money, I know she has expensive tastes." Setrag shook his head in resigned disbelief.

Megouch, Setrag's younger brother delivered the Hina tray to the Sabondjian residence at six o'clock on July 25th 1912. Peproné bowed as she opened the door to receive it as though the Holy Grail itself had been passed to her for safekeeping. "I wish you could come in to see the lovely girls lined up in my living room but I'm sorry, there's no men allowed in here today." "Pity, but you could open the window so I might just peak at them. Maybe I'll fall in love in exactly the same spot my brother did!" she winked and closed the door, then stepped carefully into the living room, holding the tray tight to her chest, and placed it on the low round brass table in front of her daughter. Friends and female cousins stopped chattering, grabbed hands to form a circle around Astra and waited. She started with the centrepiece. She unfolded the veil and placed it on her head. Then she opened an ivory box and took out the ring and placed it on her finger, it fitted. Then she lifted up the lace cloth to see an exquisitely embroidered double pillowcase on which a written blessing had been attached. Krikor the shoemaker had no need for fancy writing or elaborate words. He had written "May you both be very happy and grow old together on one pillow," and she knew he meant it with all his heart.

"Some of our Garin traditions are lovely and definitely worth keeping," whispered Astra as she passed Anoushka the tray full of sweets, nuts and dried fruits. It had been a year, almost to the day, that Astra and Anoushka had walked out of the gates of the American College for the last time. "I still can't believe you're getting married," she replied and Astra knew what she meant. "I know this sounds strange Anoushka, but I feel as free as a bird. It's as if he liberates my soul and takes it to places I could never have dreamed of before."

Astra's wedding day shone like a brilliant star in history's dead of night. She would remember it with ever-lasting vividness as though God knew when to hand out joys that must last a lifetime. She wrapped every single one of those moments in airtight emotion so their brightness could never fade. It had all started with her mother's kiss and the words, "Wake up my girl, your day has come." It amazed her how she still remembered each face in the long winding procession of relatives, guests and candle bearers as they filed by her house, sprinkling flowers at her door, in true Garin tradition. Famous writers, academics, politicians, actors, journalists, old school friends, fishermen, shoeshine boys, shopkeepers, couturiers and tailors all forming part of their impressive entourage. Silhouetted heads moving towards the huge amber sun as everyone headed for church. Her mother's bursting pride as growing numbers of strangers formed a queue to see the bride in ancient traditional costume. Her heart beating faster as she looked down at her sumptuous red and green velvet wedding dress stirring passionate images of a proud peahen fluffing up feathers just before the throws of rapturous lovemaking. The silent humming as the two Hagop brothers ushered guests into the aisles. The overflow from the church milling out in the courtyard while inside three archbishops conducted a dazzling ceremony. Her little brother's cheeky eyes turned down, holding a huge candle, his voice still clear as a bell, "Astra, I counted two thousand feet, that makes one thousand people, and they all came to see you!" The silver trays of food brought through the doors of the large hall of the Dashnag party offices, somehow enough to feed them all. Gifts from all over the world, personalized poems, songs, and a fine silk Persian carpet from Setrag's friends in Boston. The music and dancing till morning light seeped through to greet their new day as man and wife. She smiled when she remembered her three best friends who had arrived early with pots of rouge and coloured powders to make up her face, but who were later disappointed when she lifted up her veil stating, "I'm sorry, but I washed it all off. When I looked in the mirror and didn't recognize myself, then I thought that today of all days Setrag must see what he's getting. It didn't feel honest somehow." Then the most enduring memory of all, as the sound of their breathing stopped the world outside. "I'd die for you," he said.

Chapter VI

The Importance of Life's Ceremonial Handovers

FIVE months later a letter came for Setrag and Astra wondered how it had managed to find him, given the address was barely legible. The postmark said Boston, America. They had been waiting for news from Setrag's brother in America, but his handwriting was refined and well spaced and nothing like this scrawling spidery hand so she knew it was not from him. Hagop had left for Boston five weeks before and would have already attended the charity gala evening as Setrag's representative at the annual fund raising event of the Garin Compatriotic Union of America. Setrag was a founder member and in the four years since leaving Boston in 1908, the GCU had already sponsored hundreds of orphaned children through the first years of a decent education. Astra had found out so much more about her husband in the last few weeks. It amazed her that she still had not seen anything in him, however insignificant, that could make her doubt him, even for a minute. Astra was four months pregnant and although she always wanted her husband close by, she had encouraged him to make the trip himself. "You should be there, it's an honour for you, I'll be fine" she had said, but Setrag was not quite comfortable leaving Astra in Smyrna while his mother's "headaches" were still sending her to a darkened room, especially as she was expecting their first child.

The GCU had been forwarding Astra stories for her education features and even Anna Tokadjian seemed to be more approving of her articles. Astra was deeply involved in a research project with a large sample group of education fund beneficiaries, most of whom had answered her with heart-warming stories. However, when some of the envelopes came back unopened, with the stark words "now deceased" stamped across the top in bright red, her heart would sink. She wished she could dispose of the tragic evidence but instead she stored them in a large box file so that their funds could be reallocated. "Hagop, these poor children had no one left in the world, not even to answer their letters," she said, hoping it was typhoid or some other illness which cut their futures short and not the same barbarous acts which had killed their parents. "Astra I need the heart-warming stories from your survey as proof for the Union that their money is being well spent." So she collated a big pile, and then helped him write his speech, full of quotes from children as young as eight, and it made wonderful reading. "That should help tug at those wealthy heart strings, especially after a big fat dinner," she laughed. Setrag hardly ever showed emotion at work, but hearing tales of poor little orphans full of hope and gratitude as a result of his associations' financial assistance made him blubber like a baby.

"I might find the girl of my dreams in America," Hagop Tokadjian had dropped in flippantly as he waved goodbye, but now these words were keeping Setrag awake at night. It was three o'clock in the morning and he needed to unburden his soul, so he woke up his wife and told her the whole story from beginning to end. "It's about that letter that came today. It's from a woman I knew in America. "Well, she has terrible handwriting," she replied suddenly wide-awake. Then Setrag began to tell the story of how she and her sister were alone in the world and desperate to marry. "They both took it in turns to try to seduce us, first me and then Hagop, but I never told him. He was so flattered, and anyway, we were just about to leave America to come home. I completely forgot about them. They still work in the GCU offices in Boston."

There was more. As soon as he remembered they might still be there, Setrag had written to Hagop to tell him what had happened three years ago, warning him not to go anywhere near. "Somehow one of the sisters intercepted my letter and read every word I wrote!" "How did she do that?" "Well, like an idiot I sent it to the offices and obviously one of them recognized my handwriting. That letter today was from one of the sisters. She wrote and said it was too late, she and Hagop were getting married and if I so much as breathed a word of what happened to a single soul, she said that I'd never see my brother again." Astra became even more confused "What do you mean? Is Hagop's getting married in America?"

Setrag had no one else to blame so he cursed the American postal service, which put his letter into the wrong hands. "If I had gone myself none of this would have happened." "Look, you did what you thought was right so you can't blame yourself, and anyway she might make him happy, people do change." Setrag loved his wife, the hopeful peacemaker, the trusting optimist, but somehow he feared this time she was wrong.

The following week they received a letter from Hagop containing spectacular news. He started by begging forgiveness for marrying so suddenly, so far away, but it had been a whirlwind romance. He called his new bride "a special and wonderful girl," an orphan who till then had no one else in the world apart from her sister. Their wedding had been a low-key affair and of course he had missed them but promised to bring his wife over to meet them and was saving up money already. Setrag and Astra tried to appear amazed as they passed around the tiny wedding photographs. "You know, I'm sure I've seen this girl's face before, in the GCU magazine I think. She has beguiling eyes. Do you know her Setrag?" asked his mother holding back tears, barely able to speak. Her perception shocked him. "Yes, Mama, I met her in Boston a few years ago. She works at the GCU offices."

Setrag never saw his brother again. During the next few years they wrote long and private letters to each other and it gave Setrag absolutely no satisfaction to know that Hagop's marriage lived up to his expectations. Some years later Hagop and his wife and their two children moved from Boston to New York. Hagop discovered he had considerable fund raising talents and gave over a large part of his working life to the expansion of charity networks for the GCU, the organization that had changed his life so abruptly. His other passion was plant life. Within six years Hagop had compiled a complete reference book, cataloguing every species of herbs, flowers, and shrub life. It proved such a useful publication that the book was translated into seven languages. His hobby had started as essential therapy to soothe his nerves and to take his mind off domestic difficulties but soon his fascination turned to expertise, and he filled his life with the beauty and magic of silent living things, and his marriage was far better for it. He also empowered thousands of needy children of all ages, to benefit from an excellent education, courtesy of the financial support offered by wealthy American humanitarians throughout the GCU of the United States, so it was not all bad, nothing ever is.

Astra was well into her pregnancy. "Our child will be destined to live the life of a tireless literati," said Setrag, wondering whether his wife would take any rest at all before her due confinement. In the last four months her writing had become prolific, as though the speed at which her womb expanded bore a direct correlation to the output from her pen. Those hard wooden train seats to and from Cordelio had started to rock her unborn child awake but time was precious and Astra's career was on a roll. It was just as she had predicted, her marriage had given her professional freedom and a license to work amongst men, even when her husband was not present. Her confidence was flowing and she had begun to establish herself as a budding new guest speaker on the Sunday evening circuit meetings. Her swollen condition and boundless energy made audiences sit up and take notice all the more and women particularly saw her as a revelation, a living-breathing role model that gender need not stand in the way of ambition or potential.

"Education can give women everything it gives men. If our Empire encouraged training and development amongst its entire population, every one of us would benefit as individuals and as an empire. Education, employment and self-realization are the right of all men, women and children, rich or poor. It's about choice. If I wanted to visit a doctor about my pregnancy why shouldn't I be able to choose to see a female doctor, and choice breeds choice. The more we accomplish, the more choices we have to free ourselves from the inevitability of life in the kitchen. Let us look beyond the lives of our mothers and grandmothers and truly believe we have a choice." Astra had given more than a dozen such speeches. Her more radical ones were always at American school halls and each time she felt she was becoming more polished. Peproné would say more dangerous, but whatever it was, the audiences were becoming increasingly more appreciative and Peproné was becoming increasingly anxious. "I wonder what their husbands or fathers would say if they saw their wives and daughters clapping like that? I sincerely hope no government spies were hiding in dark corners. You know full well these are perilous times Astra, and what with your baby nearly due, don't you think it's about time you stopped these exhausting talks?" Peproné had been listening to her fiery speech and although the audience was virtually all female, she had noticed a couple of suspicious looking men hovering by the door. "Those men were the college caretakers," said Astra tidying up her papers, still glowing in the aftermath. "Astra, don't you understand, you never know whose ears might one day be used as weapons against you?"

Astra had never heard her mother sound so emphatic. "Mama, you worry too much. All I'm saying is that women could work somewhere other than at home. I don't even bring up female suffrage, Setrag advised me against it." "Well you and Setrag are walking on eggshells. This is hardly a place where modern ideologies can ever lead the way. All we can hope for is that our men come home safe at night, and anyway just look at what's happening abroad, women are throwing themselves under horses for their precious emancipation." Peproné stopped short of cursing Miss Jennings out loud but Astra heard her anyway. The power of telepathy, passed down from mother to daughter for generations was no longer a surprise to either of them. Astra had never kept it a secret that Miss Jennings was now writing to her at her new address and had even shown her mother a letter from the famous British suffragette Elizabeth Garrett in London. What she hadn't mentioned was that Miss Jennings had hopes that Astra might instigate the beginnings of social change in Asia Minor, but her mother read her mind. "Why can't they concentrate on their own country? Nothing will change here for centuries. Let England and America sort out their own problems first, and then maybe one day your great grandchildren will reap the rewards." Astra felt her mother tugging thick protective maternal reins and the strain was making her breathless. "Mama, don't upset yourself, all I'm doing is telling people what I believe will change their lives for the better, that's all." That evening she went into labour.

On 27th of October their first baby pushed his large head into the world. "His head is bigger than mine, and they say that's a sign of exceptional intelligence," said the proud father. "Oh, is that right?" said his wife smarting from the pains of the delivery. Grandfather Krikor had lived longer than expected and was there to pass the baton and his name to his grandson. "I think we should call him Koko until he is older," said Setrag still eyeing up the circumference of his newborn's head. "Koko will do till he becomes a little older, but after that we must call him by his proper name, Krikor," said Anna Tokadjian, relieved beyond words that Astra had delivered a boy. But he would always be Koko. Somehow it suited him.

Baby Koko was baptised two months later with the pomp and ceremony reminiscent of the ancient glory days of medieval Armenian kingdoms. It was an unforgettable day when imposing solemnity combined with glittering splendour, as though the firstborn son of the Great King Dikran (Tigran) himself was being anointed for future greatness. Five bishops representing the full complement of Armenian churches, Apostolic, Catholic and Coptic, performed a truly multi denominational laying on of hands and sacred oils. Once their holy duties were completed, the leader of the Dashnag party, Aknouni, took baby Koko, raised him high above his head, and with a powerful voice which silenced the cathedral echoes, bellowed, "I name you Gorioun, our brave new Lion Cub." And so was recruited the youngest member of the Dashnag party into the fold. Koko was baptised with three names, each one symbolizing the baptismal commitment of the Armenian Apostolic church, love, faith and hope. Krikor, Vasgen, Gorioun was hardly dry behind his ears but already he had a lot to live up to.

Grandfather Krikor Tokadjian hung on to life for a few more months until his last breath finally left him with a smile on his face, and his best shoes on his feet. Minutes before Anna had heard him fumbling in their wardrobe, "What are you looking for? Come and have your tea," she had called up from the kitchen. "Anna, I'm looking for it, you know, for Astra, we talked about it last night." It was to be a surprise, so he spoke in whispers, hearing his daughter-in-law near by. Anna listened out for his steps but it had gone deadly quiet, so she climbed the stairs to find him slumped up against the bed. She bent down to touch his shoulder. "Krikor, Krikor," but he had already left her. She knelt beside him and held his fingers till they went cold in her hand. She had loved him then and still, after all this time she still loved him. She gazed thoughtfully at the precious heirloom balanced in his open palm. "Alright, if you want her to have it, then she shall have it," she said kissing his forehead. "But why her and not your sons or daughter?" But Krikor had left this world with his final instruction, Astra was to inherit Krikor's mother's prayer book. It was intricately carved out of ancient bones, bones of what animal no one was sure, but Krikor said it was the most precious thing he had ever held in his hands. The pages were full of hand painted illuminated folios. "It's from Byzantium, it's been in our family for centuries," he had told her, but now it was too late for arguments. She went downstairs and placed the book in the hands of her daughter-in-law. "Krikor died holding this, and he wanted you to have it," she said.

They dressed Krikor in his best suit, slipped his shoes back on and laid his body on the bed. Calmness followed as welcome peace, which follows the deserved release of a cherished loved one. For once baby Koko slept soundly till past midday while Astra made herself useful, comforting Anna and Gayené, pouring cups of tea and wondering how her son of so few months knew his mother was needed elsewhere. It was his little gift to them, sensing the demands of grief must come first.

As night fell the grieving women were still alone. Setrag and his young brother Megerdich had not yet come to share the burden. Surely they must have heard the news by now, bad news travelled fast. Astra's brother Hagop had rushed to the bookshop six hours ago and Anna was becoming inconsolable. "My boys, Setrag, Megouch, for the love of God where you? I need you with me," she wailed, throwing her arms up in despair, pacing and reeling by the front door, threatening suicide where she stood. At last Megouch and Hagop came back but Setrag wasn't with them. Hagop tried to stay calm and soften his words but there was no easy way to say it. "Setrag's been arrested, he's in prison." Megouch was trembling as he spoke. "Someone warned me first thing this morning and I cleared out whatever I could before they came." Astra stood in stunned silence while Anna became delirious, wailing high pitched shrills before fainting into the arms of her youngest son. Hagop tried to put things into perspective. "Don't worry Astra, they will release him, this happened to my editor last week and they let him out the next day." They helped Anna onto the couch and the calm which followed gave them time to think. Suddenly poor Krikor's death became old news. In the light of his son's false imprisonment, it was exactly what he would have wanted. Astra picked up the bone-covered prayer book still on the kitchen table. She kissed it and asked heavenly powers for strength and wisdom, somehow sensing it had started. She willed a powerful surge of strength and resolution prepare her to take on the intolerant machine of the Ottoman warlords, and to make them putty in her hands.

Chapter VII

Fighting for Justice with a Lion's Share of Love

WITH Anna fast asleep and Krikor lying dead upstairs, the house felt startlingly empty. Gayené watched as Astra reached for a pen and paper, calm and determined, and ready for anything. She could see why Setrag adored her so. She likened her to a solitary pillar left standing after a devastating earthquake, from which a new temple would emerge with its proportions and purpose still intact. For the first time that day Astra looked down and saw she was wearing red. That morning, when she dressed, none of this had happened, but now the colour seemed offensive and inappropriate. She thought about changing but no one around the table seemed to have noticed. So she closed her eyes and sent a silent apology to Krikor, then leaned forward and waited for Megouch to recount the events, which had led up to Setrag being taken away by the militia.

It was true that the Tokadjian brothers had always hovered on the edge of political danger but Setrag had made sure that they operated within the limits of accepted boundaries. He had developed his literary style in response to established levels of national censorship, using a form of intellectually encrypted code, which his astute readers, having lived through years of tyranny, could easily interpret. Reading between the lines they understood when under-reporting and understatement masked ugly acts of brutality or religious and ethnic persecution. Innuendo and irony allowed veiled accusations to be labelled at perpetrators without directly pointing fingers of blame. Astra had heard his rationale at her first editorial meeting. "Most of our readers already know our hands are tied. They know to read between the lines and interpret truth through ambiguity. Veiled truths are still better than the official whitewash." It was the philosophy of an idealist who felt pain at being part of a world which required such a compromise. The compromise had worked, right up till then, but it was almost 1914 and local and international politics were shifting against the underdog. The Great War was about to allow full freedom for the elimination of "undesirable minorities" and it was to be a very different story from then on.

Astra, Hagop and Gayené sat and waited for Megouch to control his quivering jaw. "Setrag had stopped off at the barber's shop so I was on my own. It was about eight fifteen and I'd just put the coffee on when someone started yelling and banging on the door. 'They're coming to raid your shop, clear out whatever you can.' Then he ran off, and I have no idea who he was. So I dived next door to Spiro's to see if he could help."

Spiro, an elderly carpenter had recently been widowed and was no friend of the local officials. His wife had died under the wheels of the carriage carrying the Minister of the Interior himself, but so far he had received neither a word of apology, nor a kind word of sympathy, and as such was the perfect ally. This usually mild mannered and private individual instantly came up with a daring plan.

Megouch continued. "He was obviously out for revenge and said we should make a hole in the wall at the back so I could pass everything through to his shop. He had a mound of sawdust he hadn't yet cleared out so we used it to cover everything up. He said they'd never think of looking under there. So I ripped open a hole through the wall with my bare hands." He stopped to show them his cuts, took in a sigh and sipped some more brandy, before going on. "With Spiro on one side and me on the other, we worked like donkeys. I got rid of all our most sensitive books, newspapers, periodicals, party leaflets and even the flags, while Spiro covered them with sawdust."

Within the hour the shop and print room had been cleared of every bit of potentially incriminating material. Megouch thanked his unlikely comrade but there was still a lot to do. He set about spacing the "acceptable" international books and magazines along the shelves. Setrag had still not arrived but Megouch had tried to think positively. "We only had a stranger's word for it, and who was he anyway? I hoped it might have been a prank or even a false alarm. I stood and waited by the window hoping and praying, but then I heard marching boots getting louder and closer and I knew they were in the street." Megouch had lost the battle not to weep but carried on. "They were outside, and I tried to hide, but they started slamming their rifle butts into the door and would have smashed it open so I had to let them in." It sounded like an apology. "I ran to the back as they stomped inside, before starting to stab at every corner, plunging bayonets into books and shelves as though blood and guts were hidden within. It seemed to last forever. None of them said a word. Then, when there was nothing left to stab, they kicked their way through the shredded literature, mouthing threats of death and torture as they left. I wonder if any of them can read at all? Almost every book on every shelf was destroyed. It was though they came to perform an act of meaningless barbarism, and in that they were completely successful." He came up for air, slammed his fist on the table and grabbed the brandy bottle. Hagop poured him a top-up and he gulped it in one. "It could have been worse. They didn't lay a finger on me and took nothing away with them. Then I locked the door out of habit, there was nothing left to steal and went to find Setrag. I went to the barber's shop but it was shut. A young lad sitting outside told me what had happened. Apparently soldiers pulled Setrag from the chair and dragged him down the street with lather still on his face. Then the barber threw everyone else out and locked the doors. Just then Hagop came up the street and told me Baba was dead."

Megouch's emotions finally got the better of him so Hagop took over. "Anyway, we went back to the shop to clear up and think about what we could do next. I'm wondering if someone put a vicious note in the church drop box, but who?" The drop box was the government's only secret ballot system but as the box was placed outside the church anyone, even, or especially, government officials, could drop in accusations at any time. Threats and intimidation were a common ploy to subjugate the local opposition and exert terror without ever having to justify whatever response they chose to pursue.

But Hagop knew that holding a captive in prison often boiled down to a straightforward financial arrangement, as long as the family had enough money with which to bargain a release. He had negotiated his boss' release only last week. It was accepted that local government leaders got richer while local populations became poorer. However, in his experience, long-term incarceration of well-known newspaper editors with an international reputation, who had friends in high places, would be political suicide. Strategically, the Ottomans needed friends abroad. America and European powers were on the verge of siding as world war Allies and the propaganda machine of international affairs was still on Setrag's side. Hagop Sabondjian knew his way around official headquarters, having walked miles through the corridors of power to pay taxes, levies, and fines, even bribes if it meant they might live and work in peace. "I guessed they might be holding him in the cells under the Ministry of the Interior, but by the time we got there the doors were locked. So we asked a guard patrolling outside to check prisoner lists for that day and eventually after two hours someone came back with confirmation that Setrag was being detained on the charge of "subversion."

Megouch was shaking with fear at the thought of going back. "Those monsters murder, rape, take our land, march around like bandits, destroy our livelihood, point bayonets and rifles at us, and we're not even allowed to carry a tiny knife." Hagop added the voice of experience. "You'll see, we'll just pay them and they'll let him go." It sounded so simple and in most cases it was so. Money had a power and privilege all of its own. "If they're so keen on taking our money why did they keep us standing out there for so long? Are they trying to up the stakes?" said Megouch cynically under his breath. "I'm sure we will be allowed to open our account tomorrow," replied Hagop with a comforting reassurance.

Astra shuddered to think of the conditions her husband was enduring while they sat around the table drinking lemon tea. The thought that he might be breathing the same filthy air as a savage murderer was heightened by the memory of recent ocular accounts she had read in the American press. Two anonymous prisoners had somehow managed to escape from a Turkish jail and were now living in New York, the land of free speech. Their graphic stories of unthinkable tortures while guards attempted to extort statements, not caring if they were true or false, for the sole purpose of incriminating others sickened her. But she tried to remove them from her mind; this was not the time to dwell on miseries past or present. "Megouch and Gayené, you two stay with your mother tomorrow and I'll go with Hagop. The bishop is coming in the morning to bless the body of Baba Krikor and to organize the funeral arrangements." Just then someone knocked at the door. It was Peproné. She had hardly seen her daughter since her wedding day, though not through want of trying. It was always the same, Anna would keep her foot on the door offering lame excuses, all on the same theme, "I am sorry Madam Sabondjian, it's not a good day today," or her headache was bad, or Krikor needed rest and quiet.

"Astra may I come in, I won't stay long. I've come to offer my condolences," she said over formally. "Mama, it's fine, Anna is sleeping, you can come in." Gayené took the warm basket of food from her hand. "It's just some rice and chicken, I didn't think anyone would feel like cooking tonight." "Thank you, Mama Sabondjian, and I wanted to say this before; it's so nice having Astra living with us, she's like a real sister to me. I don't know what I'd do without her now." The young women in the Tokadjian house needed to stick together. Peproné knew what she meant. "Mama, let's go upstairs," said Astra whisking her mother upstairs to see her grandson before she heard Setrag's news. "Let her enjoy a rare moment with him first," she thought and waited till her mother was saying goodbye before telling her. Then as she closed the door and looked down into the dark narrow hallway it struck her that, at still only nineteen, she was too young for all this. She was the protector now, she was protecting her mother, protecting Gayené, protecting Megouch, a mother herself, and with her husband in prison, who was there to protect her now? In less than two short years her life had changed beyond all recognition. In a moment of realization she knew the clock could only go forward. Her innocence and youth had disappeared into a puff of smoke when she wasn't looking.

Next morning Astra and Hagop waited like obedient sheep outside the Ministry of Interior for what felt like an eternity until at last a guard summoned them to enter. The building was almost empty making their feet echo too loudly on white marble stairs as they were briskly ushered into a first floor office. It didn't take long. "Mr. Tokadjian has been quite co-operative and we have decided to let him go this time, but of course there are fines to pay but if you are able to cover our 'expenses' immediately, the matter will be settled." His craggy face grinned menacingly as he slowly flipped through the pages of a large black ledger. Hagop paid the bill and they were dismissed.

This was Astra's first time in a government building and after the danger was almost over she felt free to take in her surroundings. By the time the huge mahogany doors closed behind them Astra's eyes were wide with outrage. "Oh my God, did you see that palatial interior? It's obscene! The hard earned taxes of starving peasants probably paid for it all. They toil and sweat for years to line the pockets of these ignorant pigs." Hagop didn't reply, sensing malevolent eyes flickering through the first floor windows. Within minutes Setrag had joined them at the gates. "Did they hurt you?" she asked. "It was terrible, look, they shaved off all my hair and made me look like a criminal!" As he took off his hat to show them, she saw his hand was an oozing mess of cigarette burns.

It would never be that easy again. Setrag had been ordered to close down his newspaper but that still left the matter of his political affiliations. They weren't finished with him yet. In the months that followed, in a travesty of justice, Setrag was imprisoned and condemned to hang four times. Each time they dragged him to court on trumped up charges, not that their laws required them to explain why one man should hang while another might buy freedom. Hagop and Megouch fled town, forced into hiding to avoid the same fate, so that Astra was left to negotiate life saving deals with the Ottoman judicial system single-handedly.

Nothing could ever have prepared her for the ordeal that on four separate heart-stopping occasions she would somehow manage to save him and others from the clutches of death. Astra, the charmed winged angel from Erzeroum, found superhuman powers and did what she had to do to set him free. Amongst the images, which would last a lifetime, one kept pushing its way to the front, but it was her doing, the way she recorded it to memory. His sunken face caked in blood, his tortured beaten body bent double as he tried to drag broken limbs to reach her. The guards were always close, laughing and listening. "I'm alright," he told her to defy them and to save his friends from more torture. "Setrag, we're almost outside, please don't die, not after all this," she pleaded propping up his skeletal frame while he dug his jagged nails tighter into the palm of her hand. She had stored it into her bank of visual images by recording the day in her consciousness. "Today, the 16th of February 1914, Setrag was released for the fourth time. One day we'll wonder where in God's name did we find the strength to live through all this?"

It surprised her more than anyone to realize that almost overnight Astra had transformed herself from a dewy-eyed social reformer into a tough talking hostage negotiator. She was not yet twenty years old. With his back against the wall, and with no time to think or breath, she jumped into hostile territory to secure releases not only for her husband, but also for his closest friends, all high-ranking members of the Dashnag party. She argued with reason, pleaded with passion, threatened with caution, bargained with cunning, and they listened. She strode fearlessly into the Ministry of Interior demanding to be heard as though it was her right, she settled ransom payments at the Ministry of Finance, throwing money at them like confetti and persuaded every known newspaper contact of the international press propaganda machine to tell his story to the outside world. News spread like wildfire. She banged on the door of American and British Consulates till they let her in and agreed to negotiate life saving interventions. As the hangman's noose pulled tighter, the cost of ransoms grew bigger so she demanded help from her wealthy sister; there was no time for family niceties. Each time Setrag came home, far from basking in the glory of her achievement, the young mother turned hard-hitting prison reformer pushed to the limits of endurance, collapsed with exhaustion into her husband's beaten arms.

Astra had never needed her family's love more, so it cut her to know that not all of them were on her side. "You know that if you were to denounce your husband, your whole family would be given amnesty," the presiding Mayor had told her. "So what's so wrong with saying a few words, then it would all be over, Hagop and Megouch could come back home and life could get back to normal," said Aizennig. Astra couldn't believe her ears. "You can't really mean that; they'd hang him!" she said feeling the whole world was turning against her. Aizemnig shrugged her shoulders in reply and Astra stormed out of the house. "I know it's terrible Mama but I can't believe how selfish she's being. What on earth is she thinking of, slamming her fists on dangerous tables, threatening powerful officials on a daily basis?" Even Anna, Setrag's own mother, had muttered as much. Were they really asking her to denounce the man she loved to make their small lives more comfortable!

On this rare visit to see her mother Aizemnig was on form. "Mama, Astra reminds me of a rampant lioness on the African plain, pouncing at the throat of a charging wild beast with her precious cub in her mouth. Can't she see how dangerous it is for all of us? Who knows how many more wild beasts are lurking in the shadows." Aizemnig had just finished reading *Life on the Serengeti* and was practising her social repertoire for after dinner party soirees. She felt pleased with the parallel. Her wealthy husband had helped with ransom payments but after the four large donations to the Ottoman tax fund, Aizemnig felt utterly put upon. "It's just so typical of her. She just expects it!" Her daughter's callousness shocked her. "How can you speak about her like that? Astra has worked miracles: aren't you proud to have a sister like her? She's saved Setrag's life and the life of his friends, those wonderful men would have been hanged four times over if she had left things in God's hands," said Peproné, having felt every single stab of Astra's pain on her own skin, "Or have you completely forgotten everything your father stood for?" "Yes, of course I remember, but look where that got him! They killed him, didn't they? Mama we are all being tarred with the same brush, don't you care?" But Peproné knew the power of love and admired the passion, which drove Astra to stand up for justice with outrage and indignation. "Aizemnig, can't you see it's not a question of choice or convenience. She's compelled to do it, and anyway, a lioness that wears gloves cannot catch mice," she snapped, continuing with the animal theme. Astra was like her father. She operated with the same idealistic confidence of someone with right on her side. Armed with that alone, Astra strode upright and unyielding into enemy offices, over and over again. Whether it was her charisma or her incisive arguments, somehow she managed to persuade international strategic partners, America and Great Britain, to take up his case. Astra told them she had already smuggled out compelling evidence abroad and foreign powers were listening. "We have written to newspapers in America and England about the appalling treatment of innocent journalists in Turkish prisons whose only crime is that they are attempting to report the truth. I suggest that unless you investigate the evidence, you'll be left with egg on your faces. The world out there will know before you do what exactly is happening on your doorstep. You must intervene now and save them."

Torture in prisons was a strictly covert operation though in reality everyone, including the world outside, knew it was part and parcel of the Ottoman penal system. If prisoners complained they, or even worse, their fellow inmates, suffered even harsher punishments. This allowed the heinous goings-on inside jails to continue unimpeded. Threats served as effective deterrents against passing out hard evidence, which gave barbarous jailers free reign to go about their evil business as and when the mood took them.

Setrag had been beaten senseless but the fear that flowed through his bloodstream came from knowing that others would soon follow him into the chamber. Night after night chilling sounds echoed through his cell: high pitched squeals and muffled moans as friends, colleagues, and strangers were being given the same treatment just a wall away. He lived through it with them, every harsh lash from toughened firewood, every scorching stab from red hot pokers, as they denied their guilt and begged for mercy, till pain overload or death made them silent.

Astra's ready monies gave her access to visit her husband once a week when she would bring fresh bandages and ointment, a grudging concession granted to prisoners close to death. Visitors were welcome if they could help minimize the spread of gangrene, a medical inconvenience. They were never alone, the visits were kept short and she knew not to mention his worsening condition, but at least she knew he was still alive. The prisoners dismissed their torture injuries as "accidents," telling relatives how they had fallen down stairs, or had been "justifiably" punished after failed escape attempts and no visitors ever brought them up in conversation in case they added to the chances of even more terrible "accidents" being inflicted on their loved ones.

And so it went on till one day Setrag thought of an ingenious plan. Before she arrived he peeled off the top layer of his bloodstained bandages. Then, using a cracked nail as his pen, and the pot of his own urine as invisible ink, he gave her the evidence she needed. As she leaned forward to take them from him he whispered, "Don't wash it. Hold a match underneath it and my words will come through." So she went home and lit a match under the ragged cloth till a spidery scrawl in yellow ochre began to appear as though by magic. He had crammed every possible unstained surface with harrowing accounts of inhumanity and suffering inflicted behind locked doors. Astra gently folded up the precious rag, wrapped it in a tea towel and put it in her handbag. "Setrag, you are a genius," she thought. "Now I have more than just money and your reputation to bargain with." She ran straight to the British Consulate.

Next day the British Consul, the prison governor, and a newly arrived German officer met behind closed doors. Astra never knew what was said but she presumed that the Consul exerted his waning western influence by expressing moral outrage and the fez adorning image conscious prison governor, who fearing accusations of political 'hand washing' was left no choice but to accept some culpability. So Setrag and his compatriots were released and lived to fight their political battles another day. But by the end of 1914 American and English political power was diminishing in Asia Minor. The reason was simple. The Ottomans had made a new important friend and Germany had much bigger things on its mind.

Koko was just eighteen months old when on the 19th March 1915, his new baby sister, Adriné, fluttered open her wide brown eyes to see them all smiling down at her, all that is except for Anna Tokadjian. Anna had always preferred the male of the species and even though Astra had already delivered a son, Anna stood aghast, as the baby was wiped clean. "Oh no, Setrag, it's a girl!" she cried in anguish. From that moment on Anna refused to speak a single word to her daughter-in-law for months. Astra never understood why, but although it was hurtful, at times she thanked God for the exclusion. It gave her time to lick the wounds of the last few months and all in all it was a relief to be ignored. Silence meant peace and her heart craved it. So she took to reading novels and doing intricate embroidery as therapy from the harsh political world she'd been dragged into kicking and screaming. Whether it was the result of the worn torn world around them or an emotional valve released in their own household, baby Adriné was showered with an outpouring of affection from her parents. But Setrag could not accept his mother's alienation. His terrible experiences had made him more demanding of family harmony. He knew life was too short, but Astra, the peacemaker, preferred to bite the bullet and wait for a natural thaw, and it finally came three months later.

Setrag was still out of circulation, spending much of the day in bed waiting for his bones to heal. "You know Setrag, I think your mother's finally coming out of her depression. Today she sang Adriné a lullaby and actually spoke to me." "What did she say?" he asked. "She said Adriné is so pretty and with those dark eyes she thinks she's definitely taken after her side of the family. Then she smiled and kissed her forehead. I haven't seen her smile for so long." Setrag admitted it was an improvement at least. She hugged him gently: his ribs were still healing. "Your mother seems to have built a wall around herself and I wonder if she feels we're being irresponsible for bringing another child into this dangerous world. I worry about that too. The whole world is at war, and here we are having children. Think of it, she's already lost one son, her other son is living in America, who knows when she'll see him again, then we nearly lost you so many times, and we're still mourning your father. Her nerves are torn to shreds." Setrag, for all his philosophical thinking, had never once pondered over the rights and wrongs of bringing new life into a corrupt and dangerous world. "You know I adore children. I want us to have as many as we can, lots of them. They are our hope for the future. Without them life has no meaning." "That's all very well, I feel the same way, but have you ever considered what would happen to them if something happened to us?" Neither of them knew what to say after that. Their future was still unfolding.

For the first time in his life, Setrag had too much time on his hands and it was not sitting easy with his industrious soul, so he took to teaching two-year-old Koko to sing songs and write in four scripts, Armenian, Greek, French and Turkish. Astra could hardly believe the rate at which her son was lapping it all up but drew the line at Setrag's choice of bedtime stories. "Don't overload the child! What can he understand about the Illiad?" But Setrag sat on Koko's bed and read out aloud for hours, long after his son's eyes had closed for the day. "You would make a wonderful teacher, if a little too demanding," she said. It was a serious suggestion now that editorial journalism was out of the question. The military police had come back to make sure. Even though the brothers had shut up shop, they set fire to the office building, as well as burning down the carpenter's shop next door. No one had seen the poor carpenter since then. Setrag feared the worst. "They suspected he helped us, so they killed him, the bastards."

Chapter VIII

Exchanging Lives and Disillusionment

NONE of it was her war, nor were the images invading her dreams more vivid. Shouldering the guilt of the conscientious objector who abhorred the taking of life for any reason, she shuddered to think of the depths that humanity could reach. In March 1915, a Dashnag peace mission to end the hostilities in Van ended disastrously when the Ottoman Armenian leader Ishkhan was murdered by the government and the Dashnags were accused of treachery. "How can they blame us? We set the meeting up to bring them together, but even Constantinople has turned its back on us. Now that the British and French naval attacks on the Dardanelles have been called off, we are on our own." Setrag was terrified. "I hate to say this, but the mood has definitely changed, there's a defiance in the air. This could spell serious trouble."

In their new gung-ho mood they struck out at the Armenians. By the early hours of April 24th 1915 the "Armenian solution" was on the verge of implementation. The police arrested hundreds of leading Armenian politicians, writers, educators, lawyers, and churchmen. In Constantinople, the cream of the intelligentsia were held at a central police station for three days, before being exiled to Ayash and Chankiri prisons, where most of them were executed. By two o'clock that morning Setrag had already fled and Astra was waiting for the military police to come banging on the door. Someone had warned him and immediately Setrag set about spreading the word. He weaved his way across town, dodging curfews, hiding in shadows, and managed to alert other party members. They, in turn, did the same. The government plot for the complete ethnic "displacement" of Armenians was about to spill blood from Erzeroum to Smyrna and in every town and village in between. About the same time the police, again in the capital, arrested five thousand young Armenian men of fighting age, loyal to the Ottoman regime, and none of them were seen again. The way was clear; it was the opportunity they had been waiting for. Hidden under the blood stained blanket of World War I, their plan could proceed with swift deadly impetus. The Ottoman government had begun its systematic extermination, confidently believing that the annihilation of a whole nation would be far easier during a world war, as would getting away with such mass murder.

So with Setrag and Megouch gone, Astra tried to calm her mother. "Mama T, drink this brandy, at least they're safely away by now," though they had no idea where. When the soldiers came the house was full of women but they knew which one of them might know the answer. She tried not to flinch as a bayonet touched her cheek. "Where is your husband?" they asked her. "I have no idea where he is, but be sure I will tell him you were looking for him as soon as he returns." Her defiant tone spurred them into action. The women froze in panic as they stomped through every room, throwing up beds, stabbing furniture, smashing vases, cursing her nation. Then one of them seized Astra's arm and dragged her out of the house, "Perhaps a spell in prison will refresh your memory."

Astra was kept in prison for thirty days and was left pretty much alone by the authorities. They questioned her a few times and she wondered why if they didn't believe her, she wasn't being tortured. She shared her cell with two other women whose husbands had also failed to come in for "questioning." None of them were tortured but the fear that it might happen at any time hung over their heads like a bad smell. They were not allowed visitors and the food was stale and meagre and made them ill whenever they were hungry enough to eat it. They sat and slept on a damp stone floor, hardly exchanging a word all day. Their voices echoed and they knew who was listening. One day blurred into the next, all except for one. Astra always remembered the strained expression on one of her cell mates for the strangest of reasons; her severe constipation and that acrid smell she released when after thirty days nature finally took its course. It had completely overpowered them, until silent embarrassment turned into unrestrained hysteria. The three of them stood laughing and fanning skirts in a desperate attempt at air circulation. It was the most fun Astra had had in weeks.

Setrag's reliable sources brought him news that his wife had been imprisoned and so there was nothing else to do but to hand himself over to the prison authorities. He knew this time he was unlikely to escape the hangman's noose, but after his experiences of prison, his life was a small price to pay. Imagining her in that stinking hole at the mercy of torturers was more than he could take. "I would die for you," he'd told her a thousand times and now he was about to prove it. Then he remembered his parting words, "I'll see you soon, I promise." Setrag was a man of his word and contrived a plan. He paid a stranger to deliver a letter and within two hours it was in the hands of the prison governor. It was short and to the point. "I will give myself up at exactly 9 o'clock tonight under the main clock at Smyrna train station. Bring Astra there at eight fifty-five and give us a few minutes, please. She's done nothing but be a loving wife and has no idea where I am." He hoped they wanted him enough to agree.

At five to nine Astra was trembling, bewildered and standing underneath the central clock at Smyrna Station. The curfew was in operation and the place was deserted. A thousand thoughts were spinning in her head. They had taken her from her cell and brought her here without a word except for giving strict instructions not to move. Then they marched off somewhere out of site. "What's going on, why here, why now?" But she knew better than to question their reasons or hidden agendas. She looked down at her filthy skirt and saw how thin she had become. She waited in that dark eerie space, feeling those warning hairs on the back of her neck for what seemed an eternity. Then her heart started to thump as running feet charged towards her and she gasped clean air into her lungs for the first time in thirty days.

Fading light through the windows made it difficult to see. "Oh my God, I am going to be shot and no one will ever know. They've brought me here for my execution!" Her head started to spin and she began to run expecting the sharp burn of a bullet to hit her in the back. But her body was weak, her feet dragged along the ground, the footsteps were catching up with her with every step, he was almost there. Her heart stopped as a hand grabbed her arm. "Astra, it's me. It's me, Setrag." She turned round and collapsed in his arms. He had asked for five minutes, that was all, but the minute they touched, an army of heavy boots stomped towards them and suddenly they were completely surrounded. She knew then what he had done and wept into his neck till he lifted her face. "I need you to be strong, for me and for our children. Don't cry for me, but pray that I will be the last to die for our nation." His eyes pierced with determination and she felt his blood pumping power through her veins. He was on fire.

She listened till his footsteps were gone. They sounded strangely melodic, staccato notes echoing away as his metal-capped shoes clipped soft lyrical music as he strolled to his death. How could he have been so unruffled with eight stabbing bayonets hurrying his departure? How typical of him to have come as the prized hostage, so composed and immaculately dressed! Sixteen bloodthirsty eyes had just watched him reach into his top pocket to take out a silk handkerchief to mop up her tears. Astra had recognized it as the one she had embroidered before they had married, "To S from A with endless love." The irony turned her grief to rage. Well, he really had thought of everything! Then her rage turned to accusation. She blamed him for his expectations that she would love him forever, she blamed him for leaving her, and she blamed him for being left to break the news to his poor mother that her son has just exchanged his life for her freedom. She blamed him for his powerful nationalism, which put his precious homeland above his family, but most of all, she blamed him for walking away with an air of a man who had fulfilled his life's dream, or was it theatrical bravado? She would never know. He didn't even look back one last time. She felt punished, cheated and abandoned in a dark grim empty station and saw the future for what it was. Pushing her feet towards the one light left burning over the main door she wondered what more life could throw at her. She was still only twenty years of age.

Chapter IX

Arbitrary Fortunes in Shifting Sands

BY the summer of 1915 they were all on tenterhooks. At first it seemed that only Armenians in the East were being deported but it soon became apparent that no one was safe. The climate of fear was spreading. News of the massacres and deportations, a euphemism for mass murder, had begun to reach them but the stories seemed too terrible to be true and no one except the most cynical could bring themselves to believe it was part of a centralized plan of genocide. They thought they were protected in Smyrna, the western most tip of the Empire and still under Greek influence, but they were wrong. Murder was becoming as infectious as cholera, and was spreading as quickly. In just a few months more than two thirds of the Armenian population would be dead.

It took Astra most of the night to walk home from Smyrna Station. Anna Tokadjian was genuinely pleased to see her. "Astra thank heaven, you're back! Your children have done nothing but cry since you left." All Astra wanted to do was to hold them close but she had to get it over with. At least now she would have an understandable reason to be enemy number one. "So, what are you waiting for, you must go now, see if you can stop it again," said Anna. "I'll go but I don't know what more I can do. If I could change places with him I would, you know that."

The prison guards recognized her. "So you're back again. You must like it here. Are you missing your cell mates?" "All I want to know is if my husband was brought here last night." The guard pushed her away. "Your husband is dead, now go, and don't come back."

"My son would still be alive if he had never met you. He could have gone back to America." She didn't reply knowing Anna Tokadjian needed someone to blame, but it was time to leave so she took her children and went back to her mother's house leaving everyone to grieve in their own way. But Astra felt the mysterious powers of metaphysics stroking her neck and had no real urge to grieve. "Mama, every time I shut my eyes I can sense his breathing. I don't believe he's dead."

Three weeks later impatient gendarmes banged their rifles butts at the door again shouting "Open up immediately." It was the dreaded Ministry of the Interior. They had tracked her down. "We have a warrant for Astra Tokadjian, her two children, and Zevart Sabondjian. You have to come with us now." "What for?" she asked. "Your names are on the list. You have five minutes to collect what you need. You're going to Syria." "No, no, there must be a mistake," pleaded Peproné, but Astra had been expecting it. But why did they want her sister? Her mother stood between them but an impatient hand lashed out and she fell backwards. "Leave her alone you bullies, we're coming on your march," said Zevart. By the time they gathered a few belongings and quickly dressed the children, there was no time left for last minute hugs or tearful good-byes, which was just as well.

They had to sit on the floor, the train was crammed full. "We're stopping at Konya, then it's on foot from there," said a voice from somewhere behind them. "Then they'll make us walk hundreds of miles in the burning desert and if we live through that they'll kill us when we get to Der el Zor." Others joined in with "I'd rather die here, what's the point?" "Oh be quiet, what do you know you stupid old man," snapped a well-dressed woman thinking her gold would buy her freedom when the time came. Three hours later the train stopped suddenly in the middle of nowhere. They craned their necks to see beyond a hostile jagged mountain pass, but there was nothing for miles. Everyone was hoping the same thing, that it was a technical hitch rather than something more sinister. Soon they had the answer as a dusty cloud of smoke rose up from the depths below. A dozen or so sword brandishing bandits were charging up hill and straight at them like bats out of hell.

They were ordered off the train in orderly rows for what they were told was a head count. Zevart held baby Adriné and Astra gripped Koko's hand while sinister eyes scanned everyone up and down. A few young girls were being singled out. Suddenly she heard Zevart scream, "Hold the baby!" Astra stooped to grab her just as

Zevart let her go from her arms; it was that or taking Adriné with her. A split second later, once the baby was safe, Astra grasped the full horror of what was happening. Zevart kicked and punched with every ounce of strength in her body as the sabre-flashing bandit threw her onto his horse. He pressed down on her writhing body as though she was a lumpy saddlebag, then clipped his spurs and took off. Astra watched helplessly as her sister's chestnut hair trailed the dusty earth and she screamed out for dear life. "Oh my God, please help me, that's my sister, he's taken my sister," she cried out but no one moved. Instead, eyes were averted in resigned acceptance, as though nothing was happening as more squirming bundles were dragged down black ravines.

The girls' screams echoed through the mountains, then nothing till the order came to board the train. "How can we go and leave them here?" she pleaded to a group of elderly women who seemed incapable of speech. They just shook heads and joined the queue to be herded back on. As the train began to move, Astra wished she were dead. Adriné was two months old, too young to know, but Koko was almost three. He squeezed his eyes tight shut and clung on to his mother's skirt with both hands knowing it could have been her. Her wise little philosopher knew better than to ask why his auntie wasn't there to pop sugary sweets into his mouth. "Mama I love you so much," he whispered as the train chugged through a long black tunnel. Even though she didn't see his face, his desperate little voice stirred her soul and gave her life a new purpose, survival. She knew she must survive no matter what. They had no one else in the world.

The power of positive thought and plain good fortune converged right there, on that crowded platform in Konya to cut short her journey to the death marches to the Syrian Desert. "Mama, look at all those people," said Koko, as the train steamed into Konya station. The landscape had opened up to give a full and uninterrupted view of a massive encampment spread across open fields as far as the eye could see. The sight made their jaws drop. Thousands of people were huddled together, and even from that distance it was obvious that many were close to death. Astra focused her eyes into the distance trying to guess numbers. Possibly up to ten thousand people, their tongues and stomachs swollen, as they slumped like sick starved cattle, too weak to move. "What hell is this?" she sighed, as filthy naked children, covered in sores, reached up at the windows, begging for food as the train pulled to a stop.

Even in all of this, history would have told them to stay right there, better to die together in this decaying graveyard on the east side of Konya Station than to tackle death marches from which only a handful would survive, but they could not choose how to die. Those who were taken lost their life's savings to pay for a cup of stagnant water, only to be shot in the head as they tried to drink it. Others seeing this would walk on as their tongues swelled bigger, before they too met the same end. Others witnessed young mothers clutching babies as they held hands in rows and threw themselves into the Euphrates, preferring suicide to savage rape. Others were killed when their feet refused to carry them any further while their loved ones were forced to march on and leave the bodies of their mothers and children to be piled high onto pyramids of corpses littering the grey sands behind them, dehumanizing victims and perpetrators alike.

"Everyone get off and take your belongings! We stop here!" They left the train, praying to be moved on to the desert road, anywhere to get away from the unbearable stench. "Cover your mouth Koko, take short breaths," she said putting her hand over Adriné's face. "Mama, where are we going? I don't want to stay here, I feel sick," he said running towards the gate. Suddenly she saw a painted wooden sign perched on a rickety table by the ticket stand. She had never studied formal Turkish so it took her a few minutes to read it properly. It said, "Army seamstresses wanted. Apply here." Now that Turkey was fully entrenched in its commitment to war, mobilization was an urgent priority, and the soldiers needed uniforms.

Within an hour, she had been taken to the clothing factory around the corner, proven her skills on a sewing machine, passed her interview and was offered a job. Miracles were coming thick and fast that day but she didn't know it yet. In the factory, with heads down and busy at work, were two of her closest friends. Anoushka and Satenig had both seen her walk in, but as a move out of turn was enough to put an end to your employment, they raised astonished eyebrows at each other instead. Astra walked right past their tables without seeing them. They heard her ask Koko to sit quietly on the floor, and hold his little sister before sitting at the sewing machine. Anoushka wanted to rush up and hug her but she kept her head down, knowing output was always measured against quicker and better hands whenever the trains pulled in.

It was nearly five o'clock and Adriné craved her mother's milk and no amount of rocking by her brother silenced the need. Koko's anxious eyes caught the supervisor and she walked over to Astra. Her voice was kind and gentle and belied her stern appearance. "Yes, that's very good, we can use you. Now go and find the lodgings. Ask for Fatima and tell her you are to have the back room on the first floor. If you have money Fatima will cook you some food. We do not allow children here under any circumstances, so don't bring them back, is that clear? Be here tomorrow morning at seven sharp." She tried to look pleased but her heart was breaking. By the time they walked out of factory, the platform was empty and she caught the last of the deportees disappearing into the quagmire of pestilence and disease accompanying deportation. She sighed, crossed herself, and wept with relief. For a while at least they were safe.

She had done what she had to do, though she didn't know how. Her hands had been trembling as she threaded the machine and the stitches seemed to be wavering in all directions, but she had been fast. She couldn't get her sister's terrified face out of her mind. "How could I sit and sew trousers when God knows what's happened to my sister?" "Mama, please don't say that," Koko was distraught. "Why, what did I say?" "You said you wished you could go blind. How could you see us or sew clothes if you went blind?" "Did I say that? You know I didn't mean it. I'm upset, that's all. Of course I don't want to go blind." He wanted to believe her. "Now cheer me up with a big kiss and let's go and find our new house. You must be even hungrier than your sister."

When people met Astra they sensed she valued and understood them almost as soon as their eyes met, because she did. She exuded a rare unconditional respect and admiration for the human spirit, which inspired dignity, and self-respect, even in those who until then never knew it was in them. Her gentle aura comforted souls, and her life energy brought out the best in people. It was nature's gift to her, and she used it with judgement. It was an effortless short-cut into people's hearts, and it was with this that she was able to touch the unlikeliest of soul mates. She was tough too, and by the time they found the lodgings, emotional release had given way to an inner strength.

Adriné was still nuzzling for her mother's breast as milk dampened Astra's shirt, so she buttoned up her coat. "I have to feed her soon or she'll die of hunger," she thought as she pulled the door bell. The door flew open and a huge figure pointed them inside. The entrance hall was cool and dark, and the air smelled sweet with jasmine. The floor and walls were decorated in lavish blue, red and green Moorish tiles right up to the tall ceiling. They heard the trickling of water nearby. "Mama, look! A fountain!" The unexpectedly lavish interior soothed their spirits. Astra searched into her bag for her room ticket and looked around her, trying to get her bearings. The house was enormous. The atrium centred on a maze of rooms with a wide staircase on the right leading to floors above and below. It looked like a medieval palace. "Good evening. May I speak to Fatima?" asked Astra. The figure pointed to her pursed lips and shook her head. Then she put her palm on her chest and Astra realised that the huge figure was in fact not a man but a youngish woman, and she was mute. As her eyes began to focus in the dark, she saw Fatima more clearly. She was almost toothless, with wiry black hair, and huge red knuckles. Astra nodded her understanding before bowing and offering her hand in formal greeting. Fatima pointed upstairs, and they followed her up as she stomped and giggled silently to herself. "I think I'm going to like her," thought Astra.

It was nine thirty and Fatima had just collected the supper tray. Koko lay next to his sister on the bed, finally asleep. He had battled hard to keep awake, worried his mother might go blind if he took his eyes off her for a single moment. It was time to focus on tomorrow, and make sense of a day that had started so benignly. What about her children, how could she leave them and go to work? It was still noisy in the hallway outside, and for that she was grateful. The slamming doors, the women gossiping, even the evening chorus of birds outside the window helped her pretend she was not alone. When it grew quieter she checked her watch. Fifteen hours ago, on a day when time and space had lost all meaning, she had just woken up expecting to take her son for a stroll along the fish market.

Then she heard someone calling her name and rushed to open the door half expecting beyond hope that her sweet Zevart had somehow escaped and found her. "Astra, we're here too!" said Satenig and Anoushka in unison. She felt she was hallucinating. They were the last people she expected to see standing outside her little room in this house full of strangers. "I thought you were Zevart," she replied before a wave of bitter disappointment took away the strength from her legs. "Is she here too?" asked Anoushka. "No, she's probably dead and it's all my fault." Astra had someone to tell at last, and to unburden her guilt. They listened open mouthed till Satenig, sensing sympathy was the last thing she needed, made her rethink her logic. "How on earth can you think it was your fault they came to deport her? We're here too, aren't we? It's just pot-luck. They pick out names at random. What, do you honestly think that all those poor people in those fields are here because they support the Dashnag party or any other party for that matter?" She needed that. It was only then that she saw quirky fate for what it was. "I can't believe it. You're here too! Oh thank God!" They helped her to bed and lay down with her till she slept.

Chapter X

The Transient Nature of Hopes and Dreams

ASTRA had no choice but to entrust her children in Fatima's care. Adriné was fed mother's milk early morning and late evening. It was not ideal, but luckily Koko could eat lunch with Fatima. Communication was surprisingly easy given she had no voice at all. It worked well under the circumstances and soon Astra had no doubts about leaving her precious children in the care of those huge capable hands. When her work allowed, Fatima would sit with Koko and listen to his stories. Childlike Fatima shared his love of fables and fairy tales, and soon she knew them all, almost as well as he did. Koko had mastered the mysteries of word recognition before he was two and after this he never stopped reading. Astra would come home to hear them both in the kitchen and rather than go straight in, she would stand behind the door breathing in mouthwatering smells of Ejemi pilaf cooking in huge pots while her little prince sat on Fatima's ample knees recounting stories of kings and queens or ghouls and ghosts. Fatima pulled contorted faces as Koko screamed with glee at her rubbery face as it transformed into grotesque monsters about to get him. No one had ever read to her before, at least not that she could remember. She cuddled him at every opportunity, while ruffling his cute blonde curls in comic admiration, wondering how a child so young could decipher what seemed like random symbols on a page and make sense of them. Fatima was illiterate as well as mute. "Mama, I feel so sorry for Fatima, she can't speak or even read or write," said Koko, as though it must be the worst thing that could ever happen to a person. "There are far worse things than that you know," she replied, thinking that Fatima would never be taken to prison for questioning or tortured for information. "Well, I think Fatima is blessed. She's always so happy and cheerful whatever she does, and she has the best excuse not to have to talk to people she doesn't like. Plus, she has you to entertain her every day!" Koko suddenly felt much better.

Astra felt like a traitor working in a factory which made uniforms for the enemy. The days seemed endless and she would drift off into a fantasy world of sartorial frippery to keep sane. If she was honest she had all but given up on seeing sweet Zevart ever again, but she felt differently about Setrag. The three friends behaved like strangers during their working day, but linked arms like sisters as they walked home, starving hungry and bottom weary. At night they talked about old times and how when the war ended they would go home and try to forget the sights and smells which overpowered them every day. They would question fate, good and bad, and the power of angels who brought down miracles. "I believe each one of us has a guardian angel. How else can you explain that we're here together?" said Anoushka, always looking on the bright side. "Zevart might be living in the mountains somewhere, maybe taken in by a kind family, or she might have amnesia, you know that shock can do funny things to our memories." Astra appreciated her trying to keep hopes alive but it rang hollow somehow. Strangely, Satenig hardly mentioned Setrag except to say, "We can search for our loved ones when the war is finished, but until then, we must try to keep ourselves alive." So Astra kept it to herself, that she sensed him still breathing somewhere in this world. It was September 1915, and although it felt like an eternity, they had only been in Konya for two months. The war would not end for another three years.

In July 1915 Setrag and six of his compatriots had been sentenced to death. They were the last of the 84 intellectuals from Ayash prison to be sent into the desert for extermination in the name of nationalist cleansing. He was in good company, chained alongside two of Armenia's greatest contemporaries, Vasgen and Khajag. They were shackled together by a thick chain, which interlocked their necks and feet as they marched through the deserts of Der el Zor. As the chains tightened around their throats it forced them to move in more synchronized motion, for all their sakes, but Setrag was lucky. Their guards were reasonable people, and they were charming, polite and entertaining captives. As they marched, they sang songs and told jokes, which made their captors roar with laughter. Whenever the guards rode close by they would stroke their horses, sneak wry smiles and knowing looks, which chiselled away at the boundaries of captor and captive. It was a deliberate subtle psychological tactic and it worked perfectly and finally human empathy triumphed. After five days of banter and repartee under scorching skies, the guards began questioning their unsavoury duty. Setrag heard them talking. "These are good men, they don't deserve to die, why don't we leave their fate to Allah? If we let them go and they live, it will be God's will not ours, and who would ever know?" And so with a sudden abdication of responsibility they untied their chains. "We're going to leave you to find your own way in this wilderness. Praise Allah," they called out as they rode away as fast as their horses could carry them. Yet another last minute death defying reprieve made Setrag question whether his life was truly charmed.

The freed men rubbed feeling back into their necks, looked into the horizon and started walking aimlessly at first, then a renewed vigour started them thinking, "It would be good to stay together but we stand a far better chance if we separate," said Vasgen. So they made a pact to meet in better times, swore allegiance to their proud nation, said sad farewells, and began to make their own ways into an unknown barren landscape.

The sun had almost faded when Setrag caught sight of a figure silhouetted against shadows in the distance. He was perched against a rock; his menacing eyes wide open, staring straight at him. Setrag held eye contact until his gut instincts sensed the aura of a dead man. As he got closer he saw the man was dressed in full army uniform. Suddenly Setrag had a plan. He had never touched a dead body before and the thought of it sent shivers through his veins, but it was fate staring him in the face and he knew he had to do it. Crossing himself three times and apologizing reverently to the Almighty and to the soul of the dead man, he started to search his pockets and found more than he could have hoped for. "Poor bloke," he thought, "he was on his way home!" He read the release note. It had been issued on medical grounds just two days before. The body showed no outward signs of illness but he considered the possibilities: TB or cholera? What if it was contagious? But throwing caution to the wind, he removed the dead soldier's clothes, shook them clean, and shuddering with revulsion, put them over his own clothes. Then he put the identity documents and release pass back in the top pocket. The uniform fell loose around his shoulders but the boots fitted perfectly. "God forgive me," he said aloud, as he walked away leaving the naked corpse to hovering vultures. His luck was really in. Just a few feet away he saw a horse almost beckoning him to mount his empty saddle now that its rider was dead. "Thank you dear Lord," he said feeling spiritually exonerated. Using the sun as his compass Setrag rode for two days, always keeping a safe distance from the weaving lines of doomed deportees, praying his wife was not amongst them.

Thirty-six hours later Setrag was back in Smyrna sitting in Peproné's dining room, sand and dust still on his boots, eating the best she had to offer. Putting aside the million things she wanted to ask, she held his hand in silence while her son-in-law, back from the dead, shovelled mouthfuls of rice and meat down his ravenous throat. Everything else could wait. She hadn't recognized him at first, but even after a hot bath and a good night's sleep he still looked different. With no moustache, his wavy hair clipped short and his cheekbones piercing through cracked burned skin, he had the air of a Greek god. She watched his chiselled jaw chewing and swallowing in frantic motion and it struck her that, even famished and wounded, he exuded an aura of rare nobility. "You and your wife were both born with that, and nothing or no one can ever strip it away from you," she thought.

"Setrag, I know where they are, look!" she had said instantly, cursing her impetuosity, but the excitement of seeing him alive had caught her unawares. She had shown him the telegram and now he was about to go to find her. Setrag read it. "Dearest Mama, we are in Konya sewing army uniforms. Everything is fine. Astra." Peproné squeezed his hand in a vain attempt at persuasion. "It might be better to wait till things are not so dangerous. Konya is a big city. Where would you start looking?" But even as she said it, she knew it was useless. "Mama, you understand I must find her. She thinks I'm dead," he said adding, "please keep my coming here a secret. Don't even tell my mother, but try to find a way of letting her know they didn't get me this time either. I know you'll think of a way." He hugged her and she felt the freshly washed army uniform still damp against her chest. "Setrag, don't go yet, at least stay till your clothes dry." But he was already up with one foot out of the door. "Then at least be careful. God bless you all and keep you safe," she whispered.

She closed the door and stood there in the hallway looking critically at her own reflection in the long gilt mirror while her conscience struggled with the rights and wrongs of what she had just done. There was no one to hear her so Peproné embarked upon an audible soliloquy of moral debate, but this time she knew logic would not give her the answer. "Have I the right to keep a husband from his wife or a father from his children, even if it does mean putting my daughter's life in danger?" Then with barefaced defiance she concluded that they had just about had enough of evil intimidation. "It's about being with the people you love, that's what matters." She knew she had no more right to keep them apart than to defy the gods who contrived to bring them together. "At least the authorities think he's out of the picture now. He might well live longer as a dead man."

Setrag rode to Konya with a positive heart and a parcel of food in his saddlebag, courtesy of Peproné. His uniform gave him the freedom to patrol the streets under the guise of curfew surveillance, and before morning he was getting off his horse outside the military uniform factory. He had just seen and smelled the horrific encampment. He thought about saying goodbye to his horse but decided to tie him in a disused shed, before hiding behind a vantage point. He didn't have to wait long. Soon a long stream of women, their identities hidden behind black yashkmaks, were walking past him towards the large metal gates just a few feet away. He wondered how long he could stay there breathing in the repulsive smell of decaying flesh when he saw her. She was unmistakable. Amongst the trail of dark brown eyes, her eyes shone through like translucent aquamarine gems almost in touching distance. "She looks tired, but happy enough," he thought, angry at his selfishness at wanting her not to seem to have banished painful memories to history quite so soon.

That evening, riding his horse, Setrag followed them home unnoticed. It seemed completely bizarre that the three of them were here together, but these were strange times for everyone. Once he knew where they lived, he rode his horse into the field opposite to consider his options. Dressed in Turkish uniform, under the cover of a dead man, he was free to roam the streets undetected but it would be far better to work undercover from one safe place. Setrag had a plan. Wasting no time he rode across town to make contact with the secret army of journalists, now depleted in numbers, but ever more determined to tell the world what horrors were being perpetrated by their supposed protectors. Even with censorship, information was still getting through. He had read it himself two days ago. An undercover journalist in Smyrna had shown him a copy of the *New York Times,* and it was particularly explicit. The column was headed "No Armenians to be left alive in Ottoman Empire." Another paper had reported on atrocities in the eastern provinces in June 1915, particularly in the Sivas region where in one town, Shabin Karahissar, the entire population had been killed. "Every man, woman and child was killed by the sword." He used to have relatives there. He read about tens of thousands on forced deportations to the Syrian Desert of whom less than five percent reached their destination and about a new Ottoman law to ensure ethnic cleansing would continue down future generations. It had just been made illegal for any male Turk to marry an Armenian woman. "But it's not illegal to rape and murder them," he thought. However, if he was reading such news, then others were reading it too, and this gave him hope. The incurable optimist believed that the American and British governments could not stand by and would soon be rushing to help those still alive, but in reality the world was far too busy with their own war.

The next evening he stood in wait as Astra came out of the house alone. It was his chance. He followed behind her as she turned the corner and walked down the steps into a dark basement. His heart was pumping joy, just seconds away from showing her he was back from the grave, yet again. He tiptoed downstairs and waited till she emptied a large bundle of washing into a large tin container. Then he stepped inside and she felt a presence behind her. She turned round to see a figure in army uniform leaning against the wall. Her heart stopped. "Astra, it's me, Setrag!" His words brought back memories of another time, another place. "Oh my God! I just knew you were still alive," she said spurting tears onto his cheeks. "Shhh, not so loud, my love. No one must know I'm here, not Satenig, not Anoushka, not even Koko," he whispered, bursting her bubble much too soon, but he was like that. A pragmatist in love, no matter how deeply, was always a pragmatist.

As Astra walked up the stairs, her knees refused to stop shaking. She stood at the front door, glanced at her watch, tidied her hair and gathered her thoughts before taking a deep breath and stepping inside. "My nerves can't take much more," she thought. "Now calm down, try to be natural," she told herself, over and over again, as she nonchalantly strolled back into the kitchen to see Fatima anxiously waiting for her return. She was able to lip read a little if people spoke slowly. "Sorry Fatima, I bumped into a friend outside, you weren't worried about me, were you?" Astra had taken to helping with chores after her children were asleep. It was the least she could do for her new friend who had been doing such a good job of taking care of her children while she was at work. With Adriné strapped to her ample chest and Koko following behind her stroking the walls with a feather duster while reading from his favourite books, Fatima was still able to keep to her busy schedule. Fatima had often wondered why Astra had been offered a job in a factory whose policy was not to give work or provide accommodation to women with children, but since she couldn't speak to ask, she put it down to kismet, her and theirs. Fatima put most things down to kismet. She found it made life much simpler.

The fact was that since Astra had arrived Fatima felt an exciting liberation brewing inside her, urging her to develop new means of communication. Fairly early on Astra and Fatima had started to devise an idiosyncratic form of sign language. It was crude but effective, and it opened up a new silent language, which gave Fatima what she had needed for years. For the first time she was able to confide in someone whom she could trust, and who was genuinely interested in hearing the highs and lows of her own life. They would scrub mussels, slice aubergines, and roll out pastry late into the night while devising new words and symbols. When it was difficult, they drew pictures, or played a form of charades to communicate what they liked best or hated most. Before long their silent vocabulary became more sophisticated and Fatima knew she knew enough to be able to tell Astra her terrible secret.

Last Friday, her day off, Astra had been stirring quince jam over a low heat when Fatima took the pot off the fire and gestured her to sit down. She had something to tell her that no one else knew. It was what had made her mute at the age of twelve. Fatima had been playing by a stream near her house when two men had pulled her into the bushes and raped her so savagely that her vocal cords had ceased to work. They had kicked her face so hard her teeth fell out. They had sliced off both her nipples and before leaving her for dead, they had lit a match and burned her hair which never grew back soft and shiny like it used to be. Mirrors brought back constant reminders. Since that day, Fatima had not been able to speak one single word, not even to her mother.

Emotional exhaustion sent them to bed soon after; neither one could be bothered to bottle the jam after that. Astra lay awake all night thinking of two people she cared for. She hoped Fatima felt better after her soul baring and hoped that spilling out old wounds might bring on a new healing phase. She remembered those gnarled grubby fingers outside her house as they flicked the long string of dried nipples and how she had run upstairs to be with her little sister, but how other hands had taken her anyway while she stood by helpless. Next evening Astra needed her own healing phase and told Fatima. Their shared anguish took friendship to a higher level. "We are sisters now," they said and kissed each other.

Astra was standing at the sink washing her hands while her heart still thumped with joy. She wanted to shout it out: "Setrag is alive!" and rush upstairs and tell her friends that he was hiding in their cellar right now, but it was her secret, for now at least. She smiled at Fatima and reached for an onion, but even before she cut into the soft layers, she made up her mind to form a most unlikely alliance. "Fatima, I really need your help. It's very important and I am going to ask you to keep a secret. Please, promise me, not to breathe a word to anyone. Not even my friends or Koko must know." Astra hoped her deliberate mouth movements and sign symbols conveyed her words exactly. Fatima nodded unreservedly, put her wooden spoon down, and listened.

In the time it took to cook the stuffed vine leaves Fatima and Astra had devised an apparently foolproof plan. Setrag could stay right there in the cellar for as long as he wanted. He would need candle light, writing paper, and a pen. The large storeroom, with five concealed anterooms was the perfect hiding place where he could write away to his heart's content. As the rooms could be accessed from both inside and outside the house, it was perfect. "Promise me Fatima, it must be our secret," she said again after it was all settled, just to make sure. Fatima nodded, put her hand to her heart and raised her eyes to Allah. Then she led her to the door, pointed to the cellar, and using her two over large fingers signed, "Go to him and tell him, but don't stay long. You need to be up in a few hours."

After she left him Setrag spent the night on a cold stone floor and woke up like a bear with a sore head. "Why do I have to live like a criminal? I can't even see my children!" "I'll bring Adriné down later when Koko is asleep. He's much too young to keep such a huge secret. The war can't last forever. I have to go to work now, but be patient with Fatima. She is mute and illiterate and bigger than any man in Smyrna!" Setrag wondered who on earth had Astra chosen to take into their confidence, but as she had no time to go into details or to explain reasons of loyalty, he just had to trust her. "She has a kind heart and she loves us, especially your son." Setrag felt a pang of jealousy. A woman he had never met was able to hold and kiss his children just one floor above him.

When Astra went down to the cellar the following night, she saw Setrag had already made himself at home. She found him lying on a thick mattress, completely relaxed, arms behind his head, wearing that wry smile she knew so well. "Well look at you, making plans already I see," she said still amazed at seeing him living and breathing all in one piece. "Well, I have rather a lot to think about, but I must say I'm very impressed with the service so far!" He pointed to the opposite corner of the long narrow room. "Fatima has exceeded even your expectations of loyalty." In the dim candlelight Astra could just make out a small table, an old wooden stool and a thick wad of writing paper, as yet untouched. "She even came down to bring me tea and cake. It was delicious. Now come here and let me tell you what's happened so far." She lay in his arms feeling the thick wool of his army uniform tickle her cheeks, listening to his deep gentle voice, and wanting nothing more from the world. Setrag had left his hiding place early and by mid-afternoon had already set plans in motion. "I found him, you know, my newspaper distributor. He's still in Konya, and he's working with the network. He asked me to be their editor." "My lips are sealed," she said tickling his bare upper lip. "I so prefer you without a moustache."

Astra turned out to be an invaluable source of local eyewitness information seeing every horrific detail as it unfolded twice a day. The views around Konya station were tragic beyond belief, but as her role changed from helpless eyewitness to undercover reporter, she tried to convert the images into journalistic prose. It gave her journey to and from the factory some higher purpose, but now she felt like a voyeur, staring at other people's misery as a form of analytical information exercise. She would run the details over in her head while adding to the pile of trousers next to her sewing machine while trying to make her words more concise and less emotional as her editor would demand. At night Setrag made notes while Astra recited her reports. Her first report was the longest. "Everyone felt it, that moment of realization as we got off the train. Hundreds of people were led like doomed lambs into diseased swamps to join the thousands already there, waiting to die of starvation or cholera. The little children crying in terror, trying to shake life into their mothers' corpses, only to be flogged into silence by vicious guards." "It's far too emotional," he said, but she insisted and for once he made a concession. She went on, "The heavy smell of death seeps through our factory windows, while we do nothing, already defeated." "I can't possibly include that, they'll know there's a spy in the camp and have your exact location," he said. "I know silly, I just wanted you to appreciate what I have to live through day in day out so you won't complain so much about a little damp on the walls!" she teased him to lighten the mood before continuing, "No one camped out in those diseased fields will ever reach Der el Zor. It's organizationally far simpler this way. The gendarmes don't need to march people into the deserts of Syria to achieve their deadly plan." "Yes, that's much better, simple but effective," he said.

Within weeks the covert operation was in full flow. What the outside world did with the information is now one of history's sad truths, but for them nothing could have mattered more. Fatima played her part. Every week bundled articles of eyewitness accounts were sent from far and wide and dropped right outside the kitchen steps, concealed alongside bulky sacks of rice and wheat. She would wait for the knock at the door before rushing out like a banshee to snatch them up and take them down to the in-house editor. Her part was done. Then Setrag would spend all night editing pages, writing under a pseudonym, before passing them to Astra, who in turn passed them to a network of trusted contacts. At eight o'clock every Thursday, she and two American missionaries would arrive separately to buy their bread from the local bakery. After exchanging a few pleasantries they would pick up a package she placed by their feet and leave. The missionary network collected news from all corners of the Ottoman Empire and delivered them, via the American ambassador in Constantinople, directly to the United States of America. Within days the written word was printed and distributed to countries all over the world. Indigenous correspondents, foreign visiting journalists, and humanitarian sympathizers did everything they could. Some bought bread on Thursdays, others went to Turkish baths and carried out towels wrapped around personal accounts of mass murder. Their efforts should have changed things, stopped the horrors, saved innocent lives, but in truth no one was listening.

By early spring 1916 mass deportations had more or less fulfilled their deadly purpose so the war effort looked to conquering people outside its Empire. With the gendarmes needed to fight elsewhere, internal pressure was off and this opened the way for the three friends to go back to Smyrna. It was what they had been dreaming of so it came as some surprise that Astra was not budging. "I can't understand why you want to spend one more minute in this godforsaken hole," said Anoushka, but still they had no idea that her being there served a higher purpose. It had been almost impossible at times but somehow she had managed to keep it secret that Setrag was there, hidden in the cellar, where he was heading a major journalistic undercover operation. She quickly thought of an excuse. It was lame admittedly, but it was all she could think of. "You know why I have to stay here. If Setrag is alive, this is where he would come to find me. My mother knows I'm here and he could walk the streets unrecognised. It's safer, at least till the war is over." "Astra, face it, it's been months now, it kills me to say it, but if he had survived he would have found you by now," said Satenig. But Astra stuck firm, "I really wish I was going with you but I can't leave, some day you'll know why." Next day she helped them carry their cases to the station. "My mother must not be told about Zevart, not yet. I have to be the one to break it to her. You could say she was put on a train, and we don't know where she is, at least that part is true, and give her this letter. It was cryptic but enough. "I miss you terribly but we are still needed here." Peproné was in on the secret.

Later, those three dark years of self-imposed exile left her questioning if any of it had really happened at all. Was it really her who had worked in that foul smelling uniform factory for six days a week, eleven hours a day, breathing in smells of death in order to dress the enemy? Was it really her who ran home to her children to sing them songs and put them to bed, then finish off the housework before running down to the cellar to wrap her exhausted arms round her husband till three in the morning? Was it really her who smuggled out real life horror stories, ignoring mortal dangers, week after week? But some things flashed bright like yesterday as proof that she was there, like the night she asked Fatima if she could slip down early to cut his hair. Dimming candlelight shot tall shadows as her fingers flattened his soft wet curls. "Astra, please, don't cut it too short," he pleaded. "Why are you fussing so Setrag? No one is going to see you down here." But it mattered to him, the proud peacock that he was. More proof, in case she needed it, was that in December 1917 Astra gave birth to their third child, Christopher. Hiding her condition from her employers, in that cold winter, under thick layers of clothes, proved far easier than trying to convince Koko of the impossibly grown-up questions. "A white winged angel flew down and put your baby brother right here in my arms," she had told him. "But I thought babies were made by both mothers and fathers?" "Well, not always," said his mother, "some are brought down straight from heaven and surprise us all." So he accepted it as a moment of grown-up make believe. If that's what she was telling him, he knew she must have had her reasons.

Chapter XI

Capricious Times for the Great Healer

ASTRA was still only twenty-three when World War One began shuddering to its unstable jittering finale. More than half of the Armenian population in the Empire had died. Newspapers written in every language cluttered the cellar; at least something reminded her of home. In May 1918, Adriné and Koko had been re-introduced to their father after three years of living just one floor above him and now Astra was desperate to take her family home. But Setrag had been following Ottoman developments on the Russian fronts. "Astra, it's the news we've been dreaming of, listen to this," he read on, "now that Armenia is to be a major player in the Transcaucasian Commissariat, the Dashnag party has emerged as a renewed political force." He was nearly exploding with excitement. "We are to lead the national committee in setting out the new social order, human rights laws, education, and social welfare! It's absolutely wonderful, I must leave right now." She couldn't believe it. "You can't be serious. You're going to leave us again and put your life in danger, now that it's nearly all over." He wasn't listening. It was his mission, and nothing she could say or do would stop him. "My darling listen, you understand, I have to be there with them. This is the most glorious moment in our history since Leo the Magnificent founded the Rupenid dynasty in Cilicia in 1198! You take the children back to Smyrna as we planned and I'll join you there very soon," he said vanishing off in a puff of nationalist glory.

A single candle lit the grim cellar as she sat alone on that rickety stool, her head buried in her hands, seething with anger. "How could he just up and leave like that, after all I've done for him?" she said jumping up to kick and stomp through every sheet of newspaper he had been drooling over just minutes before. "Why didn't I leave two years ago with Anoushka and Satenig? I'm crazy. I could have been with my mother and spent my days with my children instead of snatching a few precious moments with them before bedtime. I'm a stupid victim of my own making." She felt denied, betrayed, outdone of her own personal sense of justice and she had just about had enough of putting "the cause" before plain simple human family needs. She was as patriotic as the rest of them but no cause was worth dying for, not after all they'd sacrificed.

Fatima helped her pack. She felt sad that they were leaving, but even sadder to see her friend spilling out three years of pent up frustration and anger during their last few minutes together. "Fatima, I will never understand him! Now that we can all finally go home together, he's abandoned us all over again. Is it too much to expect that for once he might put us first? He wasn't the only one who suffered; we all did, you did too, and for what? He has always expected so much from me, and he's so patronizing; the party this, the party that, I'm sure he loves the Dashnag party more than any of us, maybe more than life itself." By then she was utterly sick and tired of politics. "What is the point now anyway, most of our people are dead." The utter futility of war filled her with a sense of overpowering disillusionment. Millions had died all over the world and she mocked the high-minded ideals, which had so consumed her life till then.

Meanwhile Setrag had a job to do. On the 28th of May 1918 Armenia declared a hollow and short-lived independence, carved out of desperation and forced compromise. Land grabbing treaties between the Ottomans, Bolsheviks and Germans had left her husband's Dashnag party and nationalistic countrymen proclaiming independence on a rugged piece of hostile highland, miles from their original homeland, covering a terrain of no more than four thousand square miles. But to them it was a wonderful victory. They danced and sang patriotic songs as they planted the red blue and orange flag on a piece of land, she said was "not much bigger than a postage stamp." Maybe her reaction was over cynical, even ungrateful, but it was not just that. For the first time she saw her life as a complete over investment in self-sacrifice for such little return and it drove her to ask some hard-hitting questions about life's priorities. It was time to take control, and if this meant choosing less demanding allegiances, then so be it. She and her three children deserved better. A new life beckoned. "Fatima, do you know how I feel? I feel like a runaway slave." Fatima nodded. She had often wondered how such a charming intelligent fun loving beauty had spent so many years running between a stinking factory and a dark damp cellar. "You are right," she sighed. "That's it, from now on I'm definitely going to put us first, and he can just put that in his pipe and smoke it!" With that she slammed her case shut, dried her eyes, and they all marched down the stairs to freedom.

Fatima had been practising in private. The train was seconds from pulling out. "I love you," she said. "Oh my God, Fatima, you spoke!" cried Astra on hearing a more than vaguely discernible sound formation choke its way out of Fatima's unused vocal chords. "Mama, was it a miracle?" asked a wide-eyed Koko as they stood blowing kisses and waving frantically to an emotionally overcome Fatima on the other side of the train window. They were the first words Fatima had uttered in nearly twenty years and they were meant for Koko. He had stared at her in stunned surprise before clapping and cheering as she reshaped her lips for her second attempt. "Bye-bye, Koko," she said, swooping down to kiss him lovingly on both cheeks. "Yes Koko, in a way it was," said his mother.

A few hours later they were home. "Mama look, the sea!" said Koko, remembering. Smyrna gleamed like a curved jewel in front of them. "Didn't they have a war here Mama?" he asked as they walked through the busy port apparently untouched by world hostilities. She realized then how she had not allowed herself to miss it. Fashionable well fed people bustled through the fish market on their way to everyday normality, sucking on sugary sweets and breathing in fresh cool breezes ignorant of the east west divide which had so far managed to work its spin. By the time they reached her mother's house the bubble had already burst. She was minutes away from telling Zevart's story and from putting an end to her mother's false hopes once and for all. Her children stood to attention while she combed their hair and tidied their clothes. "Your grandmother won't recognize you. The last time we stood here Adriné was just born and baby Christopher was still in heaven."

Predictably the joys of reunion lasted till mother and daughter sat down to list the casualties of war. Zevart, Aizemnig's husband Karekin, Gayené's husband and baby, their first cousins, and whole families of aunts, uncles and second cousins living in the Eastern part of the Empire, had not returned. "It's three long years since they went on those marches and no one has heard a single word from any of them, so….." There was no need to finish. Astra felt her eyes about to spurt, but a burning anger held back the floodgates. "Well, I think it's about time I went to tell Mama Tokadjian her son is still alive, at least he was the last time I saw him."

The political amnesty of November 1918 allowed Setrag free passage home and he arrived unexpectedly one day to reclaim his family. "Well thank you so much for letting us know you were coming. I feel like left luggage, one day I'm a widow, then I'm not, then I am, then I'm not, and as I'm obviously not this time, I suppose I must leave the warm bosom of my mother yet again and take up my place as dutiful daughter-in-law in the unwelcoming Tokadjian household!" There she said it. Strangely enough that year, the two families came together in shared grief in a way that happiness had never managed to achieve. But as the black months of mourning drifted slowly by, married life began to resume its familiar themes. Nine months, almost to the day after Setrag's return, on the 16th August 1919, their fourth child Varoujan was born.

Since the 15th of May 1919 the Allies, America, Britain and France, agreed to allow Greek forces to occupy Smyrna, and the defeated Ottomans could offer no opposition. So with censorship more or less a thing of the past, but with the heaviest of hearts, Setrag and Megouch decided to carry on where they had left off. Setrag found new offices, nearer home this time, and with the help of his friends Anton Gazelian and Garbiel Lazian, and her two brothers, Hagop and Haroutioun, now back from hiding in Bulgaria, he resumed his position as publisher and editor of his second newspaper *Horizon*. Within months they had also opened the doors of the Sevan Bookshop right next door, and so everything was back to normal, but nothing about it would ever feel the same. A new business in a renewed world should have smacked of a new optimism but instead they found they were fighting personal deep-rooted cynicism at every step. Their literary vision was far tamer this time around. Personal loss and the guilt, which followed survival from genocide, had made moderates of them all.

But Astra's scars went far deeper than journalistic and political compromise. Astra, the mother, felt angry at a world which could create life with such effortless ease, only to take it away with such agonizing cruelty. At night when she tossed and turned, hiding her head under the pillow, trying to shut out Anna Tokadjian's heart-wrenching screams as she called out to her, she knew empathy had its limits. A toughened phoenix had begun to shake broken wings in readiness to rise from the ashes of precious souls loved and lost. She would never be the same again.

Surprisingly her more detached persona improved relationships in the household, especially with Anna. Fewer expectations meant fewer disappointments and so they preferred to slip silently past sunken shadows while time performed its healing process. Peace began to permeate through open doors while Christopher, now aged two, giggled and rolled his large wooden hoop around from room to room. Astra tended to her newborn while her two eldest children busied themselves with important domestic decoy tactics. She had not needed to tell them but Adriné and Koko both knew the importance of keeping grandmother Anna amused. Their comic smiles and chirpy twittering lifted her spirits, squeezing hope back in, almost unnoticed.

Working in a factory sewing uniforms for the army that had inflicted unimaginable atrocities with such relish had made Astra swear never to push needle and thread ever again, but that day the winter sun shone bright, melting away memories of Konya. They were playing hopscotch in the garden when Anoushka came to visit, carrying her usual present, a huge box of Turkish delight. "Astra, my wedding day is getting close and I was wondering, it would be so wonderful if you would make my wedding dress. Oh please say you will." Suddenly the thought of running her hands up and down soft luscious fabrics rekindled those aesthetic senses. "It would be a real honour," she replied without too much consideration. "I can see you in rich oyster silk taffeta, draped with cream lace, and the whole thing decorated with mother of pearl sequins and long satin ribbons." She unwrapped her present. "I just love pistachio *lokhoum*," she said mouthing two in one go. So you agree to dismiss with Armenian tradition and go for a modern western style gown." "I don't believe it. You must have read my mind! That's the very same dress I've been dreaming of," said Anoushka, rushing up to hug her best friend and it was settled.

Just then Astra felt a warm sweet breeze brush her face for the first time since 1915 telling her it was time to allow fun and frivolity back into her life. Her eyes sparkled as she stepped back to look Anoushka up and down. "You just wait and see! I am going to make you a shimmering fairy tale of a dress. You're going to look lovelier than Cinderella at the palace ball." The fantasy was as much for her as it was for Anoushka. Soon her magical mood had infected the whole house. "Mama you look so pretty when you smile, your face shines like the moon," said Koko, as she waltzed out of her bedroom in a powder blue dress, out of mourning at long last, and dripping stardust all along the hallway.

"Setrag, I feel like playing the organ tonight. What do you say we have a little party? You could dance with the children," she said feeling he needed it too. So bedtime was put back till their little tired feet found their own way up the stairs. Astra lay down beside her daughter, stroking her dark damp curls, till sleep overtook thumping excitement after an evening of fun. She stayed with them in the shadowy darkness, and let Setrag put the world to rights on his own that night. It pained her to admit it but her children's emotional development seemed to have been rather low on their list of priorities ever since she could remember. It was no one's fault, and she tried not to blame him, but from what he was saying at the dinner table, the war was not over yet. Turkish and Russian border uprisings and unfair treaties had been threatening the new Armenian borders and accounts of on-going atrocities were constant topics of after coffee conversations. He was still at it now with Anton and Gabriel, and it was well past midnight. "Why can't they keep their voices down, or better still, talk about it somewhere else." Enough was enough. She began to think that hate and suffering would always be somewhere close and wondered what all this might be doing to her children, especially to Koko? She had caught him hiding at the top of the stairs, with his ears pinned back, listening to it all so many times. And, as no one else seemed to care, it was up to her to make it stop.

She compared her own start in life to theirs. They couldn't have been were more different. She was born into a family which wrapped its children up in happiness and fascinating social interaction. She remembered the endless stream of parties as mouthwatering smells and infectious laughter that drifted into her bedroom whenever doors were opened. She remembered eavesdropping on after dinner philosophies, and being introduced to important guests who listened to her recitals and filled her with confidence. She remembered the Czar's glittering jewellery she had held in her tiny hands and stirred her senses. Admittedly it all came to an end when she was eight, but these memories would last a lifetime. So far the solemn Sunday lunches when Setrag invited his newspaper colleagues round for media dolma and a heated debate to follow, was the nearest thing to a good time her children had ever known. She remembered too how her mother and uncles had spoken in French when her father was murdered, ever sensitive to young minds within hearing distance, and her children deserved nothing less. The nature nurture argument had always intrigued her, and after long deliberations with herself and others she believed both were equally vital to psychological development. Whatever, bringing children into the world was a heavy responsibility and before she left her charges to their soft synchronized breathing, she promised them, and her ancestors, that if she had anything to do with it, their influences would be very different from then on.

Next day she was on a mission to educate their tactile senses. "Setrag, can you please take your nose out of that newspaper for a minute? I need your help today. Could you go in a little later this morning and stay with our two youngest for a couple of hours? I'm going shopping with Anoushka to choose the material for her wedding dress." She gave him no time to answer. "Come on Koko, Adriné, put your shoes and coats on, we are going out." She picked up her design sketches and kissed her husband on the cheek. "I fed Varoujan and Christopher is still asleep. I shan't be long."

"Where are we going mama?" they asked. "To feast your eyes in a haberdashery shop," she answered. They didn't know what that meant and were a little disappointed as they walked in. "Now take your gloves off and show the gentleman how clean your hands are so he can have no objection to your little fingers feeling their way around lovely sensuous textures." It didn't stop him from thinking she was a little more than eccentric. "Now feel this one," said Astra, rubbing their fingers along fine quality silks and velvets. "Now close your eyes and try to feel the colours this time." By then his patience had completely run out. "Madam, normally parents teach their children not to touch things. Have you ladies come here to give them lessons in quality fabrics or are you actually interested in buying something?" Astra couldn't abide small-minded people. "Everything in life is an education. For example, one should always fight petty intimidation. Come on Anoushka, I know a shop with a much better selection."

That night Koko, Adriné, Anna and Astra were playing cards in the dining room while Setrag, Anton and Gabriel were raising their voices in the living room. The Bolsheviks had apparently occupied Goris and Setrag was fuming, but so was she. "Mama T, just listen to those armchair anarchists. It's like being in a state of siege in your own house. All I'm asking is that our peaceful home isn't occupied by verbal wars night after night." Setrag needed telling but it struck her that with all their supposed earnest communication, she could count the times she had ever reproached him on the fingers of one hand. Nevertheless she went next door. "Please boys, keep it down, we're playing cards and the children can hear every word."

Minutes later the men were sitting down to join them. Koko always won at cards. "So my clever son, tell me what you did today?" asked his father. "I helped Anoushka pick her wedding dress material," he replied, reaching down to open a large box under the table. "This is called embossed satin," he explained. "Oh, very nice" replied Setrag, a little lost for words. Astra stepped in. "That's not all, today Koko taught your daughter a very long poem. Why don't you recite it for us Adriné?" Instantly Adriné jumped up ready and willing so Setrag took over as master of ceremonies. "Mama, Gabriel, Anton, Koko, Christopher, everyone, are you ready? The performance is about to begin."

Little Adriné straightened her stiff white collar, made herself tall, looked straight at her father and recited her poem to perfection. Then everyone clapped and cheered as she bowed, giggled and twirled her ringlets in feigned embarrassment. "I wonder who she reminds me of, the way she loves to perform to a crowd?" said Astra winking. "Bravo!" he said, lifting her up and swinging her round the dining room. "Tomorrow I am going to buy you a lovely pair of shiny new shoes." "Then you should buy her brother a lovely pair too. He spent the whole afternoon teaching her," said Astra. Next morning Setrag kept his word but only after Adriné made him burn with pride for a second time. "You should have seen her, bold as brass, she climbed up on the counter, cleared her voice, straightened her petticoat and with her chin pointed in the air, she said it again, word perfect, but this time in front of all the staff and customers in the best shoe shop on the Rue Franque." "That's more like it," thought Astra.

A week later Astra sat sewing sequins, thinking that nothing much had really changed. The atmosphere was so tense that Setrag felt an urge to break the silence. "Just because I go through my editorials in the evening doesn't mean I love you or the children any less," he said. He wondered at the power in those blue eyes, which with the lightest of touches could bore right through his emotions and straight to his soul. "I didn't say anything," she replied a little too quickly. Anna Tokadjian had spent the evening in her room and for once they were alone. "You know I would do anything for you and the children," he said pressing her hand to his lips and she seized the opportunity. "Then I wish you would stop bringing death and cruelty into the house. Doesn't it bother you that their vulnerable ears are always listening?" Setrag said nothing. Humility was not his strong point, but as he slowly stroked his moustache she knew his brain was ticking. "You're right, I'll keep my work on the other side of our front door from now on," he said. Suddenly huge tears dripped off Astra's cheeks but she didn't know why. Much later she understood that chastising your hero, whose own upbringing had offered him no concessions whatsoever felt unjust, like an imposition, but at still only twenty-four, life was still for learning.

It was an unusually warm spring in the year of 1919 and it gave Setrag an opportunity to spend more time with his children. It was still bright daylight when he came home, and grabbing a towel and little eager hands, he would chase them along the beach road, until they reached his favourite spot. They would stand at the shore's edge and wave him off, watching him swim away like a writhing sea snake, till his outline blurred into the huge red setting sun in the horizon. Sometimes he disappeared under water for so long they made up games to take their minds off possible dangers lurking beneath. "Adriné I bet the next car we see will come out of this road," and she would say, "No Koko, I bet it will be from that one." But so few cars ever drove past that they would sit and wait, arms around each other, staring out to sea, till their father surfaced again. "There he is! Baba, baba!" they shouted, waving back in huge relief, till he was back, reaching down for his towel to sprinkle icy water over their faces, usually before a single car had driven passed.

Anoushka was standing in front of the long oval mirror in Anna's exceptionally tidy bedroom. It was the final fitting before her big day. She gazed at her dazzling reflection in amazement. "It is just soooooo beautiful, I can't believe you made this! Astra, it's a real work of art. You are truly some kind of creative genius." In the last two weeks Astra had been working non-stop, hardly coming up for air, and she had to agree, the results were magical. With neither time nor money ever in the equation, Astra had allowed herself to drift into an over elaborate self-indulgent fairytale fantasy, but not everyone in the house was impressed. "Wherever I go, I have to pick up these damned sequins, and those tiny strands of white silk thread. It's killing my back. At least you could try to be a little tidy," said Anna Tokadjian, burning with resentment at the complete frivolity of it all.

Actually, Anna did have a point. Tidiness was not high on Astra's priority list, especially when her creative senses were in full flow. Her own mother had told her as much. Whether it was newspapers strewn across the floor whenever she wrote her articles, or the baking flour, which covered her hair and clothes with a dusty white coating whenever she baked a cake, that was how it was with her. Astra was heart and soul. "Yes Mama T I know, I'm sorry, but I will give the whole house a massive spring clean this week. You'll see, it will be spotless," she called down from the bedroom wondering why she had to wait for Anoushka to be in the house before voicing her complaints. "You know Anoushka, Zevart was the tidiest person in the world, and she was so artistic. I've framed her beautiful sketches, but Mama can't bare to have them around her yet. They're in he cellar." Astra welled up as she helped Anoushka step out of her gown. "I wish I could have made her dress like this."

The wedding dress was the talk of the town and chattering brides-to-be came to the house, budding with excitement, only to leave soon after, disappointed. Astra had been taught well by Satenig, not only in couture but also in pricing. Fairy tale dresses were beyond the average pocket, as Astra would politely point out. To produce a dress in any way similar would cost them a small fortune. But at the time, when she closed the door on potential business, she had no idea her family was in such financial trouble. Printing *Horizon* and keeping the Sevan Bookshop open was costing more money than it was making and Setrag was beginning to wonder if things would ever pick up. The Great War had vastly depleted his circulation and readership. Now that two million Armenians were dead or displaced, business was not what it used to be.

On one of her rare visits to the publishing house, Astra found a pile of unpaid bills tucked away in a dusty corner of the bureau. "Hagop did you forget about these?" she asked her brother, already guessing it was more serious. "Sister, these are hard times for everyone, bakers, grocers, butchers, printers, even governments. People have no money for food let alone for books and newspapers. Setrag didn't want to worry you, but we are in serious financial trouble. We may even close the bookshop." Her eyes grew large. "Where is Setrag?" she asked. "He went to the theatre to promote his new play." "What play?" she asked. Hagop was confused. "Astra, he's been working on it for weeks. I thought you knew." "No, but you were right to tell me. This is my fault. I've made a real issue about asking him not to bring the world's problems home with him, but I didn't mean our problems too." She waited till Setrag came back and rushed to put her arms around him. "Hagop and I have been talking. Why didn't you tell me things were so bad? If only I had known, I might have been able to do something, but maybe it's not too late. Just give me three large sheets of paper and a pencil."

Astra was always her best in a crisis. Taking a detour and sketching frantically on street corners, she set about redesigning Anoushka's wedding dress for the three brides-to-be. "This could be very embarrassing and I really wouldn't blame them if they slammed the door in my face," but this was no time to dwell on false pride, so she went straight to see them. "After you left I made a few minor alterations, but as you can see, the overall effect is almost identical. Now the dress will take half as long to make, and of course it will be completely original, after all no one wants a copy." Each one was persuaded but in her excitement, she agreed to near impossible deadlines. Three dresses, each different, all to be finished by the middle of next month. How would she do it? She would have to ask her mother-in-law to mind the children and to put up with complete strangers dressing and undressing in the house, but desperate times required desperate measures.

And she did it, although it meant working till four in the morning, five nights out of seven. The dresses were finished on time, worn and admired, and now after all that hard work Astra mused that they would already be packed away on the tops of tall wardrobes or in deep mahogany chests, never to be seen again. Sewing was so fickle, so superficial. "At least words stay in the minds of the reader far longer than it takes brides to get married, and it's far less work," she thought, handing over all her earnings to Anna Tokadjian, the frugal keeper of domestic purse strings. "You're really quite a talent," she said stuffing it in her handbag. Astra was taken aback and when her husband came home she told him. "It's not every day I get praise from your mother." "Look Astra, when business picks up, you really must go back to writing your features page again," he answered, in the way of an apology for his mother's backhanded compliment. "Yes, of course I will, but till then I'm happy to keep the orders coming in, even though, admittedly, it's more satisfying to be on the cutting edge of social change than sewing thousands of tiny sequins late into the night just to satisfy fleeting vanities." It was how she felt.

"I can't believe how many people are getting married in this town. You are always so busy," said Gayené Tokadjian packing her black wardrobe into a suitcase. Poor Gayené, four years after her husband and baby had perished in the Syrian Desert, she still blamed herself for making it out alive. She had no urge to leave them but a letter from her brother Hagop in America had persuaded her that a change of scenery in the "heavenly playground" might be exactly what she needed to start rebuilding her life. "Boston is a wonderful place. I wish we were all going with you," said Astra, meaning it. They had been talking and packing behind closed doors for hours. Astra went to dig deep into her special box and found the photographs to prove it. "You could go to see Miss Jennings. That's her sitting on the porch," she said, pointing to a gleaming white wooden house with black shutters. "I would love to meet her one day, but to be honest, I'd be embarrassed now." She put three of Gayené's black hats into a hat-box, wondering what her sponsor would think of her now. She was bound to be a disappointment, sewing wedding dresses for a living rather than fighting for women's rights. They had been writing less often and what was there to say? "I bet she's wondering what happened to that fiery young woman, bursting with a mission to change the world." "She got married and had four children," said Gayené. Astra had an idea. "I'm going to ask Setrag if I can add a last minute addition into *Horizon* this week, there's still time. Take it to her, would you?"

Astra slipped back into writing her article, "Important Issues for the Modern Woman—Learning a Skill to Change Your Life," so effortlessly that it was as though nothing had interrupted her flow, but in truth it had, marriage and motherhood. She read over it but it felt dishonest. The words were encouraging enough, but it read far too glibly. In truth there was so much more that women had to overcome, it wasn't that easy, and she knew it. She put her pen down to vocalize her ideas out loud. "These last few years have been terrible for so many women, but it won't always be like this, and I shan't let cynicism get in the way of progress. In the end it's about who we are and how we choose to live." Even then it sounded hollow. Had she let her own sex down? By becoming a mother had she somehow lost the deepest part of herself? What would women do if they were free of the powerful social conditioning she had been so dismissive of before her first child was born? She asked herself if real choice was only for women who were completely unbound by even the slightest hint of convention, or whether society should share in the responsibility of allowing them to make choices. Either way, it was too late, or too early for her, but not so for others still to come. "No, I'm sticking with it," she said passing her article over for printing.

The following Sunday Gayené was on her was to Boston with the latest copy of *Horizon* in her suitcase.

Some might say, a life which pulls the rug away so cruelly, again and again, was cursed, but in truth it happens even to the blessed. In early July 1919, Christopher, just two and a half, died suddenly of pneumonia. Astra had found him, ice cold, white, still beautiful, his little eyes unopened from the night before. "Oh my dear God, my sweet baby, how could it happen, I didn't even know he was so ill, it's my fault." Astra wished she could die. "Mama, you did say Christopher was a special baby, that the angels brought him down to us, maybe now they've taken him back," said Koko, praying it was true. Her heart was breaking, but she had precious little time to grieve before her husband too was lying dangerously ill with pneumonia. Their son's death had taken him to the brink. So fate stepped in again, forcing her needs to the back of the queue, but her husband's love meant more to her.

"Anoushka, I just don't know what else to do. He's lost the will to live. He's delirious with fever. I get the feeling Christopher is calling him. You know what they say, they take someone with them when they go." "Astra, if you want him to live, then you have to want to live yourself. Can't you see it's your sadness that's killing him?" It felt like a reprimand. "I do try not to cry when I'm with him." "You need to get him away from here before it's too late. Look, we're going to the country for a month, let me take the children with me, the air will do them good." "Could you? I would be so grateful, but shouldn't you ask Raffi first?" "My husband will do everything he can to help, you know that. There's no more to say."

"Anoushka is absolutely right, the Caucasus Mountains are known for their healing properties, and the sanatorium has a world wide reputation. It's at the bottom of the foothills, with the mountains on one side and the Caspian Sea on the other. It's absolutely gorgeous," said Aizemnig, who had become lady bountiful since Astra's luck turned bad. "You've been there but you're too young to remember." Astra did remember but had no energy to disagree. Aizemnig, now a wealthy widow, had found a new and more satisfying role in life, working with orphan charities and doing "good works" and it seemed to have taken the edge off her childlessness. "It's all organized, the travel arrangements, the sanatorium, and the treatments all paid for. I'm not saying it's cheap, but you don't need to concern yourself about that now. Telephones are so useful," she added beaming. Being needed was what she needed most. She had visited the patient daily, administering strange smelling potions and creamy green herbal treatments. "Where did you learn how to do all this," asked Astra, concerned that most of the flora and vegetation of Aizemnig's garden was being rubbed into her husband's chest. "Oh, you know, from here and there. I've read a lot about it, and from Mama too. If you had spent more time at home, you wouldn't be asking me."

Aizemnig started rolling up her sleeves. "We need to make him strong for the journey. Astra, get me some candles, some tall glasses and matches. I think we should do a 'Koupa.' It works like magic for the circulation," she said turning Setrag over. "I'll do the back first, then the front." "What do you need all that for?" asked Astra, wondering if Aizemnig was about to perform some act of ritualistic witchcraft. "Trust me, you can help if you want." Setrag had been listening with growing trepidation, especially when he heard "matches," and craned his head to see her in action. "Lie still Setrag, you won't feel a thing. I'm going to open up your capillaries," she said already lighting a candle and placing it on his back. "Now, Astra put the glass over the candle and press it down." As the flame went out, a mound of flesh was sucked up into the glass. "It's all to do with the vacuum effect," she said scientifically, working systematically across his back till it resembled a lumpy box of ripe red tomatoes. Aizemnig had her funny ways and it didn't do to dwell on them too long, but in medical terms she was a miracle worker.

After forty-eight hours of mountain air and non-stop sleep Setrag woke up with an appetite for the first time in four weeks. "You look so much better. Look at the size of this room, it's like eating in a huge restaurant," she said, mopping his chin clean of clear vegetable soup. "Setrag, do you remember how I used to beg you to take me somewhere, anywhere there were no newspapers? And here we are, our first time away together, but before you start getting ideas, they've given me strict instructions you're not to go anywhere near a newspaper. You must put every bit of your energies into getting well.

Aizemnig was right to send us here. They say the air is the best in the world. She is eccentric, but she is truly kind deep down." Astra had seen an improvement in his breathing very soon after the candle episode. She put the spoon in his hand and walked over to the window. The air was so pure it made her head spin. "My great uncle Roupen used to live up there, on that very mountain. Mama said he lived to be a hundred and thirty four, eating a diet of figs, nuts and yoghurt. We stayed with him once, that time we left Erzeroum. He must have been a hundred and twenty then, but he was still chopping down trees and stoking the fire. Perhaps in a week or so we can take a walk by the water's edge." She stood there taking deep breaths, gazing at the spellbinding scenery, while trying to count the number of times she had almost lost him.

She left the shores of the Caspian Sea three weeks later, but it was a full six weeks later before Setrag was given the all clear. When she saw him at the station, he looked like a new man. "You look wonderful, and as handsome as the first time I met you," she said, with those breathless blushes of a woman permanently in love. "Oh yes, are you referring to that evening, when I came to sit at your mother's table like a pompous puffed up penguin with indigestion, surely not! I missed you all so much, let's go home."

By 1921 their broken hearts were still healing but at least their money worries were over. The new *Horizon* readers demanded political analysis rather than social comment, so Astra took on the role of proofreader. "Your editorials read more like historical records than news," she said. "That's because history repeats itself. How can I describe the long term persecution we've suffered in fresh words?" She began to wish she had kept to sewing wedding dresses. "Surely there are other things in life apart from war," she said reading detailed military accounts of the growing crisis in the newly independent Armenia. "It's my responsibility to tell the world how east and west have betrayed us with false promises and broken treaties." She read on about how the Bolsheviks and non-Bolshevik Kemalist Turks had sided together to start a one sided offensive and how thousands of men, women and children had been killed in their continued resolve to crush Armenia again. "Do you ever wonder if your readers might become desensitised?" she asked him, wondering if anyone outside their nation had ever been sensitive to their cause to begin with.

When Setrag's nationalistic dream came to an end, it was his responsibility to record that too. His nation had been cornered from all sides and all that was left for the Dashnag party and for Armenia was to accept the offer of Lenin's protective intervention. In October 1921 they relinquished independence and became a Soviet state, but at least this meant that the inhabitants of the new Armenian Soviet Socialist Republic would be able to live in peace, though not all of them.

In the early hours of October 25th 1921 Setrag pulled himself together and pushed all the papers off his desk to make space to write a special obituary. It was his brother's. Megouch, a fresh-faced passionate recruit in the volunteer Armenian nationalist army had joined in the fighting to stop the Bolshevik invasion, and he had all but reached the outskirts of the capital Yerevan. A few days later it would all have been over, there would have been nothing left to fight for, but he died there at the foothills of Mount Ararat along with independent Armenia itself. He reread the letter from the battalion captain. "Megouch, impeccable, brave and noble to the end, took a fatal bullet at six o'clock this morning while running through enemy fire to deliver vital battle plans. He died a true and willing patriot." Setrag decided to write the obituary precisely in those words. "What do I care about his bravery? He was my beautiful baby boy and now he's dead, and for what?" wailed Anna, and Astra sharing a mother's sorrow had to agree.

Mercifully nothing of any significance happened for ten months till in August 1922, bouncing baby Arpoun was born to parents ready and needing to love him, and in that way at least he had timed his arrival to perfection.

"That's enough now, Setrag, stop smothering him with kisses, you'll be late again," she said smiling and pulling them apart as cute little Varoujan giggled and came up for air. Losing baby Christopher and his brother Megouch in such quick succession had taken its emotional toll. Over the last few months leaving his children every morning had become the toughest thing Setrag did each day. Varoujan, now three, was the apple of his father's eye, and Setrag kissed his rosy apple cheeks, again and again, as though it would never be enough. Every day he would wait till the last possible moment, till the train guard whistled its imminent departure, before starting to run. Then he flew like the wind, charging down the street, jumping over rails, landing his feet on the platform, just as the train started to move. The family stood and watched as he chased the chugging train with his arm at full stretch till he grabbed hold of the last rail of the observation car. As the train picked up speed he ran faster and faster, then with the elegant ease of an acrobat, he twisted his body and propelled himself up and over, just in time to wave back. As the train disappeared out of Cordelio station Astra smiled and shook her head. "Varoujan, did you know your father is crazy, but that's why we love him."

He always felt easier leaving when Koko came too. They would sit together like close friends on a train, telling jokes, and playing complex memory games, which Koko always won. "You, Koko, are blessed with a photographic memory," he said with pride. Koko, at nine years of age, had already read every book in the Sevan Bookshop at least once, probably remembering every single word in the process.

Chapter XII

The Welcome Clutching of Straws

SINCE the demise of the old Ottoman Empire, Smyrna lay in the bankrupt hands of the Greek army, operating as a city that for all practical purposes was still run by westerners. The British and French owned the railways, the waterworks were Belgian, and the important oil and tobacco interests were American. In 1921, when Venizelos replaced King Constantine, the foreigners decided to remain strictly neutral in the event of any private war between Venizelos of Greece and Mustafa Kemal of Turkey, but even as the ink dried on yet another disastrous treaty, they must have suspected peace was to be short lived.

And so a beacon of green light shone brightly over renewed Turkish nationalism. It was their first real chance since 1918 to turn their backs on the old Ottoman regime, become more modern, yet keep with old familiar themes: the expulsion of all non-Turkish peoples. Predictably, and wasting no time, they increased land forces on a massive scale in preparation to follow the star to senseless destruction. By the early spring of 1922, Turkish imperialism looked hungrily to their left hoping to finish off, once and for all, what they had started seven years before. In a series of death marches, apparently unnoticed by the world outside, Greeks and the Armenians who were left, were driven out into the deserted Anatolian hills, to die from hunger, exhaustion, and plain uninterrupted murder. Overpowered by surprise and sheer brute force, the marauding armies found little resistance. Regiment after regiment of Greeks threw down their ammunition and fled west for their lives.

In a rush to reach the sea, they abandoned smouldering villages, gathered desperate civilians wherever they could, and dashed blindly towards unknown ravages awaiting them on their arrival. A human disaster, kept under wraps for decades, was about to unfold for hundreds of thousands of innocents. And she was there again, Astra as sensory witness, as powerless victim, her life given and not chosen. By September 5th 1922, thirty thousand refugees spilled into the city of Smyrna, the town they called the Paris of the East, bursting with culture and commerce, with its thriving international community, its jasmine scented gardens, and its fragrant courtyards. In a matter of days that perfect crescent harbour was to reek of burning bodies as acrid smoke stifled cool sea breezes and hung heavy in the air for years to come.

In a town where scarcely a soul had any inkling of the imminent catastrophe, Setrag was in the know, though even he was doubtful at first. In the last few days newspapermen from nearby towns already destroyed had sent out warnings that the enemy was almost at the gates. By the 4th of the September he was making evacuation plans for his entire family. "The Greeks have abandoned Ushak. The Turkish army will be here in a few days. We all have to leave. Greece is bankrupt, how on earth can they deal with being overrun by the thousands of refuges heading this way. We always wanted to emigrate to America and now we have nothing to lose."

Twenty-four hours later they were on the verge of leaving Smyrna for good. Astra and Setrag hardly slept that night, dreaming of the future and closing lids on the present. Time was running out. "Once the Kemalist forces get here, our days are numbered." It was not like him to be so openly fearful. "Let's go now, forget the packing" she said, sensing that every second that ticked away might bring back horrors she couldn't forget. "We have to have money and book our passage but we could leave tonight." Within the hour she had started to gather everything that meant anything to her, before a powerful premonition made her stop.

"Wait, Setrag!" she called out running downstairs to see him putting his ambitious list of "to dos" in his top pocket. She threw her arms around his neck, and in full view of her children, kissed him with a passion which made them blush, a kiss that must last a lifetime. "I love you Setrag," she whispered. "I love you too," he smiled surprised to feel her damp cheeks. "Now I must get to the bank and sort out the tickets. The sooner I go the sooner I'll be back." She wanted to tell him that a silent little voice was warning her,

"Don't let him go," but it would have sounded foolish and over-emotional, so instead she kissed him again and he was gone.

"Mama T, please try to be packed before Setrag comes back. Just think we'll be with Gayené and Hagop in a few days," she called through to her mother-in-law who had absolutely no intention of budging and had taken to her bed in protest. Astra was sympathetic. She could truly understand why a woman who had lost two sons, a son-in-law, and a grandchild in recent memory might not relish a new start in life. "I know it's hard but we can't leave you here. Koko, you too, we can only take our very special things, everything else we can buy in Boston. Just pack your favourite books and best clothes." Her mind drifted back to the night they left one world without having another. "Garin will always be my home wherever I go," she thought. She had already been to see her mother. The Sabondjians were leaving too, just as soon as Aizemnig had organized her financial investments.

They were ready and waiting by two o'clock, but by eight-thirty that evening Setrag had still not returned. No one had said a word for over an hour and the sweltering heat was making the waiting unbearable, so Astra made an executive decision. "Come on children, it's time for bed." She went into the hallway to reach deep into bags piled high against the door and took out three of their favourite books, trying hard to dismiss those fears that he might never be coming back. "Now don't look at me like that, I'll wake you up as soon as he comes home." They knew this was no time for negotiation, so holding hands, they climbed the stairs, not daring to ask what might have happened to their father.

By September 7thKemalist forces had reached the edge of Smyrna, finding a city hushed in anticipation in resigned acceptance that it was already too late for the Greeks. Two days later the infantry marched in. First they set fire to the harbour, somehow managing to avoid the Turkish quarter, then systematically burned down every other part of the city. Defenceless Greeks, Italians, French, English, Americans and Armenians spilled out of embassies, office buildings, hospitals, theatres, shops and houses to be met by the ravages of a one sided war. By evening thousands of displaced people rolled around dazed and numb until an instinct to survive drove them into the writhing chaos of the port.

With towering sheets of flames licking the skies on one side and with the sea on the other, they were forced to jump into the burning quay. Western warships moored there, in easy saving distance, saw everything but did nothing. Grown men wept from the bridge, from portholes, from polished wooden decks as their captains followed orders. In forty-eight hours, a screaming burning wall, nearly two miles long turned into a liquid graveyard as two hundred thousand people met a torturous end. Distraught sailors begged their betters, only to be told their hands were tied. What else were they to do? It was either that or to renege on diplomatic promises of neutrality made in apparent ignorance by western governments less than six months before.

Two days later Setrag had still not returned. "Why am I living when my three sons are dead, I wish I could die too," wailed Anna as her grandchildren listened. Trapped and twitching, not knowing where to go or what to do, had all been driving them to the edge of sanity. "That's it, I have to go. I can't sit here and wait for ever," said Astra grabbing her brother's hand. "Hagop, come with me." As no trains were running, they made their way on foot. As they got closer, the overpowering stench of burning flesh became more identifiable but a curtain of black smoke hid the view. Then, within a few yards from the port, Hagop's arm cut across his sister's chest and made her stop. Through parting strands of smoke they saw the quay below them. The sea was packed with dead bodies, gruesome charred remains, bobbing hideously upright, as though in one last act of defiance, the dead crammed shoulder to shoulder with others still living. Thousands screamed for help as soldiers thrashed down swords to end their fight for life. "We have to get out of here," cried Hagop, but Astra refused. "No, I'm going through it. I have to. He might be lying half dead somewhere!" So he gripped her hand and together they stumbled into a bloody war zone, dodging burning debris, kicking through rubble, stepping over bodies with limbs freshly severed, till they saw the street on fire. "There's nothing left," she cried, trying to locate the remains of his publishing house. "This is it here," said Hagop, pointing to a pile of rubble with a few walls left half standing. They dug their way in using their bare hands till Hagop stopped her frenzy. "Astra, he's not here, dead or alive."

On September 11th Setrag was missing now presumed dead. The city was still burning, and the scorching heat was getting closer. Turkish troops had all but reached the Armenian quarter. "He may have already escaped. Perhaps they warned him in time and put him on a boat out of here," she told herself and Anna. Later that evening loudspeakers boomed out a last warning that everyone must evacuate their homes and find refuge in the protection of French soil. Adriné's French school was just across the street from their house and hundreds of local Armenians took bedding, food and water to camp out in the school gardens under the false apprehension that no one, not even invading troops, would trespass into a French enclave. Men women and children barricaded themselves under trees, until the French too abandoned them. Koko had been watching the sentry posts. "Mama look, the French guards are leaving," he said as two Turkish soldiers marched in to take their place. It was a signal for a Turkish free for all and suddenly hundreds of militia marched in. Within minutes they were leading a long silent stream of male lambs to their slaughter. No one who heard it could ever forget the pitiful cries of the women left behind. Mothers, wives, sisters all clinging on, whispering final good-byes, till arms were wrenched apart and they watched in numbed silence as stone-faced bayoneted troops led their men away. Then they waited till the sound of rifle gunfire cracked through the trees to tell them their men were now dead. With the waiting over the women collapsed into each other's arms while others passed out in anguish. Looking back it was far too easy, no fighting, no struggling, not even words of protest. By the time the French guards resumed their sentry posts, and before the women reeled home, their men were already feeding buzzards high up on nearby wooded hills.

Astra went into the garden to stare into nothingness when suddenly her eyes caught sight of something enormous sprouting up right in the middle of their lawn. "Wherever did that come from? I could swear it wasn't there two days ago. It must have grown up from seeds shaken off our tablecloth," she thought, but to her it was a sign, but of what she could not say. "Luck saves lives as easily as it takes them. At least Hagop and Haroutioun had left when they did." She thanked God for their lives and for round green edible fruits. They were starving. Then she pulled back her sleeves and pulled it out from the ground, and rolled it through the kitchen door. "Look, we have food at last, a gigantic watermelon has just fallen out of the sky."

Anna cut the watermelon into neat slices and they sat swallowing in morose silence till Aizemnig spoke. "We have to burn everything incriminating, all the books, all the newspapers, the flags, and every single Dashnag leaflet in this house, right now, before they get here." No one disagreed. Circumstances had overtaken all arguments of loyalty. Before long, Aizemnig, the practical one, was leading the speedy operation to destroy every shred of evidence which marked Setrag's illustrious career. As their black kitchen boiler consumed her husband's life's work, the flames fired up enough hot water to wash everyone in the street. As they took it in turns to get in the bath, Astra thought she saw a little too much relish in her sister's emerald green eyes.

As night met dawn in the early hours of September 13th, banging doors and screaming neighbours shocked them from sleep. "Get out, all of you, now, while you can." Astra looked out of her window to see the street in panic wondering how she had slept through it. The infamous infantrymen were almost there, ready to rape, loot and murder everything in their path. "No, I am not leaving my house," said Anna Tokadjian, preferring to die in her bed. "I don't blame her, I would want the same," thought Astra, knowing she had no choice but to leave without her. "Then at least hide yourself in the cellar," she called through Anna's locked bedroom door.

She took essentials, whatever she could carry, and within minutes they tumbled straight into hysterical crowds rushing at them from every corner, searching for loved ones, screaming out names, reaching for hands, desperate to reach freedom together. Astra pulled her children back. Even now she had to find time for words of comfort. "Nené Tokadjian is waiting for your father, and we're going to be just fine. Koko and Adriné, you hold on to my skirt, don't let go, stay very very close." She squeezed Varoujan's hand tight and with baby Arpoun, just six weeks old, tucked tightly into her chest, they moved slowly on, inching through swarming labyrinths, alongside thousands of others heading for the small Port of Cordelio. Word had spread that they had come to save them at long last. After days of watching mass slaughter, the ships had finally upped anchor.

As people pushed past her in mad panic she wondered at the sad state of humanity, which would rather step over terrified children than make way for a woman with four little ones clutching at every part of her body. The parallel was not obvious, but she remembered that night, standing under the clock at Smyrna train station, with eyes closed, waiting for the bullet that would end her life. But this was not about her; it was about four little lives they had brought into this world, who were helpless, fatherless, homeless, and stateless, and who had no one else to love them. Astra felt a surge of strength pushing her further and faster through the crowd. "Make way please, we're coming through," she said out aloud, but in truth she had never felt so completely and utterly alone.

"Can you speak English? If you can, they say you have a better chance of being taken on board," asked a male voice walking beside her. "Yes I can speak English," she replied seeing a man's face dressed in female clothing reaching down to take her baby from her arms. "My dear you need help, let me hold him," he said, but Astra shook her head and gripped Arpoun more tightly. "No, no thank you," she answered, as he cursed her under his breath and rushed on ahead.

A familiar crimson dawn was breaking as they finally reached the port. Small rowing boats packed with refugees had started shuttling escapees to a large cargo ship anchored in deeper waters, but they were not out of trouble yet. Two rows of Turkish soldiers, swords crossed in pyramid formation, lined the path to freedom. Astra had been going over her speech. "I am an American citizen but unfortunately all our documents were burned in the embassy fires. My husband has already left and we have arranged to meet him at the American Embassy in Athens." She had given her children strict instructions not to say a word till she told them otherwise, which left her praying that none of the guards would recognize her. They shuffled on a little further till a sudden blast of gunfire spread the crowd, opening up views of the horizon. Just on the other side of the checkpoint she saw a pile of bodies awaiting an unceremonious burial at sea. After that split second of panic, the queue reformed and moved forwards, knowing the same arbitrary fate could strike any of them at any time. "Don't look," she whispered, as her children squeezed past atrocities lapping the water's edge. Later Astra heard that vigilant soldiers had lifted up veils and skirts to expose disguises, and shot any men, young or old, dressed as women, as well as any babies unlucky enough to be held in their arms.

They believed her. "You can pass," said two guards, dropping down swords to let them through. Minutes later they were swaying in the back of a small rowing boat, packed full of women and children, aware that Cordelio was becoming part of their history. Her children sat wide-eyed, their lips pursed tight, desperate for permission to speak, but she shook her head, not yet ready to tempt fate until shore side perils were well and truly behind them, but she could guess their unspoken questions. "Where are we going? Where is my father, my grandmothers, what about our friends? Why are we leaving without them?" It was a relief not to be able to answer, for now.

In rocking silence, they watched the cargo ship loom larger and closer. Just then the boat swung round sharply to line up alongside. Pre-empting possible dangers, Astra stretched a protective arm behind her little ones, just as a shuddering knock shook the boat and threw everyone off their seats. As the rowing boat scraped the side of the cargo ship and scraped off rusty red paint work, it pulled off every nail of every finger of her outstretched hand.

As soon as her feet touched deck and they were safely on board, numb throbbing gave way to agonizing pain and she slumped to the floor, bringing down a large open box of cargo figs with her. Next thing she remembered was Koko, Adriné and Varoujan, and a tall handsome stranger in uniform looking down at her. "Mama, mama," cried a relieved Adriné seeing her mother's eyes opening. "How do you feel madam?" asked a sharp cut glass English voice. "You had a nasty accident," he added. Astra raised her painful arm to see a huge white bloodstained bandage wrapped loosely around her right hand. "Where is my baby?" she asked terrified that she may have dropped Arpoun into the Aegean Sea. "He's being cared for, he's just fine. Now try to sip some brandy," he said gently, lifting her head off the pillow. "I should introduce myself. My name is Captain Brandt and

I would like to offer you and your family the use of my cabin till we reach Pireus harbour. That won't be for three days," he said.

Later that evening, Astra and her children were sitting at the Captain's table, eating a delicious four-course meal while baby Arpoun slept soundly in the cabin, under the attendant eyes of a member of his naval staff. There were only two cabins on board, and it was obvious to other refugees, some of whom were very wealthy and destined to spend their night on fig filled wooden decks, that Captain Brandt had taken a special interest in the striking young mother with the bandaged hand. With dinner over, Captain Brandt wiped his chin and asked, "Madam, can I take the children for a tour around the ship?" "Yes, thank you, they would love that," and with that he put Adriné on his shoulders, took Koko and Varoujan by the hand, and together they walked out of the crowded dining room. Astra sat alone in the centre of the long table, finishing her coffee and petit fours while envious female eyes threw daggers of unjustified moral outrage straight at her. "What are they thinking, that I'm providing special favours in payment for a comfortable night's sleep? Why can't they be pleased for me, after all we've been through? They're so petty minded." She decided to take the intimidation head on, so she stared right back till their eyes blinked down and conversations resumed their normal tones.

It seemed like hours till they returned, bright eyed and breathless with excitement, Adriné still giggling on his shoulders, and all wearing sailor hats, bubbling with experiences of their special tour. They told her about the shiny polished dials, the enormous engine room, the oil covered engineer, the huge black smoking funnel, the view from the bridge, and the ship's bell perched high above their heads, which at exactly nine o'clock, Koko had stuck nine times, to ring out news that all was well. "Mama, did you hear it? That was me ringing it, I rang it myself!"

The ship waited near the island of Chios for two days while Athens set about putting up basic shelters for the millions of refugees heading for its shores. It was a time when the handsome, middle-aged Captain Brandt found he was becoming increasingly fond of his cabin guests. After their first night, Astra felt uneasy about their special privileges. "I'm feeling so much better now, there's no need to give us your cabin tonight," but he saw through her reasons. "I am not susceptible to silly tittle tattle, and neither should you be. I know you are still in great pain and your children will be far more comfortable, so please accept my hospitality, and not another word about it." So for three nights Astra and her children slept in relative luxury while Captain Brandt shared a cramped cabin with three officers. After dinner one night, Captain Brandt and Astra were playing Rummy in the cabin. "I admire your determination. It's not easy playing cards with one hand," he said showing his immaculate white teeth, thinking his admiration went far deeper. "Oh, it's not that. I was thinking about my husband, he's disappeared." He soon realized that her pain went far deeper than a flayed hand and torn off fingernails, but Captain Brand was a perfect gentleman and put personal fancies to one side. "I can check ship records when we dock at Pireus. I heard one ship did manage to pick up a few hundred people who were obvious political targets two days before the port was set on fire." Her eyes lit up. "That was the very day Setrag went missing," she said, clutching at some real hope for the first time.

With the thought of finding him alive, and with the Royal Navy's kind attention, good food and clean bandages, her spirits were high and she took the children to the top deck to show them the coastline of their new homeland before they reached shore. Six hours later they were still lined up in a long queue of rescue ships waiting their turn outside Pireus harbour while others ahead poured out thousands of refugees into an already bursting Athens quayside. The sheer numbers were bewildering. "Where on God's earth are they going to put us all?" she asked herself, remembering her husband's words, "We can't go to Greece. It's so poor, they can hardly feed themselves." Eventually they docked, and she took her place on the gangplank preparing for the inevitable. She pulled her shoulders back and prayed to anyone listening, "Give me strength." Baby Arpoun, strapped to her chest felt it first. As pounding drum rhythms fired her heart and sent thick red stripes of war paint across her cheeks, her children sensed her eyes were fixed far beyond that writhing struggle for life. They knew Mama would protect them.

Chapter XIII

The Unmovable Parameters of Dignity

CAPTAIN Brandt was true to his word. It was almost dark when he saw the family group at the far end of a crowded beach sitting under a windswept canvass canapé in front of a run down warehouse. He walked slowly towards them, his eyes pinned to her strong profile outlined against the near night sky. She was sitting on bare sand upright, motionless, dignified, the devoted lioness, surrounded by playful cubs, tumbling and preening each other under the protection of her watchful eye. As he got nearer, he saw Varoujan and Adriné taking it in turns to pull a large ivory comb through her wavy flaxen waist length hair. He knew her age. At twenty-eight she was twenty years his junior, but she looked much younger, fresh faced, dressed in white. In just three days he had drawn out stories from her that had made his blood curdle. "I've never been able to talk about all that before. You can't unburden your soul to people who have gone through the same things you have. It's true what they say, it's much easier to tell a stranger." He didn't want her to be a stranger. "She's been through so much, and she's not much more than a child herself," he thought, imagining tears dripping off her soft plump cheeks to wash away sorrows past and present.

"Hello, I see you've found a nice spot," he said, knowing immediately it sounded callous in the extreme. Astra saw his eyes and knew what he had come to tell her. "You have checked the records but Setrag's name was not there." "No, not exactly. The ship's records show that a Setrag Tokadjian was taken on board, but for some reason he jumped ship before the ship left harbour. I double checked, he was not amongst those who reached safe passage." "Jumped off? Why would he do that?" she asked. "I don't know for sure, but apparently the passengers were waiting to leave port for two days, so they must have witnessed the destruction of the city." She imagined the scene right there. He must have seen it all, her and the children at the mercy of savages burning and murdering their way across town, so he jumped in to swim back and save them. But then what happened?

It would be two months before an incidental eyewitness would give Astra the closest thing to an account of her husband's death she was ever to hear. A politician's wife had been standing on deck as black smoke filled the skies. Just to her left, a man fitting Setrag's description, suddenly looked straight at her. "I can't stay here. What kind of a man could leave his family in this burning hell?" and with that he dived into the sea. She had watched him swim fish like, long gliding economic strokes, low, almost underwater, till finally, as he came up for air, a bullet struck him in the back, and that was that.

Looking up at Captain Brandt she remembered all the other times and places she had prayed her husband had survived, four times in Smyrna, during those long two months in Konya, by the shores of the Caspian, and now in Athens. She read his mind telling her that even he must die one day. "Stop it," she said so sharply it startled her. "I'm sorry, it's just a shock, that's all," she said, and he understood. "The Turkish government has just issued a deadline that all Christians must leave Turkey, and that now includes Smyrna, by the end of October, so you should have more news by then." He had done his part. "Thank you captain, for your concern and trouble. It must have been difficult to find us here." That part was true. "No, I'm very sorry, and I really must leave now. My crew will be wondering where I am. We sail for England tonight." With that he wished her well, shook her hand, and turned to leave. "Look after yourselves, till we meet again," he said, before mumbling something else under his breath which sounded like "tickets to England," but she hadn't quite heard it, and anyway he was already making his way down the beach.

The next day unsung heroes and heroines came to the rescue of thousands of refugees, to bring food and lay blankets down in every corner of town. Displaced people were lying down everywhere, in the red velvet corners of the National Opera House, under the beautiful white marble ruins of the Parthenon, in main thoroughfares tripping up workers and school children as they stepped over huddled families in an attempt to carry on with daily routines. Within days Athens was rife with life threatening epidemics. At one point it seemed that every refugee was sick. So Astra decided to stay right where she was, on the beach, where the air was fresh and the children could play in the purifying waters of the Aegean Sea. She recognized some of the heroines from her days when feminism was the only thing that mattered. She had campaigned for the introduction of female medics at the American College debating society, and for real, at the Sunday Meetings. She had been thrilled to read in 1917 that the Red Cross and armed forces had agreed to introduce women doctors into a previously all-male profession. Now five years on, more than one thousand American all female doctors and nurses, led by two visionaries, Esther Lovejoy and Dr. C. Elliott, director of the American Women's Hospitals, were shouldering the entire burden of refugee relief operations. Now she was watching them in action, tending the sick, comforting mourners, feeding the hungry, still finding time in their impossible schedule to befriend the lonely. Here they were, providing sustenance, welfare, care, compassion, and human dignity to everyone, everywhere, old and young, Greek or Armenian, all equal priorities in their superhuman agenda. She was full of admiration.

Athens in October 1922 was unusually hot and the nights were always hardest. Teeming rows of body heat inflamed burning night fevers, killing the sick and stifling the living. Adriné was the first of her children to come down with measles. As she tossed and turned in her mother's arms, her skin was on fire, and Astra feared she might not last the night. "No, Koko, don't take them, they're my dolls, stop it, your breaking them," she screamed, lashing out at the phantom in her dreams, while Astra worried what other sinister symbols might be invading her daughter's subconscious. The smell of death, heightened by drifting swirls of frankincense, drew morbid senses to the saddest parts of the overcrowded floors.

Koko was sitting up, smiling down on his blotchy red-faced sister, thankfully still breathing. That morning he had already counted eight candles flickering in shaded corners and everyone knew what that meant. Each light marked a shrine where cruel fate had struck during the night, and by morning sobbing relatives were waiting for overworked mortuary attendants to come and do their work. "Koko, please don't point like that, it's disrespectful," whispered his mother, bringing down his index finger. "Sorry Mama, I was just counting how many 'Our Fathers' I have to say today. I say one for each person who dies." "Dear God," she thought, "Koko, my soft hearted philosopher, sending out prayers for the dead." It sent shivers through her soul. "Koko, that's a lovely thing to do but try not to be so obvious. You'll scare the little ones. We can count the candles and pray quietly together when we go to fetch the water." So they carried buckets, nodding heartfelt condolences, while Koko prayed for the dead and Astra prayed for the living. "Please, help us get out of this place alive, before I and my children go mad."

Within a week, all her children had come down with measles. Koko had it worst. Nancy Arbuckle, Astra's friend from the circuit meeting days, dropped in to see them whenever she could. "He's not showing any outward signs, it's erupted inside him, that's quite dangerous," she said, preparing his mother for the worst. The next day baby Arpoun was baptised right there on the beach. His godfather was a classical musician of some repute, a kindly stranger who held the baby snugly in his arms, apparently indifferent to the infectious raspberry rashes covering him from head to foot. Barefoot on a beach, with ragged strangers all around them, she saw her baby being anointed with sacred oils. It was all going according to plan until the priest dipped Arpoun into the sea and baptised him with completely the wrong name. "We wish for this child Apollo, faith hope and love," he said, as Koko tried to alert his mother. But she had heard it too and shook her head. It was an easy mistake, understandable under the circumstances, and she let out a wry smile. "What does it matter, it's just a name," she thought, taking sick baby Apollo back to the quiet of the shelter. Apollo the sun god, the bringer of music and culture, it seemed very appropriate somehow. "At least he's baptised," she thought.

By mid-November Astra had prayed through every hour of darkness, till miraculously all her children recovered. Somehow, without proper medication, sweating rivers on hard stone floors, they had all survived and Astra felt blessed that her prayers had been answered, but not all of them.

Necessary campsite routines denied them all the basics of human privacy, but over proximity wore down territorial barriers and brought together the unlikeliest of strangers in a way that time never would. Soon a close-knit community shared intimate ablutions and chores unabashed, and so restored lost dignities. She was sitting with a group of friends, young and old, all crocheting cream cotton blankets, while her eldest son ate a full plate of rice for the first time in six weeks. "Captain Brandt," she called, seeing him walking briskly towards her. "You look well," he said, "and it's good to see your hand back in operation." Suddenly with an uncharacteristic drop in formalities he sat down cross-legged right amongst them. She had no sooner introduced him when they started to complain, as though his smart clean uniform gave him undue influence. They protested about everything from the weather to the Greek authorities, how they had been promised shelters, even new housing, but that it was taking so long. He listened patiently, shaking his head in sympathy, finally admitting that unfortunately there was nothing he could do. Then he caught Astra's eye. "Would you come with me, there's someone I think you should meet."

She left her children in the care of the commune and they walked towards a better-equipped camp with makeshift houses, port side of the beach. A middle-aged woman wearing bright green shoes saw them approaching and came outside. She was expecting them. "This is a lady who thinks she saw your husband on the ship." Astra listened to the story, how she had been on deck, beside a well-dressed dark haired man with an imposing black moustache. "I saw him as clearly as I see you now. He jumped into the water and swam mostly underwater, but as he came up for air he was shot in the back." With a shaky hand, Astra took off her locket and opened the clasp. The woman threw a perfunctory glance over the precious photograph. "Yes, that's definitely him," she said.

They walked back in silence, till he decided the moment was right to ask her. "I have five tickets and could take you and the children back to England with me." He reached into his jacket and took out a large leather wallet as though she needed proof. "How can I leave now? I must find the rest of my family, I don't even know if they made it out of Smyrna alive," and with that she broke down.

"These tickets were given to me as a personal favour. Unfortunately England is not offering asylum to Greeks or Armenians, but of course I understand," he said. He wished she were more selfish and less in love with her husband's memory, knowing ironically that he would never feel the same way about her if she were. "You know we always dreamed of living in America, 'the heavenly playground' we called it, where Setrag could write freely, and where the children would have a liberal education. I read women have the vote in England now." It was tempting, but how could she, without the others? "Captain, I am very grateful but it's quite impossible." She took his hand only to feel it snatched back before emotions got the better of him. "Then may I write to you when things are more settled?" he asked, but he knew he was clutching at straws.

Four months later, in January 1923, Astra had become an active member of the relief effort, helping Nancy Arbuckle's nurses with their rounds for a few hours a day, washing and feeding the sick, and changing bandages, while the trusty commune minded her children. It helped her take her mind off things for a while. She could also keep an eye out for missing relatives along the way. "Yes, I did see your mother and sister, they were on our ship," said an elderly acquaintance with an oozing ulcer. "You really should go to the Armenian Church in Athens, the Archbishop is keeping records of survivors." The next morning Astra tried to ignore basic dress codes. "Refugees are entitled to look like this," she told herself, pushing out creases from her worn out grey skirt. "I have to go into the town today Koko, so take Adriné with you and go to collect some mussels. You can ask the lady at the food counter for a large tin box and see if you can fill it to the brim by the time we get back. I'm taking Varoujan and Arpoun to church."

As their mother faced the real world for the first time in three months, brother and sister scanned rock pools, picking only the best till the handles became heavy. So they dragged back the box, puffing and happy and very pleased with their catch. "Koko, look at the wide tracks of sand behind us, Mama will see them and know we've been busy," said Adriné, looking forward to her dinner. By the time their mother returned, large steaming pots of seafood risotto were feeding the small crowds along the shore.

Astra slumped down amidst her group stunned and shocked. "What happened?" asked Marie, seeing the look on her friend's face. "It was terrible. I can't speak a word of Greek, I couldn't read the road signs, and no one would help us. I'm sure they thought I was begging for money. Look at poor Varoujan, his little feet have never walked so far. It took us nearly four hours to find the Armenian Church." "Was it bad news?" asked Marie assuming the rest. "No, far from it. I found out that my mother, my sister, and my two brothers are all alive and well, and living in the comfort of a two bedroom apartment!" she blurted out, relieved and more than very slightly hurt. "You should see the Archbishop's office, it's full of hundreds of large black files, and he knows all the gossip. He told me that my sister Aizemnig's money steamrollered her way through Greek authority allocation policies. Apparently her gold investments and the ready monies in her pocket pushed them right to the top of the accommodation ladder! I thought our clergy were supposed to be non-judgemental, but as he handed me their address, apparently in one of the smartest parts of town, he actually accused me! He said he didn't approve of people who bought favours at the expense of the less fortunate, and that in a town where the local population was desperate for a roof over their heads, at least my family was firmly ensconced! It's not all's fair in love and war, well not for me at least."

Next day, Astra, her four children and Marie, who did speak some Greek, found the archbishop's travel directions were street perfect. Peproné opened the door. "Oh my darlings, my prayers have been answered," she said almost beside herself in happiness, then, when the kissing and hugging was over, they sat down on proper chairs for the first time in three months. "We asked so many people but no one knew where you were," said Aizemnig in her smart beige woollen suit, eyeing up her long lost family in refugee handouts. "Did you free the birds from the aviary when you left the house Mama?" asked Astra, wondering why of all the things she could have asked this was the most vital. Peproné was looking at her sons. "Why is it that as soon as we all come together we have to say good bye again?" It was not the answer she was expecting. "We are going to Paris next week," said Haroutioun. "I passed my law exams and a top lawyer in Paris has offered me a job, right in the centre of town, and Hagop is coming with me to try his luck in the newspaper business over there." Astra realized life had been moving on for some people. "Imagine our little Haroutioun following in father's footsteps, and to have qualified through a correspondence course entirely in French. I don't know how you did it, I am so proud of you," she said. "We all are," said Aizemnig, re-establishing her sibling rivalry agenda.

It was a bittersweet reunion. They were all grown up now, all except for Zevart, who would always be fifteen. No one had dared to mention her name, not that she was forgotten. It was just less painful. No one said it, but refugees had to look forward now, and it was clearly easier for some than others. Setrag's name hadn't been mentioned either, but Astra forgave them. It put Zevart in good company. Five hours later, when they were almost back at camp, Marie asked the obvious. "Now that your brothers are going to France, why didn't your sister ask you to move in?" She had been asking herself that very question all the way back. "It's a long story," she said, not wanting to bring her children into the 'situation' between her and her older sister. But late that night by the campfire, she wanted to make sense of it too. "You know Marie, I have never completely understood why Aizemnig has always been so competitive, even resentful of me. My mother says it's because she couldn't have children, her husband was impotent, but I don't think it's just that. I think it goes way before my children were born." Astra remembered Aizemnig's wedding day. "She was so young and naïve. When they murdered my father she became withdrawn, she loved him so much. Soon after Karekin asked to marry her and my mother saw it as a blessing. He was kind and rich, but I remember thinking he looked so old, even older than our father. She has never been to school, my mother taught her from home, but I was sent to American College. I think that's when it started. I studied literature, science, philosophy, music and sport, and I had so many friends. Then I married a national hero whom I loved passionately, and then worked as a journalist and campaigned for women's rights. It must have been hard for her and I'm sure she coped with it by disapproving of my life choices, and now she has every right to throw them back in my face. She's very clever but frustrated, so she threw herself into high society to impress her socialite friends. She was the best dressed, the best read, the best hostess. I think she would have made a wonderful doctor, she has healing hands."

Marie had heard Astra's own story and had thought it not unlike a Greek tragedy. "What on earth are you talking about? Just listen to yourself, always analysing reasons, making excuses for people. Perhaps she's just jealous of you, pure and simple." "Marie, you know it's not just about me, my decisions affected all of us. Her husband paid for Setrag's prison releases. The militia were banging on our door with bayonets so often that our neighbours were too terrified to talk to us. She thinks that I put all our lives in danger by marrying a man whose politics were too dangerous and too important to him, and she blames me for believing in him. She's never said it but I think she blames Zevart's deportation on me too. She thinks I could have stopped everything if only I had denounced Setrag in prison that second time. But even now, knowing everything that happened, I could never have done that! How they could have expected me to do that, even for a single second, I'll never know!"

Marie and Astra had only known each other a matter of weeks but burning embers and flickering fires merged broken souls in those dark quiet times. As the fluorescent sea ebbed and flowed, the commune would break up in twos or threes, each set on unburdening pains and sharing secrets of who and what they were before all this, when life was normal, affirming past identities, lest they forget. It soon became obvious that these emotional outpourings bore a direct correlation to a good night's sleep for everyone and as such became an essential part of late night camp life.

Astra was often the last to say good night. Her affinity with night skies went far deeper than her namesake. While running her fingers through cold wet sand, she beckoned the night sky to come to her. With her eyes fixed on shimmering constellations, her husband's face would begin to smile down through countless random stars, ready for her thoughts. That night she stayed longer than usual, there was a lot to say. Her family was alive, his youngest child had cut his first tooth, and stoic Koko had taken his father's place as head of the family by making sure she ate all her rations rather than pass them on. "Where is your mother Setrag, is she alive? I am sorry about leaving her, but you know how stubborn she is, there was no time, please forgive me."

It was gone three o'clock when she stood up to shake the blanket free of sand but she had decided to keep this one for last. "Setrag, do you think we should have gone to England?" A harsh wind brushed her neck and she knew he was still listening.

A week later her brothers left for France and before their sheets were cold, a large mahogany writing desk was being delivered to replace the two beds in front of the large bay window. Aizemnig fussed about preparing her large spare room for local refugee relief operations. Peproné was mortified, but it was not up to her. She had no control over purse strings. "You must agree, it's very good of her. Young mothers with their poor sick babies come to pick up milk and all types of medicines. The doctor is grateful to have a place so centrally located. She's so busy all the time. In the afternoon she goes out with the Red Cross to visit refugees, to allocate bedding and food, and then when she comes home, she gets on her knees and starts praying for them. Astra, you have to admire her," said her mother holding back tears of shame. "Mama, believe me, I do, and you must not worry about us. We're fine in the camp, and now that you know where we are, you can come to see us every day," said Astra. All things considered, it was probably for the best.

Eventually after four months, the beach front refugees were moved en masse to a nearby rocky hillside where the Greek government had just finished putting up a purpose built tent village. Peproné did come every day, dragging her swollen feet uphill in the midday sun, but it was preferable to sitting alone in a large lonely apartment while Aizemnig went out to do good works. Koko would rush down to meet her. "Nene, it's so much nicer here. Look, we have our own little tent, the water is close by, and we can still walk down to the beach whenever we want to, but Mama hates the insects," he said, helping his baby brother take his first uncertain steps on steep jagged rocks of an Athenian hillside. "God bless him for understanding the intricacies of family politics," thought Peproné.

But it wasn't just the insects which made her want to leave. This was no way to bring up a family, surrounded by stinking tents and downtrodden people, but with hardly an inch of breathing space left in the capital, the chance of a room in a stone building, big enough to sleep them all, within five minutes from the Acropolis seemed too good to be true. Anahid Hovanessian, a rich widowed violin teacher, her friend from Smyrna, was about to take her son and emigrate to Argentina. "Astra you weren't easy to find. I am leaving in a few hours. You can have my room if you want, but we have to act quickly." Astra's face beamed with joy. "Right then, get ready. You must come back with me right now and bring everything with you. You need to stake your claim on it before anyone else does. My crazy neighbour has her beady eyes on it." So they grabbed their belongings, said their good-byes, and within the hour they were standing in the room, which was to be their home for far too long. But even this came with a struggle. Astra and her children were moments away from hand-to-hand combat.

No sooner had Anahid and her son left to start their new life in Buenos Aries, someone started ramming the door, thumping fists and kicking feet, screaming obscenities the like of which the children had never heard. "Stop it Ardiro, what are you doing, you'll break the door down," said a voice in the hallway just outside. For a while it went quiet so Astra peered round the door, when suddenly it came back in her face as the wild woman snorted in like a wild bull, charging her stocky powerful body straight at them. "You and your children get out of here, now! I am warning you, this is my room. I was here first." "Get out, now!" she screeched, punching, pulling clothes, tugging hair, till finally Astra lost her balance and fell to the floor taking her terrified children with her.

The whole house arrived to see Mad Ardiro fading, more out of exhaustion than remorse. Someone went to get the police while the others held her down, delighted to give her back some well-deserved abuse. "You're insane. I feel sorry for your husband, poor man. He is so ashamed of you, he never leaves the room," said a tall refined gentleman restraining Mad Ardiro's right arm. "You greedy unfeeling cow, look, this poor woman has four young children, and what do you need two rooms for anyway?" said a young woman in evening dress, restraining her left. A policeman arrived to hear insults still in full flow. "Quiet, everyone," he shouted and set about his investigation right there on the stairs. "Mrs. Ardiro, do you have papers to prove your rights to the room?" "What are you talking about, none of us have papers. I have been living here for six months,

I was here first." "That is not a reason in law. On the other hand, the previous tenant has offered Madam Tokadjian here the tenancy, so she has the right to live here without any nuisance from you. If I hear one more complaint about you, you will be thrown out into the street." Astra knew enough about the law to know the police force had no judicial powers to decide tenancy agreements, but luckily Ardiro didn't.

It was not the entrance she would have chosen but at least the formal introductions were dealt with. "If you have any problems with that mad woman, you must tell us," said her neighbours as they left her to settle in, but as she watched Ardiro grovel back to her room, muttering lame apologies, Astra knew she wouldn't. With the commotion over, she closed her door and took a long look at their new home for the first time. It was hardly worth fighting for, but it was better than a tent. "Mama look, we have a balcony, and a stove out here for cooking," said Adriné holding up Varoujan to show him the view of the garden. "Can we go down?" asked Koko, but before his mother could answer, he saw a waddling figure holding a bucket walk right under their veranda, kick a skinny grey cat out of her way, and stop under a tree by a water pump. "Oh no, there's no running water inside!" she realized. But at least they had a stove, a rickety table, a large wardrobe and one lumpy bed. "Mama, can we cook something?" asked Adriné. In the rush to claim the room Astra had forgotten everything else, including their reliance on the handout world of refugee relief. Her children were hungry and she didn't have a single drachma anywhere to buy food. "Let's sleep first," she said. So hungry and tired, they huddled up in the single iron bed as crickets screeched outside the window, but at least they were out there and not climbing all over their hair and face while they slept.

Early light crept through cracked green shutters, waking up her hungry, thirsty children, while Arpoun sucked happily on the breast. Astra knew she had no choice but to eat humble pie. No one could blame her for wanting to take her children away from the clutches of disease and pestilence of camp life, or for craving a normal life. They had been lucky so far, but as she pulled her sister's gleaming brass doorbell she knew what was waiting for her on the other side.

"What possessed you to leave the camp? You are always so impetuous. You had everything you could possibly need there. I know how well these camps are run, I see them every day. Renting rooms is a luxury you can't afford just now, what were you thinking of," said Aizemnig, shaking her head in disbelief. "I did it for the children," said Astra, hoping her mother was awake. "Please Aizemnig, I only need enough to last us a couple of months and I promise to pay you back everything as soon as I start earning. There are a lot of rich families in my building and I'm sure some of them will want new clothes," said Astra, keeping it short, reading her sister's mind, and knowing she was just a hair's breadth away from bringing up Setrag's four extortionate prison release ransoms. This was no time to open up old wounds, with "well, you never paid back any of that money did you? And what about all the pain you put us through, all for your precious Setrag, and for what, he's dead now anyway," but the children were listening so their aunt kept her thoughts to herself. Just then Peproné's smiling face peeped around the door to offer tempting breakfasts all round and to put an end to Aizemnig's pontificating. Peace bringer Peproné went straight to work, rushing in and out with home made specialities, quince jam, vanilla sultana cake, roasted mahlebi chorek, followed by white cheese and fried eggs served up on thick slices of sesame bread. "Now chew it nicely children," advised auntie, nibbling at the corner of a sesame biscuit as Peproné kept piling their plates, knowing she had pitched their hunger to a tee.

By nine o'clock that morning the large front room was already packed full of refugees with Aizemnig at the helm handing out the daily rations. "Astra, take that envelope on the table, and we'll say no more about it, and here's a box of rations for you too," she called out, suddenly feeling generous in the company of strangers. They left soon after with Peproné eager to see where Astra was now living, and wondering if there was any room for her too. "Mama, I will call into the Armenian Church first to give them my new address." The Archbishop's secretary handed Astra a letter. "A Captain Brandt telephoned yesterday to make sure it arrived," she said, adding, "Oh yes, your mother-in-law Anna Tokadjian is alive and well. She is staying at the Holy Cross Monastery, opposite the tent village."

"Who is Captain Brandt?" asked Peproné, as Astra put the letter in her handbag. "Let's find Anna first," she said.

They found Anna Tokadjian, slumped over a stone bench, under a flaking fresco of Our Lord in a gloomy corner of a crumbling Byzantine church. "Mama Tokadjian, it is you! I can't believe it," said Astra, running to kiss her with a rush of genuine emotion. But Anna sat grey and motionless, a cold numb hollow statue, merging in perfectly with her ghostly surroundings. They could see she had nothing left to give, so they helped her up and walked her out, step by step, into the blazing sunshine. They almost carried her down the steep slopes, stopping to shade under cypress trees till they reached the house. "Mama Tokadjian, here we are at last. We can all live here together, I'll buy beds," said Astra, realizing they had nowhere to sit. "Hadji Néné, we can make it look really nice, we only arrived yesterday," said Adriné, running out to show her the wooden balcony. "Oh Dear God, I wish I was dead," said Anna. "Now you look here, Madam Tokadjian, my daughter has been through hell too you know, you're not the only one, and it's about time you finally put an end to your mother-in-law games. Stop criticizing her and do something to help. She has a family to feed in case you hadn't noticed, so unfold your arms, stop complaining, and do something useful for a change. I'm going home." She threw the rations' box at her feet, said goodbye, and left, slamming the door and years of polite repression behind her. On reflection one large bed could not sleep two grandmothers, four children and their mother, even if they did all get on like a house on fire.

Chapter XIV

A Need for Creativity and Independence

THE early warm spring helped sleeping arrangements for a while. Koko and Astra slept outside on the balcony, while baby Arpoun, Adriné, Varoujan, and Nené Anna slept indoors. "Mama, what's the date today?" asked Koko diplomatically. He knew it was the 19th of March. "This morning Hadji Nené made Adriné a doll out of twigs and grass, and dressed it up with flowers and her pink chiffon scarf." Astra put down her pen, Captain Brandt would have to wait. "Koko, you know what, with all that's happened we completely forgot poor Adriné's birthday." She finished the letter when they were all in bed. She started by thanking him for the tickets, but as he was only able to send five, she couldn't accept. She told him about finding her family, and how now that they had moved into a house everything was fine. She was usually such a prolific letter writer, words spilled from her pen, but this time she was doing some serious thinking, weighing up long term implications of turning down his offer. By the time she signed her name she was as sure as anyone could be that it was better to stay in Greece. She put the letter and tickets in the envelope, sealed it, and hoped she had chosen wisely. Their futures decided by a few words of polite rejection. It was a heavy responsibility, and it sent her heart beating, but it was done.

Next, she opened her purple velvet drawstring bag and took out the precious gold and bone prayer book, and turned to the first page. It read, "To my cherished daughter-in-law, God Bless." Krikor was like that, direct and earnest. She missed his unvarnished wisdoms. She sent him a prayer and turned over the page. It was blank and she sat upright to ready herself to write in her neatest, most formal hand. She listed her children in age order, leaving a space before adding the dates and places of birth. Her third born had died so young. Christopher, her desperately missed cherished angel with ruby pouting lips and chestnut curls. She deliberated before deciding to include him too, adding the day he had died in brackets. Five blue lines stared back at her, stark and meaningless, and she wondered if a testament of her love would be an appropriate addition but decided no. This was a true and formal record and the nearest thing to an official birth certificate any of them would ever have.

Aizemnig's loan was enough to pay rent and feed six mouths for a few weeks, but it would not stretch to a sewing machine and she refused to ask her for more. Astra waited till the early hours before taking down the hem of her brown velvet skirt. It felt like a betrayal, but if selling a few family heirlooms helped her feed needy dependants she was sure her ancestors would forgive her. She took out three shiny gold coins and put them in her purse, ready for the pawn shop in the morning. Athenian pawnbrokers were busier than bakeries. With thousands of refugees already having reached into trouser hems or secret shoulder seams to trade gold for the comfort of a clean bed, she guessed she wouldn't get much.

Still it shocked her to see what this unsavoury little man was offering. He counted it out with claw like spidery fingers, grinning through filthy teeth, enjoying every minute of other people's misfortune. "He's definitely found his niche," she observed. "I must have full payment in six weeks or I will sell the coins," he said. "Yes, I understand," said Astra holding up six fingers just to make sure. Then he handed over a docket written in Greek and it meant absolutely nothing to her, but she pretended to check it before nodding to accept the terms. "I really must try to learn this impossibly difficult language as soon as possible," she cursed.

Next she found a second hand sewing machine in a local haberdashery shop and dragged it home. They wouldn't deliver. It was a good find, even though it was old and oily and chugged like an aging steam train, but the stitching was neat and taut, so she hoped her neighbours would be tolerant. The stop and start walk home gave her time to really take in her surrounding and she saw Athens for the great city it was for the very first time. Avenues gleamed whiter, sparkled cleaner and stretched wider, now the refugees had moved on. The time had come to make this capital feel like home for all their sakes. "What is home?" she asked herself, stopping to rub blood back into her palms before heaving the machine up the last few steps.

"Well, I suppose it's different things to different people, and we must make the best of it. For me it's where I sleep, wash, eat, drink, laugh and cry, and now it's where I'm going run my dressmaking business as well!" A sense of the ridiculous brought a smile to her face. "Well it's either that or we will all starve." She brushed off the split second of self-pity and thanked lady luck for bringing rich and poor under one roof. "As soon as I clean up this machine I'm going to knock on my neighbours' doors to see how many of them are in the market for a wonderful new wardrobe." Even a journey of a thousand miles had to start with that first step.

"You can't possibly run a business from here, we have no room as it is!" said her mother-in-law. "I know it's going to be tight, but where else can I do it? At least I'm able to sew," but as ever there was no point in explaining. As Anna preferred to discourse with Our Lord in any case, Astra found out the times of services and the ladies coffee mornings at the Armenian Church which left her to get on with interior transformations in peace. As she scanned the dull cream distemper walls, creative urges began to flow and she visualized the space split into a family residence on one side and an opulent designer studio dripping with bijou baroque splendour on the other. She began by buying a large piece of red and gold brocade and made a full curtain to divide the room. Then she asked the local greengrocer for four wooden crates which she padded and covered with a rich red velvet, decorating edges with gold trim piping, and made long round cushions to match. "Oooh, I can't believe it," she said, impressed at her first attempt at sumptuous upholstery, visually at least. How sturdy her chaise longue was to be in carrying the weight of oversized customers, she was yet to find out.

Bursting with new found enthusiasm and with four children in tow, she walked the length and breadth of town. She searched in junk shops, rummaged dusty corners and argued prices till she settled on two essential items, a long oval gilt mirror, and a deep pile crimson Hatchli Bokhara rug, cheap, soft on bare feet, and easy on the eyes. "Mama, I didn't know you could speak so much Greek," said Koko. "Neither did I, but I've learned that you discover your talents when you most need to, but you have much more sense than to wait till then. You my son are a natural academic." Given what they were putting up with, they needed every ounce of praise she could give them. "Inner confidence is a wonderful thing," she thought. Her mind drifted back to April 1915, when aged just twenty one, she had stood defiant and unyielding, trying to control her knocking knees and the terror in her heart, arguing her husband's corner in front of butchering Ottoman warlords at the Ministry of Interior.

The sun was starting to set as they started the long walk back, slowly, carefully, laughing off startled stares from passers by, but it was not a sight they saw every day. With Arpoun tied to her back, she and Koko negotiated the tricky balance of the mirror, while Adriné and Varoujan ran on ahead, each holding two ends of the rolled Afghani rug, giggling and struggling with their prized purchases, all the way home.

True, their living area had shrunk by half but the new workroom had become a sumptuous space of elegant flamboyant colour. She drew fashion sketches and pinned them on the walls. She polished the long mirror and angled it to face the lush brocade curtain. She arranged the makeshift velvet seating and buffed up the cushions on which she laid out tempting fabric samples, gathered for free the day before from haberdashery shops in the Aghiou Marco. Then she stood in front of the mirror trying to emulate what Satenig used to say and do, remembering how effortlessly she would charm her customers with easy chatter and exaggerated arm movements, but she decided it looked unnatural. Feigned, flattery was not her style. "Well I can still be a couturier without all that," she decided. "I'm just going upstairs to fetch my first customer. Helena from the first floor wants a dress to wear to the opera," she said peeping behind the brocade curtain. "Please keep the noise down children. You can go and play in the garden if you want." Then, just as she was ready for the off, there was a knock at the door. She opened it to see three pompous looking men dressed in tall hats and sombre suits. "We are pleased to have found you at long last. We do hope this is a convenient time."

Years before, high-ranking members of the Dashnag Party, aware of real and present dangers, had made long term provisions for their families' futures. Clasping hands in brotherly commitment they swore promises on holy bibles that if any of them should survive, they would make it their life's work to care for widows and fatherless children left behind, wherever they might be. A daunting task indeed for that brave band of survivors with widows and children now spread across every god-forsaken corner of the globe, but still they searched undeterred, from country to country, a promise was a promise after all. It was the least they could do to honour the memory of their illustrious dead.

Astra listened with gritted teeth as they explained how they had come from afar bearing gifts, before wasting no time in telling them that neither she nor her family could possibly accept charity. It was an instinctive response, direct and final, born out of her powerful need for independence. This deep-seated horror of being beholden brought out a stubborn streak and she stood up to show them the door. "I do appreciate your coming here, but as you can see we are doing very well. Please give the money to others who really need it." Astra sounded so harsh she unsettled the men in black suits who after nearly two years of benevolent visitations had never known such ingratitude. Firm instructions from the brotherhood persuaded them to try again. "Well, in that case, can we be of any other assistance?" Astra composed herself. Actually she did have something else in mind, something much more precious than ready monies, her children's education.

Within days the three wise men had pulled some strings, dropped a few names in the right places, and returned with excellent news. Koko and Adriné had been offered a place each at the single denominational schools of Saint Joseph, the best school in Athens, situated in the grand surrounding of the Panepistimio, just by the university. As deserving orphans, the fees would be waived for the duration of their required education, and Varoujan and Arpoun would be offered the same opportunity when they reached entry age. Astra summoned her two oldest. With a simple nod of her head she prompted them to walk reverently with heads bowed to kiss the hands of their elders and betters. Then everyone listened as they embarked on the predictable pontificating which followed. "Children we do not need to tell you how very fortunate you are. You must make the absolute best of this exceptional opportunity. You must take your studies very seriously, be diligent at all times, and show the utmost respect to your teachers. You owe it to the name of your illustrious father," said the eldest of the three. Even elders had their pecking order.

Astra wondered if they were performing their solemn duty more in memory of dear departed comrades rather than for the future of living children. But whatever their reasons, her children were to receive an education her husband would have dreamed of, and right on cue Setrag's spirit swept in to let her know. She felt him brush her neck in the breeze, whispering advice she didn't need. "Dear wife, please climb down off that high horse and swallow humble pie." So she too bowed her head in gratitude, kissed that well kissed hand with perfect decorum, and showed them the door.

Two hours later Astra had a tape measure around her neck, a large pair of scissors in her hand, and was leaning across the table, cutting out a pattern for a green satin ball gown from sheets of cream flimsy newspaper. Anna Tokadjian was not amused. She huffed and puffed, tidying pins, and mumbling impatience under her hungry breath. "Yes, well, my dear clever daughter-in-law, everyone can see we are far too rich to accept charity, but do we even have a table to eat off? No we don't." Astra bit her tongue, knowing that she must try to do needlework while others slept from then on.

Chapter XV

The Wisdom of Expecting the Unexpected

ASTRA moved life on, trying to turn the abnormal into normal, hoping they wouldn't notice, but of course they did. Like the time when she came home with a roll of cream embossed satin under her arm to find Adriné and her best friend Acabi, huddled together, terrified, balancing precariously on a wobbly chair. Their eyes were fixed in horror as they stood staring at a huge green and black snake, rising straight up in the middle of the living space. Astra kept her fears to herself. She crept in, one hand to her lips, gesturing silence, the other reaching down to find the large aluminium pot by the verandah door. Then, taking a deep breath, she took aim and threw the pot and all its contents smack on target. The snake wriggled back down, somewhere under a wide gap in the floorboards, smothered in left over green lentil soup. Then she calmly walked over to help the girls down, smiling and swinging her arms nonchalantly, as if nothing of any importance had happened at all. The two girls were left wondering if it really was the most natural thing in the world to have a terrifying snake rise up in the middle of your living room at three o'clock in the afternoon. "Come on girls, let's push the rug over to cover the gaps in the floorboards. Acabi, is your uncle in? Good, let's go down and ask him if he would be kind enough to hammer in a few more planks." No drama. It helped to keep things simple, life was complicated enough.

Astra's business took off quicker than she could ever have hoped. Her neighbours rose to her bait of stylish clothes right there on their doorstep, made at lightning speed, and at incredibly low prices. She would work late into the night, sleeping only between three and six thirty in the morning when bouncy little Arpoun puckered his cherubic lips to crow with the resident cockerel outside their window with annoying regularity. Almost before her eyes had focused, his chubby legs were waddling off in search of something tasty, on a mission to eat them out of house and home, if she let him. Before the house stirred, she dared to sneak a few minutes on that ear busting sewing machine, running up and down tacked seams, timing it to the limits of tolerance, stopping just short of neighbours banging their complaints through walls and ceiling. Now and then, when she managed to finish all her seams before the banging started, she'd stop to wonder how a simple thing like that could make her smile when once she had been so hungry for everything—but at least she could sew, and she had Aizemnig to thank for that.

Once she had paid back a surprised sister and a resentful pawnbroker well before time, she felt obliged to revert back to pre-nuptial promises and out-dated customs. So, from then on, and with her slate clean, Astra handed over every drachma she ever earned to her mother-in-law, who resumed control of the family purse strings. There were obvious drawbacks however, which Astra should have foreseen. "Mama T, I need some money to buy buttons with," said Astra, finishing off the hem of a navy and white crepe suit with matching cloche hat for Helena, now her best customer and best dressed refugee in the whole of Athens. "Then why don't you ask her for the money," said Anna, not agreeing with dressmaker's protocol. "You know that I have to hand over the suit with the buttons sewn on. It's not finished otherwise, and they never pay till it's finished," she replied, shaking her head in disbelief, completely exhausted with mindless power games. "Hadji Nene, why do you always have those little devils churning inside you?" snapped Koko with uncharacteristic anger in his voice. Astra should have told him not to be so rude but instead she wanted to hug him. Anna stared aghast as Koko sat back down on the floor to carry on uncovering the mysteries of geometry, pointedly ignoring his grandmother's shocked expression. After a couple of minutes silence Anna reached into her purse. "Oh, here you are then. Is this enough money for your buttons?" Nothing was ever going to be easy inside or outside the Tokadjian camp.

Within two years Astra's name was being scribbled into smart leather address books all over the capital. When her well-dressed neighbours paraded around town, complete strangers would walk up to them and ask for the name of their dressmaker, and before long gleaming Rolls Royces were pulling up outside her most humble abode. Usually chauffeurs and husbands waited outside till fittings were over, but occasionally wives would drag their men to see Astra's creations in the making. Her heart sank whenever two sets of feet echoed up the chipped marble hall stairway. In her experience husbands always hindered operations. The men would slump down on her red velvet pseudo chaise longues, leaning forward uncomfortably close, sipping on cherry syrup, and before long were puffing boredom, fidgeting and desperate to leave. This would normally be followed by the pocket watch stage, when suddenly, remembering an urgent appointment, they would check and recheck each passing minute in an effort to speed up fussy wives and her rate of pinning and tucking.

It was Easter week 1926 and for the first time Astra had some money to make the festivities special. After four years of stoic self-denial she was ready for life's innocent frivolities, just like the rest of them. She still yearned for Setrag, but pain had given way to a constant dull ache. Now she knew in her heart she would never see him again, but others still had hope. "Mama, you'll never guess, Koko and I just saw a man who looked like Baba. He went into a house down the street," said Adriné still wishing her father would walk through the door with a bundle of newspapers tucked under his arm. Astra knew it was partly her fault but the story from the eyewitness had never really closed the door, not completely. In the early days, Adriné would imagine every man with a black moustache might be her father till he'd walk right past and she knew it wasn't him. So she dreamed with her a little. "We never know, he may find us one day," she'd say defying logic a while longer. But it was time to bolt the door once and for all. "It can't be him, we have to face it, your father must have died in Smyrna," she said.

She was expecting guests for dinner on Easter Sunday, even Fatima was coming. "Yes thank you," she had written as RSVP using three words Koko had taught her. Acabi and her uncle from the flat downstairs were coming, her mother and Aizemnig were coming, as was Maria from the refugee camp. She had a lot to do but she stood admiring her new wooden kitchen in the garden, built for her by Acabi's uncle, right next to the water pump. She had just returned from seeing Mother Superior at Saint Joseph, and was pleased to hear that both Adriné and Acabi were good students. Acabi had no mother or father and her uncle had felt awkward about entering a convent. From the moment the two girls had walked into school holding hands, Adriné and Acabi were known as "les deux orphalines," an honour they paid for in kind at lunchtime. They wiped and cleared the tables and washed up the plates of their richer and more fortunate classmates, but it was quite good fun and sometimes they got extra helpings. Koko, now thirteen, going on twenty, had started work at a smart lawyer's offices after school. His teacher had recommended him for his well-developed grasp of the Greek language and for his immaculate copper plate handwriting. Koko was paid per document, so long as it was word perfect. He was so good at it that soon he was deemed responsible enough to bring important legal documents home and so earned a few extra drachmas, all of which he handed over to his mother. At night, mother and son would sit together, whispering stories by candlelight, she with her needle and he with his pen. "You must try to fit some pleasure into your life Koko. When you're not studying, your working." But his sense of responsibility and craving for knowledge meant he was doing exactly what nature had programmed him for. "You're just like your father," she thought.

On the Thursday before Easter Astra gave her home a thorough spring clean for the first time in four years. She washed the windows and shutters and sunlight streamed in brighter. She beat the rugs and mattresses and swept the verandah. She cooked traditional savoury delicacies, baked a large vanilla cake, dyed eggs red and green, and laid everything out on the table to see if it would fit, before hiding it away in her new wooden kitchen in the garden, out of reach from little Arpoun's sticky fingers always in search of new flavours.

Lately Peproné had seen a new enthusiasm budding in her daughter and so decided it was time to pass down a few of the family heirlooms. She reached into her hope chest to take out a large lace tablecloth, two silver candlesticks and six hand made silver spoons dating back from the earliest days of the Baltadjian workshop, put them in a suitcase, and brought them round. "Astra, this is part of your inheritance, you can put them out on Sunday. We should light a candle for Aizemnig, she's worked so hard for the sick and poor and we mustn't forget that without her all this would have been lost. She knew all the right people to contact. Just days before Smyrna was destroyed these beautiful things were already being shipped to safety," said her mother, still feeling guilty about unfair domestic arrangements.

The sun was hotter than at any time that year but it wasn't the only thing that put a spring in her step. Firstly, that morning, Astra had offered a job to her friend Maria, her first paid assistant, not that she could sew. Maria was perfect for four reasons: her charm, her negotiating skills, and her unerring loyalty. Maria knew how customers, especially the rich ones, were notoriously slow payers and she was prepared to wait for her wages, and she loved to go shopping. Astra needed someone to scour shops in the Aghiou Marco in search of fine quality fabrics and trimmings at the cheapest possible prices.

Secondly, her three oldest children had just come home clasping large certificates, rolled and tied up with red satin bows, as proof that their privileged education was not being wasted. "I shall write to the three wise men and tell them of your progress. They will be pleased," she said. "Now take some bread and chicken and go and sit in the garden, I'm expecting a very important customer any minute now."

"Please come in," said Astra, as pretty young Mrs. Iouannou stepped in expectantly, shortly followed by her unusually huge husband, as wide as he was tall. He squeezed through the door, bowed his head, took off his Panama hat, started fanning himself and thumped his total body weight onto the makeshift seating with a force that shook the house. Just as he was about to stretch out his legs, they heard the wooden crate crack in half and watched helplessly as Mr. Iouannou crashed to the floor. He lay there, a giant squirming bundle, moaning and gasping for breath, barely managing to point a limp finger to a splintered spike of wood wedged into his lower back. In what felt like a moment of suspended animation, Astra and Mrs. Iouannou dived to his rescue. Fearing Mad Ardiro was back to her old tricks, neighbours banged at the door and she let them in just as the children rushed up the verandah steps to join the rescue party. It was bedlam. "Oh my God, I'm so sorry," said Astra again and again till it seemed to lose all meaning.

An hour or so later, as they helped him downstairs, Astra began to realize the full implications of what had just happened. With every step Mr. Iouannou had grown stronger and more unpleasant. He cursed Astra for her flimsy furniture, he cursed her inquisitive children who dared crowd his air flow, he cursed her nosy neighbours for laughing, he cursed his lower lumber regions for a lifetime of agonizing pain, before finally threatening her with legal action. "Madam I hold you totally responsible. This was a disaster waiting to happen," shouted the gigantic eminent politician. "You will be receiving my doctor's bills and be sure that you will never work in this town again."

The dark gloomy hallway epitomized her mood and she remembered how the morning sun had beamed false optimism into her heart. "Go on then, hide yourself behind the dark side of the moon where you belong," she said, as heavy rain hammered down on the green verandah roof. She stepped outside to let the rain cool her temper, wondering why some people are destined never to expect anything in life to go smoothly, but it was her kismet and she was still learning how to live it.

"What are you going to do now?" asked Marie, wondering if her new job was over before it had begun. "He can't stop me working, not with so many mouths to feed. I thought about it all last night. It was just an unfortunate accident. He was able to walk out of here well enough. It was his ego that was damaged rather than his back. Other large husbands have sat there perfectly safely but he was spectacularly enormous. I'm sure that's not the first time he's gone through a chair. Anyway, I am going to see him right now to tell him just that. After that I'm going to try to rent a workroom in the centre of town. Mr. Iouannou doesn't know it yet but he may just have done us a huge favour." It was like an old trusted friend, back to wrap protective arms around her needy body, firing up emotions and shaking free innate survival instincts. And so she focused on the one thing that had ever really mattered to her and to what she was born: the turning of adversity to advantage and to get on with the important business of looking after the people who she loved and needed her.

Astra stood outside Mr. Iouannou's house, surprised to see it situated right across the street from the Royal Palace. "I wonder if he knows them, he might ask for my exile?" It was a flippant aside, but it got her thinking. "Really, I ought to get legal advice first," she thought. She decided to walk on a little further to re-think her strategy. She stopped to lean against a cool marble wall and her eye settled on the shiny brass plaque beside her. "The Headquarters of the Armenian General Benevolent Union of Greece." She had never heard of it, but went inside to see what they had to offer. "Our legal adviser, Adam Sabondjian will be free in thirty minutes. Regarding your second query, we ourselves have a vacant room upstairs, if it is of interest. Do have a look and if you think it suitable, we can include it on our agenda for the next committee meeting but I'm sure your excellent reputation will secure it."

Sabondjian was not a common name, and while sitting and waiting beside large mahogany doors, her mind wondered at the possibility. Her family tree had been hacked down years before, leaving most of its roots dead or lost for good. The displaced survivors had been forced to roam from place to place and now after thirty years were practically untraceable, unless of course lady luck decided to intervene and on that day she did. The lawyer turned out to be a cousin from her grandfather's side whose parents had fled the Erzeroum massacres of 1905. He obviously wanted to delve further but professionalism took precedence and he put family reunions to one side and dealt with the legal issues first. "You have no cause to worry, dear cousin. Mr. Iouannou has no legal redress in the law whatsoever," he said, referring to a recent legal court case before reverting to family matters. "I was about ten. My father took us to see your old house in Erzeroum. I remember it was the biggest house in town. The door was unlocked so we went inside, but it was empty, everything had been looted. I sat by the fountain in the courtyard and looked at the fish swimming. They were still alive. He said that officials were persecuting you and that one night you all had to run away." "I can still remember it like yesterday," she said. Then it was his turn to look moved. "We had to leave soon after to escape the massacres. Everything's destroyed now. There's nothing left of our lovely town, just dust and rubble they say." She had guessed as much, but it hurt to hear the words expressed. "Anyway, we survived," he added, taking her hand and shaking his head in disbelief at their finding each other. Then he kissed her warmly on both cheeks and showed her down the wide marble stairway. "You really must come to see us. How about this Sunday, Mama would be so thrilled," said Astra, waving back and wondering how many lawyers past and present they actually had in the family. As Astra told her mother the news, she sensed shadows of ancestors near by. "Mama, what incredible luck to find him, and apparently my reputation as a dressmaker has reached the stuffy ladies of the AGBU headquarters of Greece! I'll know next week if I can have a lovely room on the first floor to run my business from. What a day it's been. See you at church on Sunday."

Easter Day was everything she had hoped for. "Fatima, it's so wonderful to see you, come in, and meet my mother," said Astra, wondering when she should break the news that Setrag would not be joining them. "Thank you for asking me," said Fatima in a gruff voice Astra had heard just once before at Konya station. "Oh my God, your tongue has really started to turn!" They all squeezed around the table to eat, drink and make merry, almost like the old days. Adam Sabondjian dropped by in time for the main toast. "Let's raise our glasses to absent loved ones," said Astra, who after two glasses of wine had the courage to reunite dead souls with joyous company for the first time. "To absent loved ones" they cheered, as silent clinking of crystal echoed back from beyond the grave.

Chapter XVI

The Need to Prioritise Emotional Perspectives

ASTRA and Marie moved into the palatial workroom in the Metropolis area of Athens as soon as the committee agreed a date. She took her trusted sewing machine, the red velvet cushions, and the lavish brocade curtain—a perfect room divider for the fitting room. "Mama, please can't you buy a new sewing machine now? We can all hear it from our school playground," said Adriné laughing, but it was true. At home, now that their living space was doubled in size, everyone seemed happier and none more than Anna Tokadjian. "I've heard the headquarters are open till midnight most nights for parties and committee meetings, so you could work there till late, I know you like to work when we're all asleep. I'll be here to look after the children," said Anna Tokadjian, seeing an opportunity for being the only adult in the house till her bedtime.

The receptionist at the AGBU desk had just closed the door behind a vixen of a woman. Astra waited till the door was closed behind her before coming down to explain. "I had to tell her I couldn't do it, not in four days. I only have one pair of hands and I have to finish a wedding dress and two ball gowns by Friday." It made her angry to turn away good business but she refused to compromise her high standards. Astra was an artist, a perfectionist with magic fingers and looked beyond payment. Inspired by the surroundings, and knowing her children were with their grandmother, she moulded her creations late into the night, much as a sculptress might chisel clay, weaving her dainty hands lovingly into tiny folds of delicate fabric until she was completely satisfied. But she knew she was not so good at pitching her fee, often under-pricing her work. In truth her market value was badly affected by not having that all-important diploma on the wall. Savvy customers took advantage of unqualified artisans, no matter how talented they were.

The receptionist nodded sympathetically then offered a gift of a solution. "You know, my daughter would love to train with you. I've thought about saying something before, but you're always so busy upstairs. She could be a great help, tacking hems and sleeves, and she's so neat. She asked me to ask you." Within a week, five other well to do ladies of the AGBU brought their daughters to meet Astra to offer assistance in turn for an informal apprenticeship in advanced dressmaking and embroidery. Whether these families were so rich that they found money distasteful, or whether Astra had underestimated her reputation, paying the girls, even a small amount, was completely out of the question. "No, we won't hear of it," said the ladies of the AGBU in indignant unison. Astra could not believe her luck.

It was the spring of 1928. Astra decided the master class that day would be in the form of visual stimulation and she took the girls to feast their eyes on a rare fashion extravaganza. The epitome of Bohemian Parisian chic had come to town, brought there by Lucien and Jean, the famous Fried Freres, and it was a must see for anyone involved in Athenian haute couture. The fairy tale exposition of shimmering bead dresses, gold and silver sparkling bodices, and a kaleidoscope of iridescent accessories had fired up young imaginations, but they were back now and Astra was finding it hard to bring them down to earth. "Right girls! It was out of this world, wasn't it? But settle down now, it's two thirty already." She thought about how Satenig dispersed her girls with her harsh tones when they huddled together, pretending to match buttons while whispering secrets behind wide pillars, but now she was the boss, and it took some getting used to. Shouting out orders was not her style so she raised eyebrows or cleared her throat in the hope that it might silence giggles or avert cheeky stares when clients came in wobbling enormous busts and bottoms, still set on choosing body hugging styles against better advice. But her girls had impeccable manners and all she had to do was smile and peer at them once over her gold rim glasses and the room went quiet and hands got busy again.

As more and more clients came flooding in, Astra dared to look above the parapet for the first time in five years to look beyond the putting of food on the family table, not that her children had ever complained, and in some ways that worried her. They were far too sensitive, and she felt guilty. It was obvious why they never brought their school friends home: those families were rich and they were poor, but if things carried on like this, they would soon be able to move out of that one room world the six of them had shared since the spring of 1923.

But it was a moment of unrealistic optimism, and she cursed herself for laying herself wide open for disappointment. Her mother had gone to Paris to visit her sons and meanwhile Anna Tokadjian had finally found her niche. She would dress up to the nines to meet friends, and to get involved in church society fund raising tittle-tattle, coming home later and later, but happy for the first time in years. Anna made no excuses, she felt her life's work was done, and Astra saw her point. "Look Astra, I brought up my children, three of them are now dead, God rest their souls. Now you must bring up yours. Adriné is twelve years old. Don't tell me she can't cook a meal for her brothers and keep an eye on them till you get home." Adriné had grown up before her years. "Mama, I can cook, just tell me what to do and I'll do it," she said with such confidence that Astra was encouraged to give it a try. So, after twelve hours on her feet, she would run the long journey home, frantic and exhausted, praying at every corner, "Dear God, please keep my children safe." Often by the time she reached them, the front of her blouse would be soaked in tears at the thought of what she might find.

Worrying and the long hours wore her down and when she came home ill unexpectedly, everyone was caught unawares. She heard a child screaming and looked out into the garden to see her youngest son tethered to the well pump like a dog, shouting abuse at his sister. Little Arpoun, he of the feisty independent spirit, had taken to running away, for hours at a time, leaving Adriné, now in charge, no choice but to resort to draconian methods of restraint. At first she had asked him nicely, then not so nicely, but his cheeky smile belied a will of iron. "Mama, look, Adriné ties me up here till dinner time," he said tugging at the long rope round his waist. Adriné had to come clean. "Mama, what else can I do? I can't control him. He's always running off. Yesterday I found him sitting with a shoeshine man by the fish market." "I'm going to be a shoeshine man when I grow up," he said, grinning and polishing the air in front of him. There was nothing else to do but to put their dreams on hold till the next time. So in the morning Astra went to terminate her contract for the workroom at the AGBU. She then went up to break it to the girls, "I am so sorry, believe me, but I have to work from home again, though I do have space for one of you to come and work there with me." They all put up their hands, but Lucy Casparian's hand went up first and furthest and Astra and Lucy were left alone to take down the brocade curtain. "I must warn you, you might be a bit shocked when you see where we live," she said dreading the thought of shrinking their one room home back from embarrassingly small to unbearably cramped all over again.

If only Astra had known that her mother was on her way back from Paris already, she would have kept everything as it was. Her mother could have looked after them. But as it turned out, Peproné walked in to see her hanging the brocade curtain across her living space wearing the long black dress she had worn to Krikor's funeral. "Oh my God, Astra, I just don't know how to tell you," she said before blurting it all out in one heartbreaking sob. "Our Haroutioun is dead! He died last Thursday of a massive brain haemorrhage. He was climbing the stairs to his office when he collapsed and died. His boss heard him fall down but by the time he got there he was already gone."

The circumstances were startlingly familiar. It was an almost exact re-enactment of his father's death, but this time it was nature's hand and not an enemy bullet which brought an untimely end to a young promising Sabondjian lawyer on the steps of his law firm. Haroutioun, aged twenty-seven, had literally followed in his father's footsteps, right to the grave. Peproné was hysterical. "I had to leave straight after the funeral. I couldn't stay another minute. I've got something else I have to tell you. I don't want you hearing it from her." "From whom?" sobbed Astra. "From Hagop's wife," she said, gasping for air. "Hagop is not really your brother, he's your cousin! My sister and her husband died of typhus after he was born, so I raised him as my own. I breast-fed him. I had plenty of milk because Aizemnig was just two months old then. I've never breathed a word of this to anyone, even Hagop didn't know. I'd almost forgotten myself. But I'd forgotten about my old uncle Hovaness. Can you believe it, Hagop's new bride found him in Paris. I didn't even know he was still living! She went and interrogated the old man and couldn't wait to come back to tell her husband what she found out. We had the most terrible row. She even said that as I'm not his real mother, I have no reason to stay with them. Poor Hagop, he tried everything to keep me there, but I couldn't!" Peproné had a weak heart and began to lose her footing, dark spots flashed in front of her eyes, and she spun out into the safety of complete emotional shut down. Neither of them remembered much after that, except that life was for the living, and that a brother one loved and grew up with could never be just one's cousin, no matter what others said.

By the winter of 1929 emotional trauma had left its toll on Astra's health too. Severe bronchitis and the threat of chronic asthma made her worry about the future. What would happen to them all if she were too ill to work? So she stayed home in the warmth, reading cheerful books while waiting for better health with which to raise her children. Life's rhythms beat in wistful minor keys, with her only hope being that future melodies might be tapped out in similar mundane equilibrium. "All I want now is that my children live longer than I do."

Chapter XVII

The Inspiration of Psychological Revival

AT thirty-four Astra was still a fresh-faced beauty, but as always it meant little to her except a minor inconvenience. "What on earth do they want from me, a penniless mother of four?" she wondered, wishing eligible widowers left her alone to live in peace with her husband's memories. She was never rude, offering the same rejection to each of them whenever they came calling. "I am sorry but I could never remarry. Setrag was my one true love and no one can ever take his place." Her dignified honesty had drawn them there in the first place, but they left knowing something more about her, that she was an incurable romantic who would never let their failed marriage proposal stand in the way of old friendships.

By January 1931 Astra felt strong enough to make another attempt at setting up her business outside that one room, which had become increasingly smaller as her children grew larger. She gathered up her team again and this time she rented a room on the fourth floor in a run down building in the Metropolis, as it was very central and extremely cheap. They had no toilet facilities or a drop of running water, so she made 2 litres of iced lemon tea for them and carried the bottles to work every morning. When nature called, it meant either a twenty-minute walk to the public lavatories at Syndagma or climbing up on the roof from the workshop window, then trying to balance the pot on the way down. The girls took a chance with their modesty but Astra preferred to wait till she came home. As she never ate or drank anything after breakfast, she could hold out. Then one day the Athens Water Supply and Sewerage Company slapped a large notice on her door. "Drainage systems works will start here in two weeks. These premises must be vacated by Friday." Looking back, the clues were everywhere. She had seen them digging up the whole of Athens town centre, but desperate people don't ask too many questions. And so it was back to working from home, putting up that brocade curtain, which was fast becoming a symbol of abject misery with every irritating swish.

On days when the past stayed where it was, she started to look to the future again but this time her dreams were all about seeing her children grow up into fine young individuals, each in their own inimitable way. They were so different. Koko and Adriné had completed their last year at St. Joseph, finishing their education with distinctions, leaving the legacy to Varoujan and Arpoun, though Astra the liberal would never push her children into forced academia. It was their life, their choice, and their right to freedom. Koko the polyglot philosopher had decided to reject an offer of full-time work in the law firm, possibly worried that bad luck seemed to follow the trail of lawyers from the Tokadjian clan, and surprised her by wanting to train as a mechanical engineer. Varoujan dreamed of becoming a filmmaker so she surprised him with a camera on his eleventh birthday. Arpoun, who had always hated school, dreamed of driving expensive cars, but as he was only eight, she found him part-time work polishing the cars of her richest clients. "Mama, I'm going to have a dark blue Bugatti Royale when I'm older, its gorgeous," he said, forcing himself to finish off his science homework on a dog-eared piece of grubby paper. "He's so messy," she thought, but thought it best to say nothing. After all, he was fulfilling his part of the bargain and she knew not to push it.

It amazed her how most of her clients were happy to follow her around her various fitting rooms backwards and forwards across town. They saw it as a small price to pay for exquisitely crafted clothes and still at such good prices. Then, when her team working from home expanded to four, there was even less elbowroom around the work table. Maria, Lucy from the AGBU, and "les deux orphalines" Acabi and Adriné, had just joined them on the public side of the now slightly faded brocade curtain, which after so much use had started to hint authentic baroque grandeur and looked somehow the better for it. She had taken it down for washing at least four times a year, even though it took ages to dry. This delayed the odd dress fitting, but it was either that or giving away closely guarded domestic secrets from the private side. The smell of cooked food, especially fried aubergines, hung heavy in the air no matter how many wild roses they brought up from the garden or windows they left open on cold gusty days.

On Friday afternoons Adriné and Koko would meet Peproné in the Panepistimio to pick up mail from the Athens main post office. They didn't see her so often these days; her torn heart was slow to heal. Hagop Tokadjian, Setrag's brother, was still living in America and now Hagop Papazian (nee Sabondjian), Astra's brother-come-cousin, had moved there too and both wrote every week. "Pass me your proof of identity?" said a counter clerk waiting to hand over three post cards and two letters addressed to "Mrs. A. Tokadjian, Post Restante, Athens, Greece." It was strange to see those post card photographs of valiant Dashnag Party members, now dead, being posted back to her. Peproné had given a bundle of them to her son-come-nephew, having managed to hide them in her handbag as Aizemnig shovelled every other bit of Setrag's political and literary history into the raging kitchen stove that night in Smyrna. "No Adriné, you can't buy them in America!" she laughed, "These post cards were your father's," said Peproné reading Astra's post card.

They were almost at the door when one of the most famous operatic voices in the world started bellowing behind them. Floor and walls shook as they turned to see the man with a staggeringly rich tenor voice reach his glass shattering crescendo. "Well then, is that enough proof for you? Now do you believe that I am indeed the Great Nino Piccaluga! Now please give me my letters!"

They arrived back with letters and post cards and a story to tell. "Mama, imagine the Great Piccaluga was standing just behind us in the queue! He had no passport with him so he sang an aria instead. I think it was from La Traviata. It was absolutely amazing. Everyone clapped and cheered, then he took a bow and walked out into the street dragging a heavy sack of letters behind him." Astra tried to share in their excitement but couldn't help thinking life was becoming rather dull. It was the most exciting thing that had happened to them in years.

As the weather improved, Peproné began to ignore her weak heart and started visiting again, catching them in time for breakfast with warm home made cheese pastries tucked under her arm. The mood in the house was freer now that Anna Tokadjian was spending more time in New York with her son. "Poor Astra, are you working already? Why don't you take a day off, just for once? Your children will never know what you sacrificed for them," but they did. Aizemnig was the happiest she had ever been, tending to her newly adopted children, nurturing the ready-made family nature had denied her. Following a hunch and sketchy Red Cross records, Aizemnig had left for Corfu in search of their dead cousin's three children and miraculously found them all, painfully thin, infested with lice from head to foot, and stammering from traumas of war, but alive! Astra thought how lucky these children were to have been rescued by an aunt not only desperate for motherhood, but who was also an accomplished dietician and herbalist, able to devise green sticky potions to cure most ills. Miracles did happen, she had all but forgotten, till Lucy's father, Baron Casparian, Chairman of the Armenian General Benevolent Union came to confirm it.

"Madam Astra, the AGBU committee has voted you as the most deserving candidate to benefit from our business development award this year." "But I haven't applied," she answered thinking "Why didn't I?" The charity grant could have funded her trip to Paris to study advanced couture and pattern cutting techniques at the world famous Academie Daydou. He carried on, "Nevertheless, we all agree that it would make all the difference to your career. Having such a prestigious diploma on the wall would mean you could charge the appropriate remuneration for your work, and you would be able to start a school and become a bona fide teacher of apprentices." She had spoken of it often enough but had never really believed it possible. She looked at her well-trained unqualified assistant. "Lucy, did you put my name forward?" she asked, trying to hide her excitement. "I might have done. Well, I do need you to make an honest apprentice out of me!" she laughed, winking at her father. Now that her children were older and her mother was there to supervise, it was a real possibility. "Astra, don't miss this golden opportunity. You know you've been dreaming about it," said Peproné, answering all the questions in her daughter's eyes.

After countless trips to the French Embassy, her Greek laissez passer travel documents were finally stamped so she had no reason to put it off any longer. The train was puffing out black steam on the platform. "Why are you crying Mama? You'll have a wonderful time, and we'll be just fine. It's you who needs to take care. Your chest sounds terrible," said Adriné, now sixteen and looking very grown-up in her new peach and black crepe outfit. "You've made such a lovely job of the suit, it fits perfectly," said her mother, trying to diffuse the moment. Then the whistle blew and she was missing them already, wondering how she would handle being separated from them for almost four months. "I just hope you'll cope better than I will," she said, wiping her eyes before giving out last minute instructions. "Adrig," she used the affectionate diminutive, "keep a special eye on Arpoun and Varoujan, and remind your grandmother to take her heart medicine and only take on simple orders. Don't do anything complicated, wait till I get back. God be with you all." She waved till the peach dot became invisible before sitting in her seat. The carriage was virtually empty, and with the ponderings of 'should I or shouldn't I go' well behind her, she closed her eyes to enter a different world. "Paris, here I come," she said out loud.

On the twenty eighth of May 1931, still feverish with bronchitis, Astra walked along Rue Lafayette with a black design folder under one arm and little cousin Onnig, just nine, hanging on the other. "Here it is, number 12," said her obliging young companion pointing to large oak doors framed behind black and gold art nouveau wrought iron gates. "Cousin Astra, would you like me to make the introductions?" he asked confidently as they walked up the stairs. "No, that's alright, my French is not that bad, and I have to confirm with Madame Daydou that you will be able to stay with me in class." But as it turned out the flamboyant, fluffy Madame Daydou spoke excellent English. "Mais Oui, I was expecting both of you! I have absolutement no objection at all! It is most unusual, but absolutement fine. Your letter explained everysing. Ze lessons are in French, c'est sure, but ze diploma is awarded after a successful 'critique' of your collection, so you see, it's all 'pratique,' no writing, so no problem!" Then she held out a heavily bejewelled hand to welcome her youngest ever student. "And so, you must be ze petit monsieur Onnig. How obliging of you to translate ze complexity of haute couture and pratique de coupe to your auntie. I sink It's most charming!"

So every day for the next three and a half months Onnig and Astra sat together in a crowded classroom, whispering translations and scribbling notes, "tete a tete." The afternoons were given over to practical studies, when Onnig read his book while Astra cut out patterns and moulded fabrics on a cream padded curvaceous dressmaker's dummy. "Onnig, really, there's no need to stay all day, you go home," she insisted, but he always stayed right up till class was dismissed to accompany her home as his father had instructed.

Astra was back in Athens by the end of September to see everything was pretty much as she had left it. It struck her that they had all coped a little too well without her, so it prompted her to pass round presents and recount tantalizing Parisian experiences almost uncensored. "It's such a magical city, the architecture, the museums, the shops, oh you should see the enormous glass dome of the Gallery Lafayette, and the beautiful clothes. It's really true, the women are so chic! I wish you could have been there with me." Her last few words were not completely true, but some feelings are best kept private.

She took out a delicate wooden replica of the Notre Dame and passed it to Koko, remembering lighting a large candle under its dark sacred shadows before stepping out into the dazzling brightness of the Isle de la Cité. It had been her one whole day alone and she had soaked up every blissful minute as though it must last a lifetime. She had meandered along the Rive Gauche eating ice cream and smiling at strangers. She had gazed into elaborate shop windows with mannequins dressed in exciting fashions dripping with Egyptian and African influences of the new "Mode." Feeling inspired, she had found a shady corner by the river to fill her portfolio with sketches of dresses, hats and accessories full of exotic motives and sumptuous details, nor caring if they would be shunned as outrageous in her neck of the woods. Feeling pleased with her output, she took off her shoes and stretched out her legs on the long cool grass to eat a box of cherries before running to rinse her hands under spraying fountains by the Trocadero. Then, as the sun began to set, she climbed the steps to Monmartre to watch the artists at work before sitting down at La Mere Catherine to sip brandy till the spring returned to her step. The view below her beckoned. There was so much more to see and do so she leaned over the rail and drifted into realms of make believe. "This is how every Sunday would have been if my parents were born a thousand miles west of my birthplace." On a day when frivolous and sensory overload seeped into every pour of her body, standing there, without a care in the world, guiltless and wanting so much more, she had to admit that nothing had ever felt more natural.

Her eager daughter's voice brought her back with a bump. "Mama, can we see your diploma now?" asked Adriné, already reaching for the long brown leather tube leaning against the suitcase. Astra nodded as her daughter unrolled the document. "Look everyone, it says 'Parfait.' Mama you passed with perfect marks! You are so clever!" she said glowing in a moment of role reversal. "We must have it framed and put it on the wall. Your clients will be so impressed."

Peproné waited for a lull in the proceeding before asking, "Did you go to Pere-Lachaise cemetery to see Haroutioun's grave?" "Yes, cousin Atam took me. Mama, you wouldn't believe the beautiful monument his boss has put up for him. They say he loved him like a son. It's an enormous marble angel with outstretched wings and a lovely face which gazes down on him." She emulated the angelic expression and stretched out her arms before telling her story. "We arrived to find fresh flowers had just been laid but Atam had no idea who could have put them there. He said someone had been putting flowers on his grave every day since he was buried, so the following Sunday I went early and waited. I walked about reading tombstones till I saw a pretty young French girl, probably in her early twenties, put down a bunch of irises, and then I walked over to introduce myself. I told her who I was but she didn't reply. She just looked into my eyes and took my hand, and we stood there, united together in silent grief, she with her memories, and me with mine, till she let go of my hand, kissed me and whispered, "I loved him so much." Her face was wet. Then she let go of my hand and walked away with her head still bowed. I wanted to go after her but somehow it felt wrong, like an invasion of privacy, an intrusion. She had shown me her soul and told me everything that mattered. There was nothing more to say. I don't even know her name."

Astra had easily adapted to sleeping all alone in her quiet attic bedroom with some of the best views of Paris, even without the familiar sounds of Anna snoring to her left, or Varoujan humming Gregorian chants during REM sleep. But now, as she watched her sons pushing the dining table back to make room for the beds, her home felt like a prison. "Are our cousins rich?" asked Adriné picking up her train of thought. "Not rich exactly, but five of them live in a three story house in Les Invalides, just around the corner from Napoleon's tomb," said Astra distracted, her head already full of plans. "No, that's it! I can't bare living like this any more. I don't know how we've put up with it for so long." It upset them to see their mother just back and so distraught. "Mama, we have been very happy here. We laugh all the time, and can never get lonely!" said Koko, the others nodding. "That's because we love each other. We'd be happy anywhere," added Adriné in a moment when stating the obvious was exactly the right thing to do, but still Astra had the bit between her teeth. "This time we really are going to get out of this place and nothing's going to stop me."

The next day Astra went to the AGBU to show them her diploma as proof that their money had not been wasted. "I can't tell you how grateful I am to you all. I learned so much. Paris is truly inspirational. I have so many creative ideas buzzing in my head and can't wait to expand the business. The diploma does officially qualify me to teach, so now I can start an official school." Mr. Casparian could not have been more pleased with his protégé. "A lot of young ladies have already asked about that, some of them you know from before. Of course you do need to find premises and unfortunately we have no rooms available here at the moment." It was his way of saying the rest was up to her.

For centuries psychic strands had been passed down generations from mother to daughter. It was the way of things for them, and now at sixteen, Adriné was already earning a reputation as the hot-shot negotiator of the family, but in reality it was nature passing the intuitive baton down the female line. Astra had seen it coming but as Adriné recounted a strange dream over breakfast, she knew her time was ripe. "I dreamt that too, that very dream, last night. I even saw it in those colours. Adriné was amazed. "Don't be, your turn has come Adrig," she said sensing her powers were fading, glad to be relinquishing the crown. So when Adriné asked, "Mama, would you let me look for new premises?" her mother agreed. So with an ear firmly to the ground, Adriné set about her task mindful of that little voice inside her which told her exactly where to look.

Mr. Essefian, the canny proprietor of two fabric shops in the Aghiou Marco was all ears. "I hear you have a vacant apartment for rent," said Adriné. "Yes, how did you know? The previous tenants left only yesterday. It's just across the street." So she wasted no time and jumped straight in, direct and confident, just like a young Astra. "You do agree, Mr. Essefian, that my mother is one of the best, if not the best, dressmaker in Athens?" He nodded, wondering where all this was leading. "Well, we have a proposition to put to you. If you would be able to delay our first payment for two months, we could move in straight away. It would be advantageous for you too Mr. Essefian. We could help each other." "What do you mean young lady?" he asked. "Well, if your customers ask you if you know a good dressmaker, you could recommend my mother and she'd be just across the street from your shops, so of course we would buy our fabrics and trimmings from you." Mr. Essefian smelt a viable business opportunity budding on his doorstep. "Well, I suppose it could work quite well," he said, still wanting to seal the deal with a grown-up. "Ask your mother to come to see me this evening."

Adriné tried to act casual as every pour in her body screamed out "halleluiah." A new apartment, a large workroom, in a prime location, free advertising, and with nothing to pay for two months! At last after nearly eight long sardine like years, it was time to pack up. She ran through the fruit market and picked out three pomegranates, the symbol of fertility and rebirth, and gathered up as many large empty boxes as her hands could carry. "We're moving house," she told friends and strangers along the way. It was like sweet music to her ears.

Chapter XVIII

The Power to Challenge the Impossible

ASTRA remembered the twenty sixth of October 1931 almost as vividly as her wedding day. It was just as life changing and almost as sweet. With the brocade curtain now stuffed deep into a dustbin along with any other tangible evidence of their refugee existence slammed shut behind them, life suddenly took on a new dimension. It was the eve of Koko's eighteenth birthday and Arpoun couldn't wait to invite his wealthy friends to his new home, right in the heart of commercial Athens. "I've asked a lots of my friends to Koko's birthday party tomorrow," he said assuming they were having one. "This is the best birthday present any of us have ever had," he added, usurping the event before it had been decided, but who cared, it was true.

They struggled across town, each with bundles and bags slipping from their hands till Astra opened the front door to squeals of delight and to the sound of crashing plates. After carrying it for miles Koko had dropped the box of crockery. "Oh it doesn't matter, the Greeks say it's good luck," said Astra, walking over to the window to call down to Mr. Essefian standing outside his shop. "This is going to be my workroom. I won't even have to come down, I can give you my orders from up here, it's going to be so easy!" Varoujan leaned behind her, already clicking his camera into the busy Aghiou Marco as workers came out of shops to welcome their new neighbours. It felt like heaven. "We've got nine rooms, we could get lost here!" he said, turning round to snap away at Arpoun's rear end as his ecstatic brother turned somersaults on the dusty floor. "Just look at you, you're filthy already!" said immaculately dressed Varoujan, as he chased him round from room to room while Arpoun attempted to break the land-speed record, just because he could.

Two months later Astra paid her rent and had more than enough business to take on two trained workers and four apprentices. Things were up and running. "Madam Astra, he's just getting out of the car, the Russian prince is here!" screeched Marie, dashing upstairs, clutching a box of mother of pearl buttons. "Pick up your jaws girls, he's not that good looking, not now with that broken nose," said Astra, trimming the last of the cotton threads off a bright red satin boxer's robe. The dashing prince, now middle weight boxing champion, was enjoying new celebrity status and the thought of him coming up the stairs any minute now had sent her girls into a frenzy. "No peeking," whispered Astra as she showed the Russian prince into the fitting room. Within minutes he was strutting amongst them, flirting outrageously, and lapping up the attention while dripping suave elegance from every pour. "Madam, it's perfect, I thank you," he said, kissing her hand with a smouldering passion. Then he paid her, took a bow, and left. "You look very happy Madam," said cheeky Ourania, one of her new trainees. "Yes, I am, it was the easiest money I've ever earned! It only took me two hours and he paid me twice what I asked him for. If only all our customers were like him!"

By the autumn of 1933 Astra's work force of thirty-five were working from two of the largest and brightest rooms in the apartment. This still left a very large living-dining room, four bedrooms, and the luxury of an indoor bathroom and kitchen. With forty-one people making use of the facilities, toilet cleaning was an essential end to every day. "Please Madam, you must not do that," said Acabi, trying to take the large bristle lavatory brush from her hand. "No, it's my turn today, and I would never ask anyone to do anything I would not do myself," she replied, taking it back. Astra had a profound respect for human spirit; everyone was equal, and her girls respected her for it. But even with her army of seamstresses taking turns to wash and brush up at the end of the hallway, the house still felt like a palace. Koko and Anna had a bedroom each, while Astra and Adriné shared, as did the two youngest boys. It felt so wonderfully normal, not that any of them would ever take it for granted, which was just as well.

Astra invested everything, heart and soul, into her business in a country which felt increasingly more like home, and there was nothing to tell her otherwise. As her reputation grew, so did her confidence, encouraging her to explore new boundaries of haute couture, especially when night skies fired up creative energies: that was always her time. Sometimes her creations worked and sometimes they didn't. "Girls, we must always try to be innovative," she would say with that radical heart of hers. "That is how we discover new techniques and allow our talents to develop," and her class listened, knowing that their mentor, who had reached the pinnacle of her career, was still not above parading her mistakes in front of them.

What she didn't know then was that in a matter of a few years she would be looking back at these halcyon days as pearls passed to history. It would not be her war, it never was, but by the winter of 1943, they would be struggling for life, homeless refugees, wondering through war torn Europe, reliving a cursed nomadic destiny, yet again. But for now, blissfully ignorant of the future, and with her business and school bubbling over with orders and new ideas, Astra was the talk of the town.

In the hot summer of 1935 Astra was still basking in glorious oblivion. "Come here Penelope, I need you to help me today," said Astra beckoning her newest recruit. Most girls would have already found their niche amongst the giggling fold, but this was Penelope's second week and she seemed forlorn and isolated. "Look, leave the beading today, come and sit by me. I want you to look around the workshop. See what we do and how we do it, then tell me if you have any ideas on how things could be improved." Penelope looked startled. "How would I know Madam, I'm new here." "Yes you are and that is exactly why I'm asking you." Astra believed in fresh eyes, that they might see what old eyes might miss.

At five o'clock Penelope looked down at her notes. They didn't look much for a whole day's work and she felt a little embarrassed. As soon as Astra started to scan the page the word "Hollywood!" jumped out at her. "Tell me what you mean?" she asked. "Well Madam, it's just an idea, but I thought it would be wonderful if we could make copies of the lovely clothes worn by famous film stars. When I get home from the cinema, I try to draw the clothes from memory. I could show you some of them you if you like. Anyway, imagine Madam, making exactly the same dresses that Marlene Dietrich, Ginger Rogers, or Katherine Hepburn wear. You could call it 'The Hollywood Collection.'" "That sounds like a very good idea," said

Astra loudly so everyone could hear. "Right girls, who wants to go to the cinema this evening?" she asked reaching for her purse.

Soon Astra led her team in the exact replication of dazzling clothes from the Golden Era of Cinema glamour. "Why on earth did I agree to this? Some of these dresses are really quite vulgar and the detailing takes forever. No one in Paris would be seen wearing them in polite company!" she said, semi tongue in cheek. Penelope smiled, as she sewed the twentieth row of tiny pink tassels on the bodice of a Dolores Del Rio copy. "This one's quite elegant compared to that bright yellow Hepburn garden party dress we covered in gigantic daisies last week!" she replied, much happier now that she had been instrumental in helping her boss hit on a gold mine. Grecian stars of stage and screen were fighting each other for fittings. Sometimes the finished results were so exquisite that the girls would gaze in wonder at their own work. "No matter how beautiful they are, remember they are copies and nothing can ever replace your own creation," she would say, unveiling an original design hidden under muslin drapes. If the Hollywood Collection was bread and butter, then her master classes were champagne and caviar.

Being on first name terms with well-known celebrities, or pinning up hems for members of the Greek Royal Family gave them more than job satisfaction. Busy happy artisans began to see themselves as heroines of an exclusive dressmaking fraternity, able and willing to satisfy public demand by fulfilling apparel fantasies of the rich and famous. "Varoujan, please put your camera away. Princess Marina is coming to try on the negligee for her trousseau, not to have her picture taken!" Her words sounded so pretentious, even preposterous, and it made her stop in her tracks. "When did all this happen Varoujan?" she asked him, incredulous at how far they had come in just four years in the Aghiou Marco.

Nothing was ever predictable, and that's exactly how she liked it. "I hope I'm not disturbing you at this ridiculously early hour, but I really need to talk to you before Penelope arrives, I'm her mother," said a stunningly elegant woman catching Astra in her nightdress. "My daughter is so depressed at home. She's so moody and hardly ever talks to me. She took it very badly when her father and I separated. I've met another man you see, and she absolutely detests him. Anyway, I know she's very happy here. Her friends tell me she's always telling funny stories and making everybody laugh. Would you mind if I hide myself behind the door of the workroom just for a bit and listen to her voice? I need to so badly, I haven't heard her happy for nearly two years!" So they agreed to a plan, a little contrived, but it worked. "Penelope, tell me that joke, the one you told the girls yesterday," said Astra. Penelope never needed much encouragement and once she started she couldn't stop. After half an hour of joke telling the front door clicked shut and Astra noticed the shadow behind the opaque glass door had gone. "Thank you Penelope, that was most entertaining, but it's quite enough for one morning," she said.

Other moments stood out from that crazy world of dressmaking for far more tragic reasons. "Oh Mama, to see her lying in that white coffin wearing her beautiful wedding dress, it was unbearable," said Adriné, flooding tears after the funeral. A beautiful young vivacious client, full of hope at a life just beginning, had died suddenly of an unknown illness just days before her wedding, but her mother had asked for the dress to be finished anyway. She would be wearing it to meet her maker. Adriné was given the grim task of sewing the very last thing she was ever to wear. "It was heartbreaking. Her mother was so hysterical with grief she could hardly stand, and she kept saying how lovely the dress was and how she must pay for it! I must have said, 'No Madam, thank you, it's really not necessary,' a hundred times."

Later that year Adriné fell off the balcony and broke her back. She had been leaning out of the window to reach down into the Aghiou Marco ready to catch a box of fasteners being thrown up by the lady from the haberdashery shop opposite when she lost her footing and landed into the path of shocked passers by. The doctor gave the wrong advice. "You, my dear, are suffering from rheumatism! You must try to touch your toes at least twice a day." And that is what Adriné did, till one day the pain was so unbearable she collapsed. Koko ran to get a second opinion. "Rheumatism! What utter rubbish, her back's broken! She must not move," said the bone specialist, immediately booking her into a seaside orthopedic hospital in Voula. "I am very sorry to tell you Adriné that you may never walk again. Each time you were trying to touch your toes you were making it worse. Now you have to lie completely flat and see if time and iodine from the sea will heal your bones. We can only wait and pray. I'm afraid there are no guarantees where the spine is concerned."

So for three years Adriné lay completely flat on her back in hospital, only able to move her arms. She kept sane by counting her way around tiny stitches to create complex geometric embroideries, which impressed even her. At first Astra went to see her every day. "Mama, let me tell you something funny that happened here last night," she'd say to cheer up her mother, but it never worked. "I should be cheering you up, what's the matter with me?" she'd say crying guilty tears. "How could I have trusted that stupid doctor. I should have known better. It's all my fault," and Adriné always felt worse. "Mama, it's such a long journey for you, and now that I'm not in real pain, you don't have to come so often. To be honest, it upsets me when I see you like this. I'd much rather you stayed with the girls and got on with the business." Astra understood. "I'm sorry Adrig, I'm not as tough as I used to be. Perhaps I will just come on Sundays."

"What's wrong with these mothers, they're always crying and making us feel terrible," said Marika, lying in the next bed. "My mum's exactly the same." Adriné and Marika, who were both unable to move, became the closest of friends. Then after two years of lying three feet apart, Marika, more than seven feet tall and only seventeen, died of pituitary gigantism. Immediately after the funeral Marika's mother took over where Adriné's own mother had left off, visiting every day, desperate to be with the one person who really knew her daughter during those last two years. "Adriné, tell me what you talked about the night she died," she pleaded, crying buckets over Adriné's part finished handiwork. "It wasn't anything very important. The German pilots from the camp in Voula had brought in bags of parachute silk that afternoon and she was saying how nice they were and how young they looked in their uniforms. One of them had taken a real shine to her. Then she said good night, and she just fell asleep. She was her usual happy self. I'm sure she didn't suffer. I miss her terribly too," said Adriné, meaning every word. "And how are you now Adriné?" she asked, already knowing the news was bad. "I'm not so good. Tiny bone splinters have travelled down from my spine to the top of my thigh and opened up a wound there and it doesn't seem to be healing. I heard them talking about possibly having to cut off my leg to stop gangrene spreading." Marika's mother burst into tears again, "She always told me how brave you were."

That very night Adriné had a visitation. "Oh my God, Marika, is it really you?" she asked in abject terror as her friend fluttered around the flying buttresses of a huge cathedral with tiny pink angel wings. "Adriné, don't be afraid, it's me and I'm really happy here. As today is the 15th of August, my name day, I'm allowed to ask for a special favour. Guess what I asked for? I've asked for your leg to be healed." Adriné watched shocked and terrified as Marika flitted from one holy picture to another. "Would you do something for me? It would mean so much to me. Tell my mother you saw me. Tell her I'm very happy here and ask her to stop crying. She's always crying." Adriné listened wondering how a life surrounded by holy pictures might be every young girl's dream when she suddenly heard her own voice calling out "Marika!" and woke up in a cold sweat. "It's all right, you must have been dreaming about her," said the nurse, mopping her brow. "I was, but it seemed so real, like she was here."

Every morning between seven and eleven, Adriné was wheeled out onto the sea-facing verandah for her daily dose of iodine and vitamin D, just as soon as her bandages were changed. "Is it worse?" she asked at seeing the nurse jump back in disbelief. "I can't believe it! Where is it? Where's the wound? Adriné, it's completely disappeared!" Then defying her own logic, she checked the other leg just to make sure. "No, it's definitely that one. Matron come here as quickly as you can, it's a miracle!" she screeched after discounting every other possibility. Within thirty minutes sceptical nurses and doctors from all over the hospital were crowding round Adriné's bed examining her top thigh. "Tell us about your dream," they begged, instantly forgetting years of scientific training. By the afternoon every member of staff and most of the patients had already knelt down to cross themselves in holy reverence to Saint Marika of Voula, somewhere in their midst.

By four o'clock, Marika's mother, a Greek Orthodox Archbishop and Astra were pushing through crowds to reach Adriné's bedside.

"Leave us now," said a solemn deep voice in a long black robe holding up a huge silver cross, shaking frankincense in all directions while sprinkling the bed with holy water. Adriné, desperate to fulfil her side of the bargain, wasted no time. Marika's mother was already smiling. "I really saw Marika! She told me to tell you that she is truly happy wherever she is and that all she wants now is to see you happy. She doesn't want to see you crying for her," said Adriné, lifting up her top sheet without a blush, well used by then to showing off her miracle leg to all and sundry. "This may well be a miracle but we don't canonize saints in the Orthodox Church. However, you might do well to ask the Catholics," said the Archbishop, pulling down the sheet to cover Adriné's modesty. "Your daughter will always be a blessed saint in my eyes," said Astra, bursting with joy and gratitude.

Next day Koko took time off work to see the miracle with his own eyes. "Koko, what if it comes back, say if I do something nasty to someone? I'll have to be good all my life now. Maybe I should join the Carmelites?" said his sister still reeling in awe. "You know Adriné, there could be another explanation. It might be what they call psychosomatic. You might have wished so hard to get well that your body healed itself. But I'm sure it won't come back, and anyway you could never be anything but kind," he said, offering comfort in case of either possibility. "Koko, I really need to take my mind off things. It's nearly three o'clock and the third episode of *Les Miserables* is about to start on the radio. I've been following it. It's so good, stay and listen to it with me." Koko turned on the radio, but no sound came out. He fiddled with the knobs, checked the wiring, shook and thumped it as a last resort before giving up. "Oh what a shame, it's broken, but don't worry, I'll bring you a new one very soon." But Adriné closed her eyes and made a silent wish. "Please radio, come on, work for me for just one hour, till the play finishes." Then she asked him to turn it on again and to his amazement it started working. "I made a wish that it would work till the play ends," she said. They listened for the hour till the play ended for another week, when the radio suddenly went dead again. Koko smiled knowing his angelic sister deserved every miracle she could get.

By the summer of 1939 Adriné was bandaged up like a mummy from ankle to thigh, a safeguard against a sudden blood rush after three years lying on her back, and was pushing small steps along the slippery marble floor of the cool hospital corridor, heading for her mother's arms. "Thank God," said Astra deciding to hold back the news of Anna Tokadjian's unexpected death till that precious moment fulfilled three years of prayer and hopeful expectation. A lot had happened that week, but after the surprise of seeing her daughter up on her feet, Astra decided everything else could wait. "Your daughter's back has healed in much the same way as a darned sock! Her spine has woven so tightly it's now probably the toughest part of her body!" said the orthopaedic specialist, without a single reference to the possibility of heavenly intervention. Two weeks later Astra and Koko were helping her step into their grand new, even bigger and smarter apartment and workrooms in up-town Syndagma, right bang in the centre of Athens.

Chapter XIX

The Importance of Strategy and a Mother's Love

IT was November 1940. "Mama look, the Italian troops are marching straight past the window. Let's go down and see what's happening," said Adriné, unable to hear her own voice above the sound of thousands of ticky-ticky open backed wooden sandals marching leisurely into Syndagma Square. "I never knew soldiers wore zoccoletti, how on earth can they fight in them?" "Well, you know what they say: Germans, they know how to die, but Italians, they know how to live! Compared to other marching soldiers I've seen in my time this is more like a Latino carnival than the arrival of an invading army," said Astra, and very pleased about it. The square was alive with handsome dark flashing eyes in search of home grown female talent as Adriné walked up to the steps where a group of soldiers were proudly showing off the contents of their suitcases. "Look at what they've brought with them, salami, cologne, wine, mandolins. I bet they don't have a single gun between them!" Mother and daughter watched the fun-seeking soldiers lying back to lap up their moment of glory. War was the last thing on their mind. Soon they were strumming tunes, singing love songs, dubbing their necks with fragrant colognes, and passing round slithers of speciality salami and smoked hams which their doting mothers had packed lovingly in grease proof brown paper bags.

It wasn't till Greece surrendered to the Germans in April 1941 that the Second World War came to Greece with its appropriate mantle. "Did you know there are eight million people living in Greece, and with our main export being olives and tobacco, most of our food is imported. We ought to start stock piling," said Astra, reading about predicted food shortages in the press. She had never lost her love of reading newspapers from cover to cover, even though she now had no part in writing them. Koko was reading the works of Karl Marx, preferring to fill his head with socio-economic philosophies, but she continued, "I often wondered why you and

Varoujan were so keen to learn German at evening classes. Well, it looks as though it may come in very useful now that we are to be overrun with them." Although the past was never far behind, no one could say she wasn't forward thinking. At forty-five Astra had learned that war was always just a hair's breadth away.

"Mama, listen to yourself, you're a born survivor!" said Koko, putting down his book at last. "I've had a lot of practice," she replied wistfully and that got him thinking, and he sat up to review her wartime experiences. "It's true, you've lived through some very dark days. First they murdered your father when you were eight, then you all fled Erzeroum and ended up in Smyrna. Then in 1914, during the Great War, you escaped the massacres and deportations from Konya in 1915. Then, when the war was over, you went back to Smyrna where you lived for four years till in 1922, when the Turks destroyed Smyrna and Baba was killed. Now you're thinking up strategies to survive the next war." She was about to rebuke him for totalling up life scarring experiences as though they were impartial facts on a page, when he added, "I don't think we would have survived if it wasn't for you Mama." She realized he meant it. "We all survived for each other. At least your two grandmothers aren't here to see this one," she said, needing her mother's comforting arms. Peproné had been too ill to visit Adriné in hospital but hung on, finally letting go of life eight days after she had come home. "Adrig, the time has come for me to leave you now, I'm so tired now, and I'm no use to anyone." Then she referred to the famous visitation. "I know you're terrified of seeing dead people, but you must not be scared of me when I die. It will still be me, even in the coffin, and if I can, I'll try to visit you in your dreams," so Adriné hoped and waited but it was never to be.

Astra's sons were now young men. Koko was a trained mechanic and worked as an aviation engineer. Varoujan, so handsome the girls swooned whenever he walked through the workroom, had just opened a photographic shop, but dreamed of becoming a filmmaker, and Arpoun, well, he wanted the world. So in 1941, aged nineteen, he and a few wealthy school friends left Athens bound for Vienna. "Mama, stop him please, how can you let him leave with the war on," begged his sister, but Astra saw it differently. "At his age your father was already in Boston working as a deputy editor of a daily newspaper. Of course I wish he would stay with us but it's his life and he must decide what to do with it," but it didn't stop her crying with worry when no one was looking. "Arpoun, please try to write regularly to let us know you're alright," she asked in desperate understatement.

During the early years of German occupation things stayed almost normal and even proved unexpectedly lucrative for the Tokadjian family. Koko was the first to benefit. "Two German commandants came into the aircraft factory today 'asking' if any of us would 'prefer' to work on their cars and trucks. They need mechanics and someone to translate from Greek to German when they diagnose faults, and my boss told them I could speak some German so they told me to start tomorrow morning. Apparently my salary will still be paid by the Greek government and I am going to get a pay rise!" Next was Varoujan. German film crews were looking for translators to join a production team to make propaganda films showing how the occupying armies had actually improved job opportunities in the local area, and again the Greek government was to pay his salary. His first day of filming was at a local ice cream factory and Varoujan wished he'd paced himself more sensibly with the free tasters. "I'm never going to eat ice cream ever again!" he said groaning over the toilet. "Tomorrow we're in a glass factory." It was hardly the glamorous world of filmmaking he had expected, but it was wartime and it was a start.

While Italians and Germans were attempting to run the country, and with most of the Greek bourgeois politicians already in exile, a Stalinist led communist national party, ELAS, was beginning to drag in support from all sides. By 1942 ELAS had successfully carried out a number of sabotage missions aimed at ensuring communist domination by drastic measures. This gave the Germans serious security concerns, especially when trying to comply with Berlin's policy of mingling with the local civilian population. With so many now recruited into the partisan resistance, the Third Reich had no idea who they could or couldn't trust.

Since the end of 1940, Astra's business had seen a mild downturn in orders, but considering the world was at war, she couldn't complain, even though keeping up with the latest fashion trends had caused its own problems. Merchant ships from Europe and America laden with newspapers and magazines were being regularly sunk, but the cinema matinees before curfew meant her Hollywood Collection was as popular as ever. Really, for the Tokadjians, apart from the unavoidable shoulder brushing with soldiers on the streets, life went on pretty much as before, but things were about to change. It was Friday and Astra was leaning over the cutting table, preparing for her weekly master class, when Koko put his head round the door. "Mama, is it alright if I bring a friend home for dinner tonight? I met him at the garage. By the way, he's a German soldier." "Alright, why not," she said, already thinking of a few reasons.

None of them had ever sat eating their evening meal with a soldier carrying a gun before. "I think I should remove it while we eat," said Johann, a young delicate soul who sensed it was doing nothing for the flow of amiable conversation. By the second course, Johann was in tears. "I hate guns, I even hate to hold them. I could never kill anyone! I was a philosophy student before the war started, but my father encouraged me to take a commission in the Wehrmacht," Koko translated, while Adriné found a handkerchief. By the time they were tucking in to feta cheese and black grapes, Johann had begun to feel like part of the family. In the months that followed Koko and Varoujan both came home with others just like him, all young, all desperately home sick, and all wishing the terrible war would come to an end.

By early 1943 the soldiers from the Third Reich had become more than foreign occupiers, they were now the hated enemy, especially after carrying out brutal threats that they would execute fifty Greek men for every German soldier killed in ambush. So far it had only happened in remote rural areas, but shock waves had already reached Athens where the mood was noticeably hostile and forced Astra to rethink social commitments. "Look, I honestly have nothing against these boys. Individually they're fine young men, but they're part of a regime that's slaughtering entire villages. I know you can't imagine your friends doing such appalling things, but this is wartime when unimaginable things are done in the name of patriotism. They trust us because we're foreign, were not Greek, but that's exactly the problem. Now that resistance groups are being swallowed up by the communists, I'm terrified they'll see us as German sympathizers or even collaborators."

Astra had already felt accusatory fingers pointing at her from unexpected corners. "A few of my clients have noticed that we're not joining queues at the food markets. They must be wondering where we're getting it." Blown up rail lines had severely interrupted food supplies and thousands of Greeks were dying of hunger. "It only takes one innocent comment from one of the girls about the ample contents of our larder and we could all be shot." They knew their mother was not prone to melodrama. The Wehrmacht had abundant food supplies and their dinner guests never came empty handed. "I know they're just boys in uniform driving their commandant's cars in for a service, but people resent that too. Let's not forget, those cars don't even belong to them, they confiscated them off wealthy Greeks as soon as they arrived."

The war was not usually a topic at dinner time, even when they ate alone, a house rule left from the time when her children were young, but this could not wait. There was more. "I read something shocking today. They're thinking of bringing in a new law that all unemployed Greek males will have to work in labour camps, either here or in Germany. "Well, we have jobs Mama, so don't worry about that," said Koko, but Varoujan picked up her thread. "That won't make us too popular brother, think about it. ELAS is becoming a real force, and now with Sarafis in command, power seems to have gone to their heads. They're terrorizing the countryside, ambushing boys as young as fifteen and executing anyone they call cowards or traitors, and that's basically everyone who doesn't join them."

Astra began to relive scenes from her past: fanatical nationalists, evil intolerant barbarians, brandishing bayonets and guns in the name of ethnic cleansing; she had seen it all before but decided to stop short of voicing her thoughts out aloud. She knew then their days in Greece were numbered. After twenty two years of having struggled so hard to make a good life for her family and a renowned sartorial reputation for herself, and with war raging in all corners of Europe, they would have to leave everything behind and venture blindly into no-man's land. What else could they do when her sons were deemed guilty by association? They spoke German, fraternized with the enemy, and were trusted employees of the hated occupiers. It was either a choice of leaving their new homeland or becoming prime targets in bloodthirsty communist reprisals. In a climate of terror when both sides shot first and asked questions later, no one would be interested in asking immigrant Armenian pacifists their preferred patriotic allegiances.

She shuddered at the thought that if anyone stripped away all peripheral layers of her life so far, they would uncover the same old theme, like Koko had said, escape and survival from war. Suddenly it struck her that this time even escape might be beyond them. Strict border controls meant that no one could even travel from one city to the next without official documents, and they didn't have a single passport between them. "How much disillusionment can one person take?" she asked herself with genuine curiosity, wondering if she would ever find out. Even her one unshakable belief in the unconditional advantages of education had begun to disintegrate. If only her sons had not studied German at evening language college they would not be on the ELAS most wanted list.

In February 1943, as freezing rain soaked hundreds of protesters gathering in Syndagma Square, Varoujan was pointing his camera out of their living room window, trying to find that perfect angle. "It's only nine o'clock in the morning and it's already getting ugly out there," he said watching a defiant crowd punching clenched fists and screaming in passionate unison, "No Greek workers for German slave camps." He hadn't yet noticed German and Italian security forces pointing machine guns from the roof tops of public buildings all around them. "My God, look up there, don't lean out of the window," said his sister pulling back his brand new Leica, "it looks like a gun." They watched as the crowd joined hands to sing the Greek national anthem before shifting on mass towards the government Labour Building. Just as Varoujan stepped back, hidden marksmen started firing shots into the air. Some ran for cover but most marched on. Then in a moment of defiant nationalistic fervour, the crowd taunted their enemy, gathered up speed, and stormed inside. For a few minutes everything went quiet before black flames and acrid smoke started to choke the air, plunging everything into darkness. They guessed the rest. As protesters ran out of the burning building, joyous screams turned to cries of terror as indiscriminate bullets shot across the square. By the time the Labour Building was burned to the ground, over a hundred dead and wounded were being carried away in van-loads. Diehards would say that the protesters were victorious in that the labour law was never implemented, but the massacre in Syndagma Square marked an important watershed in Athenian history. The Greek Civil War, which was to devastate the country for a further six years, had just laid its first devastating seeds in the capital.

Seeing so many slaughtered from the gaps between her shutters confirmed Astra's worst fears. Athens was now in the imminent danger zone. Astra, the matriarch, resumed her life's mission to abandon everything to protect her family by whatever means she could, even if it meant allying herself even more closely with the enemy a little while longer. She knew it was their only means of escape. Plans came to a head soon after, just as time was running out. Koko's Greek garage boss, now less happy about increased business than worried about political repercussions, decided to tip him off. "I shouldn't be telling you this but a couple of weird looking characters came here last night asking for you by name. I'm sure they were communists. Be careful." "I saw a gang of wild looking types walking up and down the street this morning," said Adriné. Koko hadn't left the house since then. As veiled threats turned into narrowest of escapes, a rare opportunity presented itself. Divisions from the German Military Command from the South Eastern Division were in the process of being relocated to prop up the Balkan front. Was it a lucky coincidence or divine intervention? No one was in the mood to ask.

Astra never worked on Sundays, so they had the house to themselves. This allowed clandestine operations to go ahead unhampered: the girls need never know Johann and his friends were coming to celebrate his twenty-first birthday party at the Tokadjian residence. After all she had said to warn them, the family was stunned to hear her invitation. "Johann bring some of your friends too, and would your commandant like to join us?" A pin dropped off the table. "I'm not sure Madam, he's a very busy man, but I will ask him," he replied smelling a pungent rat, but said nothing. This wise, kind-hearted woman had taken him into the bosom of her family for over two years, and he knew she must have her reasons.

As mother and daughter prepared far too much party food, Astra's mind was elsewhere. "Oh no, we forgot the cake, look it's burned," said Adriné, taking out the charred remains. "No, that's just the top crust, it actually tastes much better like that," she said indifferently. There were far more important things on her mind. By eight thirty, six young soldiers and their commandant were admiring the impressive spread, sipping local wines, helping themselves to olives, and tapping their shiny boots to Strauss waltzes on the gramophone. Astra had decided to wear her dark grey satin dress for the first time since Arpoun's sixteenth birthday and it complemented her silky hair to perfection. As she walked in and out of the living room, bringing out yet more trays, she oozed the style and confidence of a glittering society hostess.

Her efforts had not gone unnoticed. After finishing his third retsina, the commandant's appreciative eyes flickered over the gold rim of his wine glass and he strolled nonchalantly towards her. "No more please Madam! This is too much, too much already. Are you expecting the whole of the Twelfth Army! Please let me help you." He bellowed out a laugh so hearty it almost pushed back the half empty serving dishes with the pure force of its decibels. Luckily his English was far better than her German so she seized the opportunity to set vital evacuation plans in motion. Varoujan stood aghast as his mother fluttered vaselined eyelashes at a complete stranger. "I am delighted you were able to join us Herr Kommandant, it's a real honour to have you here, especially as your schedule must be so demanding at the moment." She noticed his eyes were bloodshot, probably from over work, and following her instincts, she went straight for the sympathy vote. "I feel so sorry for those poor soldiers from the South Eastern Division who have had to leave Athens. It was almost a safe haven for them here. I understand they're being sent to the Balkans to put down partisan uprisings on the eastern front. This must be such a difficult time for you." "Well yes Madam, it is. We are having to transport our units during the night in case of air attacks but some of our personnel have been killed even though the Luftwaffe are constantly patrolling train lines." Astra had already had her family conference as to whether it was preferable to risk being blown up on a train somewhere in the Balkans or being captured by marauding communists in Athens, and everyone had agreed on their preferred option. With the Wehrmacht bleeding to death in Russia, and with the British bombing Berlin with increased intensity, it would not be long before the German army was in massive retreat. "Alright, so it's now or never," she said decisively, "while the Germans are still in control."

"Oh Herr Kommandant at times like this you must miss your family," she sighed, taking the nettle once they were comfortably ensconced in a deep brown leather sofa, then immediately deciding to steer the conversation to broader military operations of post Italian withdrawal. It would not do to appear too obvious. "Those poor soldiers, they must be exhausted by the long marches and barbaric fighting. I hear they have met terrible resistance while trying to regain the vacated areas from the guerrillas." "She's quite the military strategist, and a very handsome woman to boot," he thought as she proceeded to confirm his opinions. "I understand major anti-partisan operations are also under way in Yugoslavia and Albania. How unsettling for all of you, one day here, one day there, weaving through rugged terrain in mid-winter. I can only imagine what their poor mothers must be going through. I wonder, do letters reach families back home?" She had personal reasons for asking. It was months since they had any news from Arpoun. One of her sons was missing; she should never have let him go. A tear slid down her right cheek. "Oh no, please Madam, you must not upset yourself, tonight is for celebration. We must try to be joyful." Then he jumped up, clicked his heels, and swirled her round the living room while his soldiers clapped and cheered, but her sons and daughter knew better than to fear the potential budding of an unholy alliance.

By one o'clock, the party was twittering on the edge of conclusion. Astra knew she had to time her final move to perfection. So she waited patiently till Adriné carried out a tray of charred birthday cake and ice-cold ouzo, and for Johann to finish his slurred over emotional appreciation speech before confiding "deadly secret concerns." As the others told each other jokes, which lost something in the translation, Astra and the commandant started to take plates out to the kitchen. She felt strange asking for domestic help from a high-ranking German officer, but she had to get him alone. "I hope you don't mind, but I must speak to you in private," she said hoping he wouldn't misread the situation, so she began to scrape off left over food just to make sure. As dishes piled high by the sink, she told him that her family had been labelled collaborators, that they were in imminent mortal danger from their common enemy, the communists, and that if only they could leave Greece and join her son in Vienna everything would be so wonderful. "Well, if you are really sure Madam, I can arrange travel passes for all of you within forty-eight hours," said the commandant, realizing that a woman who was so in touch with political and military operations world wide could hardly be mistaken about clear and present dangers aimed directly at her own family. Checkmate. "That went rather well," she sighed, squeezing her daughter's hand as the last black leather boot stepped out into the cold night air. "We could be out of here in a couple of days."

As they cleared away all evidence of a fun night in, Astra went over travel plans. "He said something about an infantry division being transferred by train to the Balkans, and said we could go with them, but after that we'll be on our own. The train is taking HQ personnel too, so luckily they won't all be soldiers. We have to be ready when they come, and they could come any time in the next two days." They looked at each other in amazement, each asking the same silent questions. What, so soon? What about the house, the business, the girls, our friends, the camera shop, everything we own? She had just the one answer. "We can only take one suitcase each, everything else we have to leave behind," much life changing words said with hardly any emotion. How else could she have said it? Whatever despair tugged at her heart-strings, this was no time to tell them. Dangerous bearded men were hiding God knows what under thick grey coats right outside their house and Astra was not going to sit about making pretty clothes while her two sons were sitting targets for a bullet in the back.

The Commandant had said they were most likely to come at night-time. Next morning she went to the bank early and cleared out all available funds, then she rushed around buying up whatever gold coins she could before making it back just as the girls had begun wondering where she was. "I have a nice surprise for you all," she said handing over a generous performance bonus and an unexpected week off work. "We could all do with some time with our families, this war has taken its toll on all our nerves," she said, hating herself for the deception and for not saying proper goodbyes to those who loved her, but that would have made the journey harder still. "Penelope's brother is one of the leaders of ELAS, what if she suspects something?" said Adriné. "Well, for a start, they don't get on with each other, and we just won't open the door to anyone who's not in German uniform," replied her mother, knowing simplicity always worked best in a crisis.

Initially, it took no time to pack, except that they kept finding ever more essential things that wouldn't fit into one suitcase. Businessman Varoujan had sneaked out to his shop at daybreak and had already filled a suitcase with the best of his photographic equipment, which hardly left any room for clothes at all. Sentimental Adriné filled her case with a few of her favourite outfits, which left plenty of room for treasured photographs and letters, and esoteric Koko didn't really need anything except the book he was reading. "There's plenty of room in my case," he said, pushing a couple of trousers and sweaters into a corner to make room, and they all rushed to him with their last minute "must takes."

Astra emptied out the whole contents of her wardrobe before putting most of it back. All she really wanted was tucked away in a folded wedding sheet in her deep bottom drawer. History stared her in the face. A pair of her husband's embroidered slippers, never worn, an antique silver dressing table set, ancient silver spoons, candlesticks and priceless jewellery crafted by her ancestors, a few gold coins, two lace tablecloths, and every piece of hand embroidery in the house, including those made by her daughter while lying prostrate in hospital. Then she went in her workroom to soak in memories that must last a lifetime. She listened for the chirpy echoes of thirty-five giggling girls wrapped up in unfinished garments dotted around the four long sewing tables. She picked up a pair of Betty Grable pink culottes from behind her chair and wondered if Adriné might wear them. "At least we weren't in the middle of making any wedding dresses, now that would have been cruel," she mused, but hardly anyone was getting married at the end of 1943. The oval gilt mirror she and Koko had carried across town in those early days was hanging in pride of place above her desk, but there it would stay, no matter how much she cherished it. "How can such a delicate thing have stood the test of time and so much transportation? It survived far better than I did," she thought, catching the back of her chignon, now almost pure white in places. A haunting maritime parallel stared back at her. "I'm still only forty eight but I feel like an old sea captain about to go down with my beloved ship, a ship I built all by myself with these little hands." Her conic fingers looked tiny and insignificant in the reflection so she swirled her wrists to register something of their intrinsic value. "Will I ever have the will to start again?" she wondered, trying to remember every single item of clothing ever made by her on those and other shores since picking up her first needle.

She unlocked her top desk drawer and pushed aside unpaid bills to linger over her favourite press cutting, now yellow and flimsy after five years, "Astra, dressmaker to the stars." The second drawer bulged with copper plate script "at home" cards, including the one belonging to her worst ever customer who had brazenly marched out with three completed outfits, refusing to pay a bean. The third drawer was packed with a thick pile of thank you letters from delighted customers, dating back eight years. Some of them were embossed with the royal crest, but she pushed them all back before reaching down to the bottom drawer. There it was, the large black diary of fitting room appointments almost completely full with scribbled dark blue spidery ink. "Well, I had no time to worry about being neat as well," she thought, stepping into the fitting room one last time. There she saw them all, clients standing in their stocking feet, hems half pinned, one sleeve tacked in, darts pinned in strategically to accentuate shapely curves or conceal unwanted bumps, breathless in anticipation about forthcoming glittering social events, whispering secret family intrigues, divulging physical insecurities, all knowing their trusty confidant would keep it from the outside world. "I must say goodbye now, but don't you dare forget me! Right now, stop wallowing!" She had decided what to take. She reached up for her Parisian diploma and took it out of the frame. Then she opened her green velvet work-box and slipped her favourite well-used silver thimble onto her right index finger. "What use are they to me now?" she cursed, suddenly wondering if any of it had been worth the pain of leaving. It was done, so she closed the door of her golden cage, and slammed a lifetime's work behind her. "The end," she sighed.

She wrote short notes to her sister and closest friends. Marie and Acabi's family were the only ones who knew and Marie had instructions to tell the girls next week. Then she sewed the cold coins into her hem, put the thimble into a purse, and stuffed her handbag with bank notes. However, with the value of the drachma falling each day, the bulk felt more like paper stuffing than money. Then she placed the purple velvet drawstring bag encasing her precious bone prayer book on top. Contaminated currency and reverent meditation both at hand for whatever the future might bring.

Then they waited in tense silence till that knock came bang on midnight, before filing out in orderly sequence, straight into the path of jumbled flashing images from a crazy dream before you wake. Only twenty-three hours after Johann's celebrations were over, he was back again, this time in a far more professional mode, with two unknown colleagues, hurrying them up and handing over green documents. "You must leave right now, the train is in the station. The papers will take you as far as Vienna." The three soldiers accompanied them, almost standing guard, right up till the train steamed down the tracks. "I think you will have to change trains somewhere near Salonika and then again in the Balkans." It didn't sound too arduous.

As silhouetted buildings flickered past, no one spoke, there was too much to say. Astra kept her misty eyes below the wooden seats staring at four brown leather suitcases, tangible proof that they had lived a life somewhere before. She had kept an iron hold over emotions till then, for her and for them, but as Athens too was filed away into a black box of memories, along with every other town she had been forced to leave with almost nothing, she started to blink her first tears. "Oh my dear God, where to now?" she cried, unable to hold the seven seas back one second longer. And as their mother cried, they cried too; it was to be a far longer journey than any of them could have imagined.

Finally after twenty-eight days of crossing wild terrain, remote craggy peaks and fathomless gorges, as guerrilla bandits ambushed others before and after them, and with air bombardments crashing down metres away from whatever carriage they happened to be in, they finally pulled into Vienna main line station. It should have taken three days at most, but war journeys don't necessarily bare any relevance to distances travelled. Their carriage had weaved in and out of so many borders, dodging so many burning bridges and exploding track lines that most of the time it was impossible to guess what countries they were travelling through. "They said we were going to Zagreb, but I think this is Balaton in Hungary," said Astra, but by then no one really cared. They were stopped beside a beautiful lake and neither December's icy waters nor possible sniper bullets was going to stop them jumping in to wash off two weeks' worth of grime. Strangely, food was never a problem. While hundreds of thousands were starving, warm tasty meals were brought out from checkpoints every six hours. "How on earth do they know where we are?" they wondered, as large wicker baskets fed scores of passengers, even when carriages were concealed behind railway sidings in the middle of nowhere.

Two days after the Germans left the forty or so civilian passengers to board the next available carriage, somewhere outside Zagreb, everyone was sure they must have reached Austria at last. For once the train had travelled at high speeds throughout the night, but as they wiped steamy windows to peer out into the breaking dawn, the view seemed depressingly familiar. "Look, we're back in exactly the same place we were yesterday evening! Adriné, look, there's that hay barn we stretched out in. Remember how soft and comfortable it was? We could go there again," said Koko. Adriné was distraught. "Oh no, it's terrible to think that if your train doesn't have its own engine you're at the mercy of any locomotive dragging you anywhere along the tracks." The seats were rock hard and her mother's legs had begun to swell. None of them had ever sat in one place for so long. "I wish I could be like him," she thought, knowing her brother could genuinely brush off bitter disappointment with the serenity of the Dalai Lama. "We're like aimless shuttlecocks flying through the swaying breeze. Who knows, we might even end up in deepest Russia at this rate," he said smiling, having no real objection to that possibility either.

Chapter XX

Chance Favours the Brave

IT was to be a whole ten days later when forty travel weary passengers rubbed blood into their legs before stepping down into pandemonium. "Mama, why are you crying, we've arrived in Vienna in one piece," said Adriné. But Astra's shoes didn't fit any more and her swollen legs refused to carry her. Other trains were spilling out, the hotels were full, and the station was a sea of chaos with hoards of people growing ever more willing to kill for the bed they'd been dreaming of for weeks. After resorting to offering outrageous amounts of money for just one night's stay in any part of the city without success, they began to survey filthy corners of the station. "Oh well, I suppose it's better than nothing, but we have to be quick, everyone's grabbing their corner," said Astra. Years after throwing away the brocade curtain with such relish, she had dropped straight back into refugee speak. Standing there, remembering that diseased warehouse on the beach, and looking down at her filthy crumpled skirt, wondering whatever next, she realized she was still fluent in it. "Once a refugee, always a refugee," she thought in resigned acceptance.

A handsome middle-aged woman dressed in a long sable coat had been watching events further down the platform while weighing up her decision. She had warmed to the mild mannered family talking a foreign language she couldn't recognize. How they had kept their dignity while others pushed past them in panic to get to the front of the queues. Adriné had seen her looking at them through the crowds, but it was actually her intuition throwing a lifeline. "She's got a nice kind face, I'll go and ask her if she knows of somewhere we could stay." Astra felt an asthma attack coming on. "I'll stay here," she said leaning against iron railings to take deep breaths while Adriné went over. Almost immediately her daughter's eyes had grown to the size of saucers. Astra watched as the woman unclipped her clutch bag, took out a huge set of keys and calling card, and placed them into her hand. Suddenly Adriné become ecstatic; she hugged and kissed this perfect stranger, then helped her board the train, before tripping over a pile of suitcases in her rush to get back with incredible news. "She said we could stay in her house! She's going away for three months!" "How could she do that? She's never seen us before in her life!" said Varoujan. "She's a Seventh Day Adventist," said Adriné, as though it explained everything. Half an hour later they were standing in a Rococo palace marvelling at Madam Trachtenberg's marble statues lining the entrance hallway. It was time to tell them the story. "First she asked me what language we were speaking. I said Armenian, and then she asked me if I spoke French! She said she watched Mama crying and short of breath, and she felt so sorry for her. She said we seemed like nice honest people, and that she was sure she could trust us. Her daughter is about to have her first baby somewhere in the country, and as her house was going to be sitting empty, she would much rather have us living in it than German soldiers setting up camp in her lovely ancestral home." Adriné ran her hand over a heavily carved bishop's chair, one of a set of twelve tucked under a highly polished Jacobean table. "She said we can eat whatever food we find in the cupboards. We should just take whatever we need, but she did ask us one thing: We must not go into her bedroom, that must be kept locked. Other than that, the whole place is ours till she gets back!"

Even with full permission of the owner, putting your hands into other people's cupboards took some getting used to. They had just dared to open the cutlery drawer when a huge air bombardment sent them diving under the dining room table. For three hours, from 11:00 a.m. till 2:00 p.m., sirens wailed, as thousands of planes throbbed overhead. Varoujan crept out to look out of the window. "My God it looks like the skies are full of giant black flies," but they were Messerschmitt planes roaring back threatening power. "Whose bombing Vienna?" he asked. No one was sure. "Nothing broken," said Koko, as the Bohemian crystal chandelier rocked slowly back into inert mode. By evening they were soaking like prunes in deep fragrant baths, stretching out on cream satin sheets, and eating off solid silver crested cutlery. The whole experience felt utterly surreal.

By mid-afternoon black smoke was still rising in the distance. "Let's go and see if we can find Arpoun. I've got a feeling the bombing has stopped for today," said Adriné. They usually went with her hunches. Soon they were walking along the elegant Karntnerstrasse, breathing in delicious aromas seeping through mahogany glass doors of Viennese coffee houses, feeling deliciously normal for the first time in months. "This is his address right here," said Astra, gazing up the tall spire of St. Stephen's Cathedral. She checked again. "Surely he can't be living in a church, perhaps it's a postal address?" They went in to ask but the priest had never heard of him and couldn't offer any clues. So they tried the Armenian Church, keeper of congregational records, official and unofficial, who had heard of him but thought he had left the country some time ago. "Please take our name and address in case you hear anything," said Astra. They did find out that air raids were targeting railways and factories and not civilians, and they only lasted from late morning to early afternoon. "I suppose they fly home for tea," said Astra, assuming wrongly that the planes were British. "I have a strong feeling he's not in Austria," said Adriné, steering their thoughts to where he could be rather than to what might have happened to him. It was slightly more bearable. Their next stop was the Office for Registration of Foreign Nationals. "Why do we have to register there anyway? We don't even have a nationality," said Astra, beginning to hate everything Viennese, including wafting coffee aromas. "These streets smell of burning rubber. What are we doing here anyway? We've travelled through God knows how many countries to find him, and now he's disappeared off the face of the earth."

What they didn't know was that early in 1943 the Third Reich had started to recruit foreign nationals to top up on diminishing army personnel, so Arpoun had escaped Austria to dodge the draft and was heading for home. After ten months of hiding in abandoned houses and haystacks by day and stepping over dead soldiers by night, picking unripe fruit off trees for food, while praying to reach the bosom of his family alive, he was at that moment back in Athens, listening to his aunty Aizemnig giving him earache. "Your mother didn't even have the decency to tell me she was going. I had absolutely no idea till I got this." She read the three-line note. "We all have to leave. We are going to Vienna. I will write as soon as I can." "That's it! That's all I'm worth to her, can you believe that?" said Aizemnig smarting. "Auntie, perhaps they were in danger," he said, coming up with the only wild guess that made any sense. Poor Arpoun, he had nowhere to go now except back to where he had come from, except that now the Russians were almost tasting German blood, they took no prisoners, and worst of all, millions of them were heading his way. "I have to go back and find them," he said, too exhausted to show fear, but he knew that if the Russians got there first, he might never see his family again. "Well my darling playboy nephew, there's nothing quite like close-up bloody war to shift life's priorities," she reflected. After a good night's sleep Arpoun was fully resigned to relieve the nightmare. "Good luck and may God be with you," she waived. There was no point trying to keep him against his will.

About the same time back in Vienna Koko and Varoujan were stepping out of the Office for the Registration of Foreign Nationals scanning through reams of employment instructions. The women were already outside. "You won't believe it, those official thugs have actually given us jobs. We have to work for them here!" Money was not their problem, they had plenty for now. "Varoujan has to go to Graz on Thursday to process films in a photographic laboratory and I'm supposed to sit about here in coffee houses to see if I can pick up on subversive activities!" A few things did upset him after all. "You mean they want you to spy for them?" asked his sister, wondering what type of recruitment procedures they were using that had so managed to misread Koko's motivational triggers. "You know that interview room they took us to, it was full of filing cabinets holding thousands of files. God knows what else they know about us." "What do you mean?" asked his mother. "Well, they knew I could speak six languages and where I worked. They knew Varoujan had a camera shop and that he's a whiz with developing equipment. I'm sure it must have been the charming Herr Kommandant. I bet he told them everything about us," said Koko, defending his lower ranking German friends. "Mama, try to remember what you said to him." "I didn't say much about us. Mostly we spoke about the war. When I showed him the workroom, I did say that Adriné was a very talented dressmaker, and I told him about our Hollywood Collection." "Well, you two are lucky. Just imagine, they could have summoned you both off to Berlin to make copies of Marlena Dietrich's sexiest numbers for the SS floosies! Come on, let's go for coffee and Sacher Torte. I might as well get some practice in."

Varoujan left for Graz and Koko started reading Nietzsche in random coffee houses around town, completely oblivious to any conversations going on around him. Sometimes he would ask Adriné to accompany him just to break the monotony. "Don't they wonder why you haven't overheard anything subversive so far?" she asked. "Well, they haven't said anything. I just have to fill in a form every Friday listing where I've been drinking my coffees, and at the bottom I just write 'Nothing to report.'"

For the first time in her life Astra had very little to do except walk the streets searching for her missing son, cook Austrian recipes (her only concession to progress this time around), polish up silver, and reflect on her chaotic life which seemed to have vanished into the void. She had no interest in learning German, even if it meant she could read newspapers. "What's the point, it's obviously all blatant propaganda," she said, still able to smell rancid journalistic censorship at a hundred paces. Anyway, after uncovering Mrs. Trachtenberg's radio under leaky bathroom floorboards, following a particularly shuddering bombing raid, she preferred to listen to the BBC World Service versions of events. "As soon as it's over we can go back to Greece. Arpoun might be there waiting for us," she said with real hope. But no one knew that even after the German army surrendered to the British, the Greek Civil War was to keep the Allies and communists polarized on opposite sides long after the rest of the world had laid down arms.

Frau Trachtenberg returned to her immaculately kept home on April 1st, 1944, to find Astra alone at the long kitchen table almost polishing the silver off a pair of eighteenth century candlesticks, thinking of her lost son, her lost identity, her lost life, her lost everything. "Bonjour," she said jumping up, but both women knew it wasn't. "La guerre est vraiment terrible," said Frau Trachtenberg, walking over to wipe black soggy streaks of tarnish off Astra's face with a crisp linen handkerchief. "Mille merci, pour tout que vous avez fait pour nous" said Astra so many times that even with the language barrier, Frau Trachtenberg was left in no doubt as to her eternal gratitude. Astra washed her hands and reached for her purse. "No merci," said Frau Trachtenberg emphatically, pushing the purse away. Her daughter had delivered a beautiful baby girl, no soldiers had moved into the house, which looked cleaner than when she had left it, and her religion would not allow the taking of money for an act of kindness. There was more kindness to come. Her neighbour, also a devout Seventh Day Adventist, was coming to stay with her for company, so they were welcome to move into her friend's apartment— although it was a little small—for as long as they needed. What did it matter whether it was a rococo palace, a small apartment, or a Turkish jail, it was all the same for a prisoner in exile.

Chapter XXI

The Rewards of Endurance

BY the end of March 1945 every German soldier was fleeing back to the fatherland. Bulgaria had liberated Macedonia and Serbia from the Third Reich and was virtually brushing shoulders with the awesome Soviet army pushing at the gates of Vienna. It was definitely time to leave. They still had no news from Arpoun, but still no one dared to think the worst. At least Varoujan was back. After his miraculous escape from a straying bomb meant for an oil refinery in Graz, which had left a gaping chasm outside the phone box he was standing in, he was in fine fettle. Adriné had heard him say "hello sister," just before a massive boom nearly blew her eardrum. But two days later, there he was, alive and well and still plucking out tiny slivers of shattered glass from his slick back quiff, more handsome than ever. "Did you know that in celebration of the Germans capitulating, the Bulgarians and British played a friendly football match here yesterday? Apparently the score was one all, but I think it was a fix," he said swinging his legs off the back of an armchair while studying the map of Europe with Koko. "I know, let's stick a pin in it, and go wherever it lands." But it was all bravado. No one was laughing inside. "A little birdie tells me that you're undercover missions were a great success!" Koko had to agree. "Yes, I am delighted to say that I am without exception the worst spy this world has ever known. I managed to write 'nothing to report' every week for fifteen months! In fact, the last time I went to file my report, about two weeks ago, the building was completely empty. They must have known their days were numbered."

After fifteen months in a foreign country, the thought of escaping to nowhere in particular had made them a little hysterical. "Woof woof woof! Don't you think the English language sounds like dogs barking?" asked Adriné as her mother hung on to every word being broadcast by the BBC World Service. "They seem to be using some kind of coded wording but listen, here's the news about Greece," she said, putting her ear closer to the radio. They listened not understanding much, but her expression dropped enormous clues. "They say its getting worse. British soldiers are being sent there to deal with the communists, who apparently have amassed a terrifying store of arms. How can we go back now?" After having followed the news avidly every day, it was no great surprise and anyway she had already been thinking of an all-together different destination. "We could try to get to northern Italy. They've already been liberated. The Germans left to defend Berlin and the Allies have left the borders open to allow refugees in. What about Venice? Your father and I wanted to go there once. Did you know the Armenian fathers have had their monastic headquarters there since 1717? They own a lot of land actually in Venice. Emperor Napoleon gave it to them in 1815." They stared at her in disbelief. "No, really it's true. The monastery is on an island in the lagoon called San Lazarro. Isola Dei Armeni they call it, your father told me all about it. It's a famous cultural centre for literature and archeology, the famous English poet Byron studied Armenian there. We had a book with photographs of the world famous library, full of ancient religious texts and Byzantine manuscripts, and they also store at least one copy of every newspaper printed in Armenian from all over the world. Your father's papers would be there." It suddenly seemed worth going to Venice just to hold one of Setrag's newspapers in her hands once more. Venice it was then. They caught a filthy train packed full of foreign refugees of every nationality who had suddenly crawled out of the woodwork to escape yet another occupying army. Bulgaria had declared war on Germany in September but now with the way clear, Bulgarians were crowding Austrian skies with deadly stuka bombers.

"We are becoming very widely travelled," said Koko crouching down to admire the beautiful alpine scenery chugging past them from a long narrow crack in the animal transportation carriage. Just then a stuka bomber screeched down, the train slammed to a halt, and Koko found himself in the lap of a smiling Hungarian cellist. "I'm sure that hit the track," said the distinguished conductor from the Budapest Opera Theatre Company sharing their floor space. The group chatted amongst themselves in pre-performance mode while waiting for the train guard to return with a track update. "So, do tell us sir, is there time to perform a play?" he asked in perfect German, excited at the prospect of being held up for hours while mechanics patched up the rail line. "Not this time, it's minor damage, the bomb hit the trees, they're putting the fires out now, so we should be able to leave in about an hour," he replied. "Well in that case we have time for the chamber quartet to play some cheerful tunes," he said nodding at the musicians to take out their instruments. With stukas dropping at regular intervals, this journey was no less perilous than the one before, but so much more entertaining. Time permitting, and at almost every stop, the conductor invited passengers to leave their carriages and form an audience outside while they played beautiful music, staged theatre plays in full costume, and even put on a puppet show for the children. Three weeks of travelling amongst courteous talented people, all hell bent on not letting evils of war get in the way of culture and fun-filled promenade shows all the way to Venice Opera House, was nothing but an unexpected privilege.

"We're booked to play at La Fenice till the middle of May, so you must come to see us, even though you have heard most of our repertoire al fresco!" said the conductor, shaking hearty hands with the Tokadjians as he led his performing company off the vaporetto at the Rialto Bridge. "We will," they waved back, as the motorbus continued to glide through the Grand Canal, forcing deep green ripples to lick moss tinged cellar walls of Renaissance palaces all around them. "Arpoun will absolutely love it here," said Adriné, always there in her mother's thoughts, although she decided not to breath a word to her about her dream two days before. She had dreamt that they had received a letter from Arpoun. It was dated the twenty first of April 1945 and in it he said he was on his way to find them. But she did tell her two brothers. "It was so vivid, I actually felt the letter in my hands," she told them.

By two o'clock the Tokadjians were camped in an open-air cinema, along with hundreds of other refugees who had come to Venice without documents or work permits. With the lagoon and Piazza San Marco right behind them, they were still admiring the view. "Look over there, I'm sure that's the Armenian monastery," said Astra remembering the book Setrag had shown her in 1913. A little bit of Armenia in the near distance, his newspapers just a boat ride away. She couldn't explain it, but somehow it felt like coming home. Varoujan read out a post card he had been writing.

"Dear Auntie Aizemnig,

It's so familiar, so divine, Yes the weather's really fine,

Crumbling monuments, ancient voices, crying against pollution's grime,

Decaying decadence exposed, these gondolas really do get up your nose,

But still we wish you could be here, before the whole thing disappears!"

"Its very good, but you know it won't disappear. It's actually forbidden to bomb Venice, we're finally in a bomb free zone!" said Koko. "No, I was referring to the sea. This tour guide says Venice is sinking at the rate of four centimetres every hundred years." They all signed the card and Varoujan went in search of a post box and better accommodation and came back with vital commercial information. "Apparently cigarettes are the best currency at the moment. We could rent a shop for a whole year with this," he said, throwing down eight long cartons. "How about we start with a room for a couple of weeks first," said Astra knowing that if it was up to him they'd be living in an open air cinema indefinitely, while he'd be setting up shop to sell film and cameras to American soldiers. Venice was crawling with them.

They weren't the only Armenian family sleeping out in the open air on the Lido that night. "Let me read your cards madam," said a pretty dark haired Armenian woman in green shoes, laying out a multi-coloured fringed shawl on the damp grass to sit down between them. After turning over just three cards, and not knowing a thing about them, she suddenly stopped and drew her index finger right across her throat. "I swear I will cut my head off if you don't see your son here in three weeks!" Astra started to weep, wondering why only women wearing bright green shoes were destined to tell her the whereabouts of her missing men, remembering the moment a politician's wife broke her heart on a crowded beach in Athens. "Who are you?" she asked. "It doesn't matter who I am, I just say what I see," she said. Even then Adriné said nothing about her dream, knowing her mother's waking dreams were too fragile to lay bare.

Two weeks later they were still camped out, waiting for officials to stamp "right to remain" on their laissez passé documents. "I've a feeling it won't be long now, why don't we go over to the monastery today? They can't expect us to sit here like prisoners forever, and anyway, they can see every move we make from the gate. We could squeeze into that rowing boat about to take their food over. Come on, he's about to leave," said Adriné. Within five minutes they were walking up the stairs on the other side, handing over packets of wrapped cheeses to a group of amiable elderly monks with impossibly long beards. "You can see the Abbot in his office, and later we can give you a tour of the museum if you have time," they said. The tiny Abbot put down his thick magnifying glass beside an ancient illuminated manuscript and welcomed them in. "I am constantly reminded of our tragic history," he said gazing at their refugee camp across the lagoon. "We all feel so guilty living in such relative comfort so close by, please do sit down," he said, realizing a history lesson might lighten the mood. "Emperor Napoleon recognized the special scholarly mission of our Mekhitarian Order and in 1810 irrevocably decreed our monastery to be classed as an academic institution," he said pointing to the actual decree in a glass cabinet by the window. "That is how we still have a small piece of Armenia floating like a jewel in Adriatic seas. Now I believe you need somewhere to live, and luckily I can help." He opened a drawer, took out a map, and proceeded to offer them very cheap rented accommodation in a prime location right on the Lido. "This is the very first time in my life that being an Armenian has brought privilege," said Astra. "Welcome to Venice," he smiled.

They hitched a ride back with the food delivery boat just in time to join the long queues for residency interviews. "If we had gone to see your father's newspapers in their archives we would have been too late," said Astra, hoping for an opportunity to be alone to relive her past with him in private, when time didn't matter. "Are you Adriné Tokadjian?" asked an official well before it was her turn. "Then if you give me a carton of cigarettes, I have something very special for you. Come with me," he said, mysteriously leading her across the street. "Where are you taking me?" she asked, as he marched her into a dingy storeroom, piled high with refugee bedding and expecting her to scream with for joy at any second. "There's nothing here except dirty laundry," she said, glancing at the person she took to be a rather unsavoury bearded laundry attendant slouched in the corner. "Don't you recognize him?" he asked. Adriné went closer as the man began to stand up. "Adrig, it's me," he said almost collapsing with the effort. She knew that voice. "Arpoun? Oh my God, is it really you." As she ran to prop him up, she felt his sharp bony shoulders, shocked to realize how hideously thin he had become. She pushed back his matted black hair to see his face. His eyes were oozing a nasty yellow liquid. "Don't you know me sister?" he sighed, making her hug him with a force that only four years of agonizing worry could inflict on the battered body of a long lost loved one. But the expression in his eyes was what shocked her most, haunted, soulless, and totally unrecognisable. As they dragged him out into the sharp sunlight, he had one thing on his mind, "Mama, where are you?" With the harrowing long road now behind him, all he had to do was cross the street. He squinted painful eyes to live the moment that had kept him alive, while millions around him died, but he took a few steps, slipped through their arms, and drifted into black oblivion. So came one more moment to last a lifetime: Astra's daughter kneeling beside a semi-breathing bundle of bones she knew was her long lost son.

"Astra Sabondjian," her maiden name was being blasting out of the loudspeaker, it was her turn. As Arpoun would still be in view, she left his brothers and sister to drip love and water with their charmed touch, and got up to walk over to the desk where officials were waiting with their round red seals to stamp down Italian immigration formalities, which would last a lifetime, or whatever life she had yet to come.

By the end of May 1945, Arpoun's body was making a speedy recovery, though his mangled spirit would take a while longer. They had been officially accepted into the Italian fold, the abbots had graciously handed over house keys, the war was over, and evil dictators were dead. The stage was set.

Adriné had been shopping but came back empty handed. "It's great here, you don't have to carry a thing. They're going to deliver everything right to the door by boat before six. Oh Mama, everywhere you look, it's all so exquisite. I know we're going to love it, and we can invite our relatives and friends over for holidays, Acabi, Anoushka, even Fatima, everyone wants to see Venice." "We never did get to see the Hungarians play La Fenicé," said Astra, finally deciding it was time to unpack her suitcase and put away things from a previous world to make way for yet another new one, but this time it felt different. She had done everything life had asked of her and now it was her turn to summon the forces of destiny so others would carry the baton. She had primed them for this moment, Koko, the kind-hearted philosopher, Adriné, the loving psychic pragmatist, Varoujan, the suave canny businessman, and Arpoun, the insatiable wandering survivor, in the best way she knew how. Above everything else she had achieved in her life, she had managed to raise four individually wonderful children and for that she was most proud.

As always, Adriné was somewhere deep in her thoughts. "Mama, do you think it's better to be happy at the beginning or at the end of your life?" she asked, as though we could make the choice. "That's like asking me how many pips there are in a single pomegranate. If I told you the answer is six hundred and eleven, would you believe me? And if I counted one pomegranate, why would I count another?" "Because they're your favourite fruit, and because Mama, now you can." Her own time had finally come.

GOMIDAS INSTITUTE
42 Blythe Rd.
London W14 0HA
England